THE HUSTLER'S HANDBOOK

THE
HUSTLER'S

HANDBOOK

by

BILL VEECK *with Ed Linn*

IVAN R. DEE, *Chicago*

www.ivanrdee.com

The G.P. Putnam's Sons edition of this book was previously catalogued by the
Library of Congress as follows:

Library of Congress catalog card number: 65-20692

ISBN: 978-1-56663-827-2 (pbk : alk. paper)

To Ruth: Whither thou goest ...
be it hither, thither or yon

Contents

⊜ ⊜ ⊜

THE HUSTLER'S HANDBOOK

1

⊖ ⊖ ⊖

Come Fly with Me
or
The Art of Promotion

YOU don't have to be a hustler to be a promoter—which is fair enough since you don't have to be a promoter to be a hustler either. But it helps. Noah Webster, a man known in every pool hall in the nation as a *?'*# *'?#¢ *¢#'? conservative (he died in 1843, which is about as conservative as you can get these days), offers as his preferred definition for the verb *promote:* "To exalt in station, rank or honor; to elevate, raise, etc."

The best he can do for promoter is: "one who causes the above to happen."

The only unsavory definition he can dredge up, in fact, is: "a person who alone or with others sets afoot and takes the preliminary steps in a scheme or undertaking for the organization of a company, the floating of a bond stock, etc., or the carrying out of any business project."

So *that's* what a promoter does? I never did feel you could trust Merrill, Lynch, Pierce or Smith, but I used to have a warm spot in my heart for Fenner.

As the first assignment, class, we will now all burn our dictionaries and get on to the real definitions, complete with illustrations, gesticulation and grimaces:

An eminent Professor of Egyptology recently deciphered the quaint markings and scrawlings on a wall in Syracuse, which depicted the stirring saga of one Tuttutantutt, a prehistoric promoter who was forced to beat a hasty exit from that normally hospitable city when half of his bear-baiting team failed to show up. He did manage, it seems, to maintain his composure well enough to take the day's receipts with him, which resulted in the complete destruction of the arena by his irate customers. Tuttutantutt not only kept the receipts, he had his customers provide their own show. *That's* a promoter, Noah!

Some years later, in Rome, during the lively reign of Emperor Hadrian, we read of two promoters who had somewhat worse luck. These boys not only lost the entire day's receipts, they ended up in the show themselves when their regular jobber ran short of unrepentant Christians during the May-day rush. We are indebted to Tacitus for this fascinating insight into early-Italian merchandising, and since neither he nor any of his fellow gossip columnists thought it necessary to make any further mention of our boys, we must assume that the lions were a big winner that day.

That's the way it goes in the promoting business, class. Win a few, lose a few.

What is the difference between a promoter and a hustler? Well, let's look at it this way. Neither of them is an advertiser. An advertiser pays for his space. A promoter works out a *quid pro quo*. A hustler gets a free ride and makes it seem as if he's doing you a favor.

The hustler's contribution to the total national product is that most ephemeral of all commodities, ideas. When Mike Todd wanted Marilyn Monroe to appear at some extravaganza or other, he told her, "Have I got something great for you? You're going to come into *Madison Square Garden* sitting on a *pink elephant!* Get it? A PINK ELEPHANT! The symbol of illusion, unreality and dreams!" (A hustler's language, you will note, consists largely of exclamation points and CAPITAL LETTERS!)

Miss Monroe was in the middle of Madison Square Garden,

shivering daintily, before she realized that an elephant, of any hue, smelled just as bad and that riding him was no fun at all.

So now we're narrowing the ground a little. An advertiser, traveling cross-country, buys his ticket from a reputable commercial airline. A promoter travels on any line where he can work out an exchange. A hustler travels by magic carpet and says (shouts, cries, coos), "Come fly with me."

The only rules I can think of, offhand, are that a sense of shame is to be avoided at all costs, and there is never any good reason for a hustler to be any less cunning than more virtuous men.

Oh yes, one thing more. Whenever you think you've got something really great, add 10 percent more.

It isn't enough for a promotion to be entertaining or even amusing; it must create conversation. When the fan goes home and talks about what he has seen, he is getting an additional kick out of being able to say that he was there. Do not deny him that simple pleasure, especially since he is giving you invaluable word-of-mouth advertising to add to the newspaper reports.

It's no secret that I have always felt that incongruity is the soul of laughter in a ball park. Ideally, then, a gag should be incongruous, amusing and—since we are not dealing here in pushcart peddlers—it should involve a ballplayer.

Let us begin with a simple example. If I were to present a player with a check I would probably be helping his budget mightily. But I would be doing very little for myself promotionally unless I were content with a smattering of applause from the audience, a brief mention at the bottom of the notes columns and a perfumed thank-you note from his wife.

If, on the other hand, I give him a check that is 20 feet by 50 feet instead of the customary 2″ x 5″, I have established grounds for picture-taking, for laughter, for comment. I have even established the wholly unjustified feeling that since the check is so big *physically* it is somehow bigger monetarily too.

There is also going to be a certain amount of curiosity about whether the check is negotiable. I will *see* to it that there is a certain amount of curiosity. This will give me the opportunity to pass on the fascinating information—just in case the question should ever come up over your breakfast table—that the size of checks is regulated solely by custom and convenience. I will even have an official of the bank standing by—looking friendly— to assure the eager sportswriters that there are no restrictions as to size, shape, color, material or national origin.

Promotions are not without their drawbacks. For one thing, they cost money. That's deplorable. The cost itself, however, can become part of the promotion. There is something about the crisp, crackling sound of money being thrown away that brings the color back into the cheeks and brings back memories of those happy boyhood days down on the farm. Why, people will come from miles away just to see money being thrown away.

A hustler should always be scrupulous about having some-body else on hand to pick up the check.

Whenever you find that you *have* to spend money around the ball park, you create a promotion. To your unsuspecting ad-mirers it must appear as if the promotion were the sole reason for the expense.

Example: In Chicago, the concession trucks were having so much trouble squeezing through the narrow path under the park that we decided we had better bypass the whole conces-sion area and bring the trucks in through the exit gate at the corner of the right-field bleachers. To do this we had to widen the gate, rip out the old runway and footings, excavate and lay down a newer, lower runway.

Now construction work may provoke some mild interest down at the union hall but it is, alas, of no great interest to the press, the public or even the Bureau of Standards.

Unless we could tie it in with a promotion.

Easy. All we had to do was to hold a Night for a player and present him with a gift that would just barely squeeze through the new, expanded entrance. Would it really harm anybody if we passed the word around that in order to get the gift into the park we had—at incredible trouble and incalculable cost— torn down the old walls?

As for the player, it was quite apparent that Nellie Fox was most deserving of the honor. He deserved a Night because he was on his way to becoming the Most Valuable Player of the American League. Furthermore, he deserved a Night just because he was Nellie.

The only problem became the purely technical one of find- ing a gift that would fulfill the basic requirement of sheer size and would also be incongruous enough to call forth gasps of awe and gales of laughter. What was wanted, in short, was a token of esteem that would look ridiculous in a ball park and be equally incongruous as a gift for Nellie.

Since Fox lives in inland Pennsylvania, far from the water's edge, it would be rather difficult to find anything less useful to him than a sailboat.

You will never guess what we surprised Nellie with on his Night. Darned if we didn't give him a sailboat. You may not be- lieve this, but we even knocked down the exit gate out in the corner of right field, tore up the footings and—at incredible trouble and incalculable cost—built a whole new runway just so we could get it onto the field.

Actually, the boat was delivered through the good offices of Ed Scherick of ABC, who was a phantom partner in a Toledo sailboat company. It was shipped to us on 24-hour lend-lease, so I bought some land in Pennsylvania, worth roughly the same amount, and told Nellie I'd trade it to him for the sailboat. Nellie was more than willing, which was just as well since the sailboat was already back on the truck and heading on the open road back to Toledo.

A promoter deals in illusion, and illusion is a distorted mir- ror which can throw back your own reflection. Once you have established a reputation for being original and imaginative, you will find that anything you do—no matter how unoriginal or unimaginative—becomes fun just because it is you who are doing it. When Bob Hope tells a joke, his audience enjoys it far more than if it were being told by a comedian of lesser stature, not simply because Hope tells a joke exceedingly well but because his audience *expects* him to be funny, *wants* him to be funny and is rather flattered that he is being funny for *them*.

Once you have absorbed that invaluable lesson, you become aware that you are entitled to steal from yourself by taking one basic, identifiable idea and playing as many variations on it as you can find—like Hope's endless jokes about Crosby.

I have one favorite category which I always think of as "The Name's the Same," since I first used it for Al Smith's benefit in Chicago by inviting everyone whose name was Smith—or any variation thereof—into the park free to sit behind him and root for him. (Actually I had used the same principle much earlier in such stunts as inviting all mothers into the park on Mother's Day, with a picture of their offspring—or any reasonable facsimile thereof—serving as the ticket of admission.)

The Mother's Day promotion is in a slightly different category, though, because there is no way of wrapping it around a player unless you don't mind being terribly mawkish. By wrapping a promotion around a player, you are bringing the ceremonies out of the stands and onto the field, providing a focal point for exploitation and giving everybody at the game the added pleasure of having somebody special to root for.

Example: If you put your mind to it, I have every confidence that everybody in this room could come up with a legitimate reason for inviting all left-handers into the park. All you have to do really is find some reason for honoring one of your own left-handers. (As a left-hander myself, I can assure you that we are a particularly abused, particularly sensitive minority, thankful for all small kindnesses. If Barry Goldwater had promised to defoliate those forests with left-handed flamethrowers he'd have carried at least three more states.)

Consider that Milwaukee almost never started Warren Spahn,

the greatest left-hander of all time, against the old Dodgers, because the old Dodgers had a lineup that chewed up all left-handed pitchers, great and small. If, under circumstances such as these, you could somehow drop a hint to your manager (particularly when his contract comes up for renewal) that it might be helpful to start Spahn against the Dodgers one time, the possibilities become endless.

We could present Spahn with an English car (so that he could drive on the left side of the road as nature intended) and have special left-handed wristwatches, telephones, eating utensils, etc., made up for his convenience. We could intone the names of all the great left-handers from Alexander the Great to Harry Truman—not to mention Johnny Torrio who, while shaking hands pleasantly with Dion O'Bannion, pulled out a gun with his left hand and killed him. That's what I said, we won't mention *him*.

For we are not only giving Spahn his chance to uphold the sacred honor of the downtrodden left-hander, we are honoring all the left-handers in town by showing the hardships they are forced to endure in their daily lives.

Despite the inflationary spiral, incidentally, a ballplayer can be honored quite reasonably. Department stores, automobile agencies and other sportsmen and philanthropists are more than willing to donate gifts in return for the advertising and goodwill.

With a little thought I'm sure that each of you is perfectly capable of coming up with a "Name's the Same" gambit yourself. In Washington, you have a President named Johnson and a club owner named Johnston, a coincidence so freighted with significance that it almost demands that you invite all Johnsons, Johnstons, *et al.* to the Opening Game. We are not only going to let them into the park free, we are going to present each of them with a baseball so that he can join the hallowed line of Presidents, governors, mayors, aldermen and beauty queens who have thrown out the first ball.

The extra added ingredient you have going for you can be

found in the question: How many of them are going to throw away a new baseball in order to be part of the Opening Day ceremonies and how many are going to tuck it into their back pockets to take home to the kids? Try though I might, I don't suppose I could prevent the writers from conjecturing about that. Or even of reporting on it afterwards. As our own contribution toward the free and unfettered flow of information we might even be persuaded to provide an official accounting.

Some of you smart alecks who are familiar with the situation in Washington may be protesting that we are letting people in free on the only day in the entire season when we figure to have a sellout. If your mind runs along such choked and dreary channels you had better either reprogram your entire thinking or go into a less chancy business—like, say, running for Mayor of Chicago on the Republican ticket.

The very fact that everyone knows you could have sold those seats makes them more valuable and upgrades the whole promotion.

I cannot stress this point too strongly: When you give something away, give it away. Freely and openheartedly. The mistake so many so-called promoters make is that they want to get away with giving away 10% or 20%—or, in some cases I could cite, 3.5%. I want to warn you right now that if anyone in this class ever runs one of those affairs in which he *splits* with a charity, his diploma is automatically revoked. If you're going to do it, do it. If you are not willing to do it, then operate for the only important charity, yourself.

A hustler's thoughts should be long, long thoughts. He should be thinking not for the day, but for the year, the decade, the era. Don't worry about letting people in free. Seats you have aplenty. Anything that brings people into your park is going to help you, one way or another, in the long run.

Besides, an act of charity bathes you in the light of respectability, and respectability is the best blind a hustler can have.

To this point, the only element lacking in our Opening Day promotion for Washington is the tie-in to a ballplayer. If I were planning this promotion, I'd try very hard to buy Bob Johnson from Baltimore or Ken Johnson from Milwaukee. To get him, I'd be perfectly prepared to pay a premium price—mostly because I know I'd have to.

Along the same general lines, I have always wanted to find a ballplayer who was born on Christmas Day, because that would mean that all his life—poor chap—he had been cheated out of a birthday. We would do our pitiful best to make things up to him—and to all the similarly afflicted—by holding a birthday party for him on July 4. All other Christmas babies within sound of our voice would be admitted to the park as our guests—to receive special solace—upon the display of birth certificates, legitimate or reasonably well forged.

Never mind the rest of it. Just think of the "Christmas in July" fireworks display we could put on!

The common denominator in all these promotions, then, is that we are honoring a group of people who have one common characteristic. The only trouble with it, though, is that it is necessary to let the people know what's going to happen in advance. Generally, that's a mistake. The big kick is to be surprised. What we are trying to do is to get the whole city in a frame of mind where they are asking, "What's that screwball going to do next?"

Promotion is a state of mind long before it becomes a state of action.

Man survives because he is the most optimistic of animals. Every time he leaves the house, he is hoping to find that elusive, magical something that is going to upgrade his life. We can't come right out and promise to transform his personality, since that would be poaching upon territory already staked out by the deodorant, hair lotion and cigarette cartels, but we should be able to make him understand that he is going to experience something enjoyable and, if we are all very lucky, memorable.

The business of baseball is characterized by two things: First

of all, you are dependent to an extent that will probably surprise you on REPEAT BUSINESS. If you break your attendance figures down over a period of time you will find that on a
total attendance of 1,000,000, less than 100,000 *different* people
are involved. Most of the repeats, need I say, are season ticket
holders. If you can sell 10,000 advance seats, you have assured
yourself (taking into account the varying plans) an attendance
of 450,000.

The average customer comes to the park no more than two
or three times a year. If you can put on a good-enough show to
get him to come five or six times, he has become a source of
pride to you. A source of revenue, too.

Since baseball is working with such a tiny portion of the
population, the latitude for increasing your attendance once
you have swung into high gear is almost unlimited. If you can
hit the right combination of fun and victory, victory and fun,
then, boy, your attendance can explode!

Here is where the second challenge comes in. Although you
are dependent upon repeat business, you have NO PRODUCT
to sell. The customer comes out to the park with nothing except
the illusion that he is going to have a good time. He leaves with
nothing except a memory. If the memory brings on either
yawns or head pains you have lost him until next year.

With its unfailing instinct for merchandising, baseball has
sold its customers on the idea that they can only enjoy themselves if the home team wins. This is great for the two pennant
winners, but it is not very rewarding for the ten teams in the
second division. If you have a particularly bad team, you are
faced with the considerable problem of coaxing your customer
into the ball park that first time. The next problem is to make
him want to come back.

Listen to me carefully, now, because if you are a hustler,
you are going to start out with a bad team. A bad ball club is
generally the available one, the cheaper one, and the one you
can best bring your talents to bear upon.

You must start out, in the face of baseball's most hallowed

traditions, by selling the customer on the idea that win or lose, you are putting on a good show.

(Pro football has done this remarkably well. While the base-ball hierarchy talks pompously about "giving the fans a team worthy of their support," the football mob has sold the slogan that "any team can beat any other on a given afternoon." Through nothing more than hard, long—and give them their due, brilliant—promotion, the footballers have created the feel-ing that their teams are so evenly matched that the game will be great no matter which team wins. I can assure you that they are not that evenly matched. As a matter of fact, the bottom teams in major leagues defeat the top teams far more often—percentagewise—than the bottom teams in the NFL.)

The question before the class, then, is this: How can we guarantee this great mass of disinterested fans that we have dedicated our lives, our fortunes and our sacred honor to giving them a good time if only they will come out to the park to taste of our wares?

Well, the only way you can guarantee something, students, is by guaranteeing it.

Guarantee it, you say? But that's impossible! You're not pre-senting Elizabeth Taylor in *Fiddler on a Hot Tin Roof*. You're not even presenting the Three Stooges in *Fiddlers on the Roof*. You are presenting an athletic contest. About the only thing you can promise the fan, without running afoul of the Securities Ex-change Commission, is that you don't know *what's* going to happen out there.

Sure you can guarantee it. You can give them a MONEY-BACK GUARANTEE. You can tell them that if they don't have fun, you want them to march, singly or *en masse,* upon your box office and demand their money back. No stalling, no box tops, no questions asked.

To prove that you are not making this offer frivolously, it would be well to grab the public-address microphone the first time you have been soundly trounced and insist upon every-body coming back whether they want to or not. "No one," you announce, your voice throbbing in agony, "should have to pay good money to see this kind of a monstrosity. I implore you to come back as my guest if only to give us a chance to make a comeback with you." If the fireworks should happen to fizzle, even after a particularly exciting game, give the money back too. What you are offering, you want to make clear, is a totally satisfying, stirring and ear-shattering afternoon of entertainment.

The MONEY-BACK GUARANTEE is a natural because it meets the ultimate test of any promotion—it helps the customer have a better time. Every time some humpty-dumpty strikes out, one guy can turn to his buddy and groan, "Come on, let's get our money back." Any time a fielder blows one, the cry will most assuredly arise, "Watch it, you bum, or we'll *all* go get our money back."

Nobody really wants to shuffle up to the box office and ask for his money back, of course, but it flatters him to know that you are that solicitous of his patronage and goodwill. You have made him a participant, in the same sense that sportswriters are participants. He can watch, he can judge, and when the game is over he can either stop at the box office or keep on walking.

As much as I hate to inject a discouraging note into such a stimulating subject, the first rule of promoting is to get yourself a good product. Without it you are stone, cold dead in the marketplace. You can shoot off your fireworks, hire your clowns, pull off your stunts; all that is only the frosting on the cake. The game of baseball is the thing on which, in the end, you will have to live or die.

If I have been a self-starting Cassandra shouting "Doom," it is because the game has become too slow for the modern pace of life. You can keep telling people what a great time they are having, but people have this infuriating habit of believing what they see. Baseball officials fight the idea that baseball is part of the entertainment business, because they confuse entertainment with show business per se and they look upon show business in much the same way a middle-aged wife looks at her husband when the belly dancer goes into her act. They cannot quite get it into their heads that show business and sports are two completely *different* branches of the entertainment business.

It is entirely possible, and we had better face up to it, that baseball has no more relevancy in our day and age than cricket. But I don't think so. I think baseball is the greatest game on earth. I also think that it is filled with air pockets, and that we had better get to work to squeezing them out.

Let me make one thing completely clear at the outset. I am not talking simply about elapsed time. I'm talking about the long stretches of time in which nothing happens. Three pitching changes, in a single inning, can clear out the ball park. Which is why we instituted the practice of getting the relief pitchers in there by car. If, on the other hand, you have a red-hot relief pitcher whose entrance is eagerly awaited, you would do well to leave that car in the garage, and let him stroll out there while the tension builds. Satchel Paige walking in from the bullpen was one of the electrifying moments of baseball.

The same thing is true with umpires. An argument with the umpires is part of the entertainment of the day and should be encouraged by every defender of our national character. It is, predictably, the one part of the game that the officialdom, which takes the game *so* seriously, has gone out of its way to discourage.

For our purposes here, we are not going to discuss how the game itself could be made more compact. As hustlers, our main interest is in how we can use the arts of promotion to keep the fans totally involved in what is happening on the field, even while nothing is happening. Because, and you had better believe it, they are not going to pay to sit out there and daydream when they can sit home and daydream for free.

Let us consider the uses of the scoreboard:

The scoreboard we put up in Chicago was intended for

greater things than mortar fire and fireworks. It was to be a bottomless magic box out of who-knows-what-marvels might fly.

Among the marvels of our modern world were to be electronic instruments which, hopefully, would not only entertain and inform the customer but also serve to keep his mind riveted on the ball game, pitch by pitch.

The great portion of any ball game consists of the pitcher holding the ball or throwing it to the catcher. Anything that can somehow turn that frozen tableau into a scene fraught with drama and excitement has solved about 75 percent of your problems.

According to the rules, the pitcher is supposed to deliver the ball within 20 seconds when nobody is on base. Anybody who can tell me when he last saw an umpire call that one wins a free trip to Leo Durocher.

We had a timer built into the scoreboard, which I called—with characteristic corniness—the Pitchometer. (It is well to keep nomenclature simple and to the point. Save the cute and the clever for the gag itself.) The Pitchometer was set up to tick off the seconds for us. When the hand hit the 20-second mark it activated a siren that was guaranteed to knock the pitcher's hat off and startle lovers in the downtown hotels. With luck, it might even call the umpire's attention to the violation of the rule.

In any good promotion (or, for that matter, any good publicity idea), timing is everything. It is essential to pick the spot that will merit the widest possible coverage and bring on the most delighted (or inflamed) comment. I wanted to find the right pitcher to unveil the Pitchometer against, a pitcher who was known for his sensitivity, for instance, or a pitcher like Camilo Pascual, who is particularly good and also particularly slow. You want to annoy, upset and maybe even cow the opposing pitcher, but more than anything else you want to surprise and delight the crowd. And, as in all gags, you want to make the rest of the world kick themselves for not being there.

I was so intent upon getting the maximum value out of my Pitchometer that I got no value out of it at all. Before it was unveiled, I was unhorsed. The Pitchometer still sits there, like a coiled tiger, unheard, unseen, unleashed.

Once you begin to think in terms of scoreboard clockings, the possibilities are endless. You can install a giant stopwatch to time the batter's speed to first base. (The clock would be run by an old scout who has been timing runners in the bushes all his life.) On extra-base hits, he has only to let the clock keep running and we have the time it takes for each man to run out a double or a triple. The fun comes, obviously, when a triple is hit by a man who is either lightning fast or dreadfully slow. You are involving the fans in a whole set of new arguments and establishing a whole new set of records. Who *is* the fastest man on the team? Who is the best *base runner* on the team? (Not necessarily the same thing at all.)

The electronics industry, having advanced to the point where it can bounce pictures off a satellite, is quite capable of developing anything you want. There is no reason whatsoever why an electronic system could not be set up to enable you to chart each pitch electronically on a scoreboard screen. The screen would record the speed of each pitch, the kind of pitch (curve, knuckle ball, sinker, etc.) and a profile of the exact path the ball followed, so that everybody in the park would be able to see how much the curve broke, how high the fast ball hopped and what part of the plate the pitch hit.

The announcer passes this information on to the viewer at home, not always, to be sure, with exacting accuracy. Why should the viewer at home have more information than the paying customer?

One of the myths by which we live is that the "real" baseball fan loves a 1–0 game and abhors a "sloppy" 8–6 game. Even the most cursory studies show that fans love 8–6 games and are bored to death by classic 1–0 pitchers' battles.

When a great pitcher is at his best, his strategy and his control are things of rare beauty and his stuff is wondrous to behold.

Unhappily, the guy up in the stands can't see the brain whirring, nor can he see the stuff breaking. All he sees is hitter after hitter popping up or sending little ground balls to the shortstop. The pitcher's part in it all is taken on faith.

The electronic screen would put the knowledgeable customer inside the pitcher's mind; it would follow his strategy and nail down his execution. It makes the fan a participant in his performance because it allows him—like the batter—to follow his pattern and guess what the next pitch is going to be.

There are scores of other things that can be done with the scoreboard. By setting up a closed-circuit television screen, you can very quickly rerun all disputed plays, giving the fan a chance to check his original view of the play against a slowed-up or frozen rerun. It would allow you to give your customers a second look at a brilliant catch or a key hit. It would, in short, fill up those empty spaces for you. It would keep the fan's mind engaged over something more than a fractional portion of the game.

The scoreboard can also be an aid and comfort during those long, dreary passages when the game is delayed by rain. While I have known people who enjoy taking long walks in the rain, I have yet to find the man who gets any pleasure out of sitting in the rain, waiting for it to stop.

In the scoreboard you have a prefabricated fresh-air theatre, built for rainy-day entertainment. All you have to do is set up a closed-circuit television screen and you can entertain your audience with anything from a follow-the-bouncing-baseball Community Sing to the pictures of last year's World Series. You can run interviews from the dressing room or from the press box. You are bound by nothing except taste and imagination.

In Chicago, we had plastic rain capes to pass out to the customers when it rained. (Since we had a contact in the Weather Bureau we were usually able to get information far enough in advance to have the capes distributed by the time the rains came.) This was a great promotion, because we were showing the fans that they were human beings to us, not just a damp and sticky mass. Still, if you are going to be a hustler you must always be looking for somebody else to pick up the check. In this case, it was Pepsi-Cola, which proudly emblazoned its name across the back of the capes. The fans were happy with their capes, Pepsi-Cola was happy with the advertising and I was happy because I had touched all the bases. I have very little use for any man who would knock universal joy and happiness.

The advertising doesn't detract from the gift. It adds to it. What you have to understand is that we are living in the age of Television, which means that the smallest child is aware that "sustaining" is a synonym for failure (they'll be off the air in 16 weeks), while to be sponsored is to have achieved the ultimate success.

The same situation obtained when we gave away bats. Originally, we gave them away ourselves. In the end, they bore the Coca-Cola label. The kids were delighted with receiving a gift from both the White Sox and Coca-Cola.

Bat Day has become the biggest promotion in baseball of late. We started it in St. Louis back in 1952 when a guy who dealt in bankrupt firms came around with a shipload of homeless bats. I foisted him off on Rudie Schaffer, and Rudie worked out a deal in which we paid 11¢ for every finished bat, and the guy threw in all the unfinished ones for free. This gave us some indication why the firm had gone bankrupt, since the wood alone was worth more than we were paying.

Rudie came back and suggested that we give them away on Father's Day, and it has only taken the Yankees 13 years to do the same thing. (If there were a cruel and malicious critic in the house he might point out that this could be the first year they have been in a position to give bats away, because it is the first year they are not using them themselves.)

In 1965, Bat Day has drawn record crowds in Detroit, Minneapolis, New York and Kansas City. It is a surefire promotion, and it will remain surefire so long as they don't get greedy and try to repeat it on alternate weeks.

They probably will.

Suppose you have no electronically treated scoreboard, though. Now how are you going to provide fun and frolic in the rain? Well, what have you got to work with? The first thing that happens when it rains is that a marching band of poker players runs out to pull a tarpaulin over the field. A tarpaulin is, to all practical purposes, a horizontal billboard. If you can get a sponsor for a rain cape, think what you should be able to do with a tarpaulin covering an area of 110' x 110'!

Logically, it would only seem to be a matter of figuring out the best possible tie-in. At least that's what I thought. When I was in Chicago, I offered the Morton Salt people exclusive tarpaulin rights for their slogan, "When it Rains it Pours," which I thought was a cute idea. They somehow didn't. Ah well, there must be a tie-in somewhere with Diamond Salt.

If you were looking for a sponsor today, how about those people who make the cereals from Checkerboard Square? We could print a checkerboard pattern on the tarpaulin and have the checker champions on each ball club battle it out from their respective dugouts. To keep the game from dragging, we would have pretty girls in bathing suits hopping around from square to square to represent the checker pieces.

If we really wanted to go highbrow we could make it a chess game. Hey, we could hire a roving band of midgets and dress them in costumes that would be exact replicas of the chess pieces. Gee, wouldn't that be great!

But, again, never advertise what you're going to do. Let them wonder. Have them hoping it will rain just to see what you've dreamed up for them this time. And maybe the people who didn't come to the game will look to the skies, as they sit in their lonely offices, and wonder too.

Now that we are well versed in the fundamentals we can proceed to individual promotions:

DATE NIGHT: This is a promotion that is designed partic- ularly for Washington. Government work has been luring single unattached females into Washington for countless years, and neither the New Deal, the New Frontier nor the Great Society has been able to solve the problem of Washington's shortage of eligible—or even available—males.

Washington also happens to be a city whose social life revolves around embassy parties, which leaves the average working girl and the average working guy without very much to do. It is the manifest destiny of the ball club, as they say around that State Department, to fill the social void. The mechanics of bringing them together are simple enough. On the designated night, single men will be sold only the even-numbered seats, and single women only the odd-numbered ones. For those timid ladies who prefer to come in pairs, we will have a few sections where they can buy two seats together with the men's seats flanking them on both sides.

Once they're in the park they're on their own, although it should be perfectly evident that the prevailing spirit of gaiety and adventure will make the encounters natural and the introductions easy. As hosts, we just might feel called upon to provide party favors and entertainment. And, of course, the dance we will hold on the ball field after the game should provide ample opportunity for all new friends to test their congeniality.

LIGHT TOWERS: I have already mentioned that I had projects galore to present in conjunction with the scoreboard. Its main identifying feature, the small war that follows a home run, was designed to make the home run the grand and noble event it used to be. Everything loses its novelty, though, and you have to be alert for the time when the fireworks are dismissed as just another border incident.

The inspiration for the exploding scoreboard came, as I have publicly confessed, from the rousing pinball finale in Saroyan's *Time of Your Life*. Back when Saroyan and I were both boys, I was impressed just as strongly by the tremendously imaginative stage effects in the play *All Quiet on the Western Front*, wherein they were able to create the illusion of a battle by flashing the stage lights off and on in weird and remarkable combinations.

Well, we have lights in the ball park too. They sit atop those huge light towers and seem to look down over the park like great birds of prey. By attaching a rheostat to each tower we would be able to feed prepunched tapes through the circuit and have the lights flashing on and off in any pattern we desired, even to the spelling out of names. With those lights flashing on and off against the dark background of the night, and the bombs and the sound track blasting away from the scoreboard, it would seem as if the whole city were under attack.

I had something else worked out in conjunction with the flashing of the park lights. I was going to have a siren attached to the bottom of every light post, each one in a different key.

As the batter hits a home run and starts around the bases the first siren sounds, then—a pitch higher—comes a second siren, and then a third and a fourth until—as the runner heads for the plate—he is accompanied by a full siren concert, a wild and exultant chord. If it is done right, we should achieve nothing short of pandemonium.

This is a good promotion, as I think you will agree, but it is not yet a hustler's promotion. It's too expensive. Before it becomes a promotion that will heat up the cockles of a hustler's heart, you have to find somebody who will quietly pick up the check while you are sitting by, being humble but taking all the credit.

Well, I don't think it would be very hard to sell a few advertisements on your light towers, since all eyes will automatically be turned to them (to say nothing of the devouring eye of the TV camera) as soon as the ball disappears and the lights begin to flash. Experience tells me that we'd have to call in reinforcements to beat the advertisers off.

TICKETS: Tickets are the one thing you put into every customer's hands. There is no reason, therefore, not to have the tickets working for you. When I was operating in Chicago, I latched onto the picture-collecting madness that hits all kids of a certain age by putting pictures of the White Sox players on the backs of all our tickets. The old man brought the picture home to his kid, the kid had a collection going and we had an advertisement in the house.

(That's why you give out schedules. Schedules are conveniences to the fan, but they are an advertisement for the ball club. It is also why you should try to make your scorecard so interesting that it will be taken home as a souvenir instead of dropped in the aisle among the peanut shells.)

The pictures caught on so nicely that the kids began to go for the whole set. Their parents wouldn't call to ask for a seat in their favorite place, they'd ask for a seat in "the Nellie Fox section."

Once you begin to look upon the backs of tickets as space on which you can doodle, other ideas have got to come to you. Like, say, a legalized pool? On the back of every ticket, you list all the games for the coming week and invite the customers to guess the scores. What do you mean it isn't legal! You've made it legal by setting up an arrangement with some gentlemen sportsmen in Las Vegas. The customer has only to fill out the form, which is detachable, and mail it to the indicated address.

Look what you have accomplished. You have not only got the fan to study the entire schedule for the upcoming week, you have got him involved in the outcome of each game. You have, through your devious devices, made him happy by giving him something extra, and you have made yourself happy by getting your ticket into his home.

The tickets could also be used as ballots for various contests or public opinion samplings. With all the talk about finding a Commissioner who can fill the legendary Ford Frick's shoes (who can *what?*) wouldn't it be a capital idea to ask the fans to suggest a candidate of their own? There is a widespread feeling abroad in the land that baseball doesn't much care what their customers think ("Just leave your money at the box office and shaddup"). There has never, it would seem to me, been a better time to try to con them into thinking that they have a voice in the naming of the Chief Executive. (In the naming of the *what?*)

If universal suffrage is a good enough way to elect the President of the United States, it ought to be almost good enough for baseball.

HOME-RUN DERBY: In Baltimore and Washington, the National Brewery Co. has a television promotion I had a little something to do with. It goes like this: In every game, one inning is designated as the Home-Run Derby inning. In order to participate, the radio listener or TV viewer sends in the bottom of one of the beer sponsor's six-packs along with the inning in which he wants to be represented. Since the H-R Derby moves from inning to inning, day by day, you *know* that everybody is going to send in 9 entries so that he will be in the running no matter which inning is designated.

On the designated inning, each batter is hitting for a viewer whose name has been picked out of the box. If the first batter steps up and hits a home run for Mr. Smith, then Mr. Smith has won $1,000. If the batter does not hit a home run, Mr. Smith is entitled to 10 tickets to any game of his choosing, and the next batter comes to the plate to flex his muscles for Mr. Jones.

If nobody hits a home run during the inning, the prize goes to $1,100 the following day.

OK. A good promotion if you happen to be the beer company sponsoring the ball game. If you are the operator of the ball club, nothing. Less than nothing. The guy staying home watching the game is getting more out of it than the customer in the park.

So why not do the same thing inside the park, using the license-plate numbers of the customers? You hire a reputable auditing firm to send a representative around the parking lot to jot down about 100 different plate numbers from widely scattered sections. As each batter comes to the plate in the Home-Run Derby inning, somebody from the same firm will draw one of the numbers out of a hat.

Now you have some real excitement. The guy hearing his name called out at home has nobody except himself and his immediate family to get excited for him. In the park, a guy jumps up and shouts, "That's ME." The announcement of each license-plate number is awaited with great anticipation, followed by the groan of disappointment and then the renewed buzzing as everybody looks around to see whether he has a winner in his section.

Each guy will have his whole section rooting for him. If you don't win yourself, you can at least go home and say that a guy only a few rows back from you did.

Got the idea? All right, your homework for tonight is to bring in three new and highly stimulating promotions of your own. You can forget anything I may have said about a hustler being entitled to steal other people's ideas with impunity. Just remember that neatness and originality count, and we don't sign any waivers.

2

⊜ ⊜ ⊜

Image, Image on the Wall
Which of Us Took the
Greater Fall?

A HUSTLER, as I'm sure you understand by now, would rather be taken in a game of three-card monte than be caught out in public thinking negatively. Who says wishing can't make it so! If you think something is going to happen, you will act as if it is going to happen and every once in a while —do you know what?—it actually happens.

On the other hand, it is always well to leave yourself an avenue of escape, in the unlikely event that through some unthinkable and unforeseeable contingency—such as your own inadequacy—your project should collapse. It does your reputation no good at all, students, to paint yourself into a corner. Rowdies smirk, gentlewomen blush and small children avert their eyes.

As long as you have been foresighted enough to leave yourself an escape hatch, you can scoot out, grab your high hat and cane and do a couple of turns at the old soft shoe, a splendid diversionary tactic. You weren't painting at all, see? You were really polishing the dance floor for the Mardi Gras ball.

(Sportsmen—who inhabit the other end of the spectrum—are entitled to paint themselves into corners at will. The true sportsman is expected to be lovable and inefficient. And rich. His function is to finish in the second division and lose as much money as possible. This gives him an air of austerity and makes him a public benefactor. We don't want no public benefactors around here.)

If you cannot get out gracefully, the recommended alternative is to turn the situation inside out and make a big promotion out of *not* being able to get out gracefully. At times such as this you have to be prepared to eat not only crow, but sparrows, sparrow hawks, roadrunners and even an underslung ostrich or two.

When everybody all around you is shouting "Drop Dead," don't. Turn humble. That will fix them.

I was faced with just such a deplorable situation in Cleveland in 1947 when I tried to trade Louis Boudreau for half the St. Louis Browns' ball club. Although the deal collapsed on me, the story broke as if it were still in negotiation. From Cleveland there came cries of fury at the thought that I might deprive them of their beloved Boy Manager.

I had to leave the World Series and go rushing back to Cleveland to let them talk me out of a deal that had already collapsed. I had to go marching from mass meeting to mass meeting, chanting *mea culpa, mea culpa* as I went.

In the long run, you reap grand profit from such exertions in self-abasement because everybody comes to realize that—misguided though you undoubtedly were—you were only doing what you thought was best for everybody. I didn't appreciate Louie? Me? Me? What other player in baseball, fellow fans, could possibly be traded for an entire club?

The fans are perfectly willing to forgive and forget because you are admitting to them that they are smarter than you. In Cleveland, I could only hope that Boudreau would live up to their expectations so that each of them could think, That silly jerk Veeck would have traded him if it hadn't been for us....

It was perfectly all right to let it be known later—much, much later—that the deal had already collapsed, because by then it had become a family joke and we could all laugh about the fun we had all had together.

In St. Louis and New York last season, you had the curiously reversed situation where both teams failed to protect themselves against the off-chance of winning. Having planned on the worst, they were painted into the corner by success. There was no avenue of retreat and both operators were notably lacking in the ability to turn humble.

If you cannot turn humble, you had better learn how to turn the other cheek, because harsh and heavy blows are about to fall upon you from the great, unseen world.

The 1964 World Series, baseball's annual version of the Coronation, was followed by some highly amusing moments of low comedy and high intrigue as pennant-winning managers went bouncing around the landscape with an abandon not seen in these parts since Frank Lane departed the scene. The analyzers and second-guessers haven't had so much fun since the Bay of Pigs.

Needless to say, fiascoes of this dimension do not come about unless there has been some high-powered brainwork going on in the higher executive echelons. What had happened was that the duly commissioned thinkers, in both St. Louis and New York, had both quit cold on their teams a couple of months before the season had come to an end. Branch Rickey and Gussie Busch had forsaken all hope for the Cardinals, and Ralph Houk had written off the season in New York. Fall Guys were badly needed and, in baseball, the manager has historically been assigned the duty of exposing the jugular before he exits, bleeding. Otherwise, the operator might have to blame himself and that might shake his confidence in his own infallibility.

The trouble really began when the players on both teams—a cranky lot of positive thinkers—neglected to quit on themselves. The repercussions were terrible to behold. Before the carrousel had stopped spinning, all the riders were so far out of character that Gussie Busch, the last living patroon, came very close to joining the humble rich. If this kind of thing isn't stopped at once, the meek *will* inherit the earth, and then what's left for the Democratic platform committee to promise us?

The hero emergent was Johnny Keane, a certified member of the meek and humble. Keane entered the month of September holding an empty hand and walked out of the first week of October holding everything any mortal man could reasonably wish for, including the universal esteem of his countrymen. He also held his own little secret.

With all due respect to Johnny Keane, if there was a hero in this latest chapter of labor-management relations it was Bing Devine.

The darker side of this morality play was very brilliantly represented, in the popular accounts, by Gussie Busch, who rides lead horse for Anheuser-Busch, and our old friend Branch Rickey, the man who taught Machiavelli the strike zone.

Morality plays are for children, converts or true believers. They carry the thrilling message that we are right and you are wrong. Life, thank goodness, is more variegated than that. Life is the interplay of personalities, the strains and stresses of conflicting friendships and loyalties, the graspings of ambition and the clashes of pride. Life was busting out all over St. Louis during the last six weeks of the 1964 season.

Gussie Busch is an old friend and I like him. But one thing you've got to say about Gussie—he's got that certain indefinable insensitivity. Item: I decided I had better get out of town back in 1952, after Gussie bought the Cardinals, because he was smarter, handsomer and he had better posture. He was also richer, wealthier and he had more money. The American League in its assembled wisdom had other plans for me, though, having little to do with making me as rich or as handsome as Gussie— or even with improving my posture. In my final year in St. Louis —known to lovers of freedom everywhere as the Year of the Bastille—I devised a grand design. Put simply, my grand design was to stay alive. As part of this devilishly clever plot, I sold

Sportsman's Park to Anheuser-Busch for $1,100,000 and all the repairs they could find.

One of the minor inconveniences of this transaction was that my wife, my son and I had to evacuate the apartment we had built right into the park.

Gussie, being a nice man, decided to help us by buying whatever of the furnishings he could use. He came to the door with that entourage of yes-men and sycophants who surround him wherever he goes, clearing away all pockets of air resistance and breathing up any loose smog lingering in the atmosphere. Well, I really shouldn't say they're all sycophants; I haven't met them all.

Gussie was sensitive enough to the delicacy of the situation that he instructed his entourage to wait out by the entrance while he wandered through the apartment, buying this and buying that. I stood by, somewhat startled, shuffling my feet and clearing my throat in my usual dynamic and forceful way. I knew that he was trying to be a good guy and that I should have been suitably grateful but—broke though I was—I hadn't really intended to auction off my home. I mean my posture didn't improve at all during the subsequent half hour.

I tell this story here only to make the point that it was this same insensitivity that turned the Keane affair into a complete debacle for Busch.

The story of that fiasco really began one night in Hollywood in the fall of 1962, when Busch dropped by the Brown Derby to say hello to the innkeeper, his old friend Bob Cobb. Cobb also happens to be a close friend of Branch Rickey. Cobb was president and principal owner of the old Hollywood Stars in the Pacific Coast League when Rickey was running the Pittsburgh Pirates, and Branch had entered into a working agreement with him and provided enough useful players to keep the club respectable.

As Cobb commiserated with Busch upon the evil days that had befallen the Cardinals, they began to reminisce about the grand old days when the Gas House Gang were running over everything in the League.

"You know the fellow you need to restore the old tradition?" said Cobb, a loyal man. "The old master himself, Branch Rickey."

Branch was no more than a rising eighty years old and in semiretirement, but when Cobb saw that he had Busch interested he contacted Rickey, who expressed interest. Busch himself then contacted Papa Branch, and before you could say "A bottle of Bud" a hundred times fast, Rickey was on his way back to St. Louis as Gussie's personal adviser.

From that moment on, there was blood on the moon. The only question left to be answered was whether Busch was in for a mild embarrassment or complete disaster. I'll give you a hint: Don't go to Gussie Busch with any new programs for putting senior citizens back to work.

Busch already had a general manager in Bing Devine. Since Bing had somehow conceived the idea that his duties included advising the boss about running the ball club, he may be forgiven if he didn't exactly view the triumphant return of Rickey as a personal testimonial to the grand job he was doing. Especially since Bing could not help but be aware that Busch, who likes forceful, dynamic figures like . . . well, like Busch himself, had always felt that Bing was too soft, too nice, too easygoing.

Hiring Branch Rickey is not quite the same as hiring a passing stranger to keep the books in order. Everybody in baseball except Busch and a few other equally well-informed owners was perfectly aware that Papa Branch is constitutionally incapable of moving into any kind of an organization without maneuvering to establish himself as the dominant force. Better to have asked Winston Churchill to run to the corner to get Lord Attlee a Coke than to have expected Papa Branch to subordinate his personality to Bing Devine's.

This wonderful situation had come about because Busch had faithfully followed the advice of a saloonkeeper. What a splendid way to run an organization!

To make things even better, the relationship between Bing Devine and his manager was unusually close. Both had come up the hard way, through the Cardinals' minor league system. Keane had been kicking around, it seemed, almost from the beginning of time. Devine had run across him in his own early days when he was running the Rochester club for the Cards and Keane was his manager. When Devine was appointed general manager of the Cards (following the departure of Frank Lane), he brought Keane up as a coach and, as soon as the opportunity arose, surprised everybody by making him the manager.

Or maybe it wasn't so surprising after all. With the front office doing everything these days except flashing the hit-and-run sign, the anonymous, colorless organization manager has become standard equipment. Still, if anyone ever looked like an interim choice his name was Johnny Keane.

It is not that he isn't the kind of manager Rickey himself might have chosen, either. Keane's great defect in Rickey's eyes was that he was Bing Devine's man.

Rickey started right out by making himself as popular in St. Louis as he had been in his final days in Pittsburgh, where the loyal fans had to be restrained from honoring him with such tokens of their affection as a fully paid trip back to the Brown Derby plus a full carload of tar (with optional feathers). His first suggestion was that Stan Musial should retire for the good of the team. To encourage those players who remained, he announced that they could not possibly finish in the first division.

It seemed that Branch's thinking had undergone a radical change in his latter years, proving that his mind had not grown rigid with the passage of time. The man who used to go from town to town, convincing National League operators that the only way to build a contending team was by trading with the talent-rich clubs—such as, it happened, his Cardinals—was now of the opinion that the structure of the game had changed to the point where it was impossible to build a pennant-winner through trades. It was really a stunning coincidence, one notes, that when it came to trading, the quickest gun in baseball happened to be Bing Devine's. Before Rickey came to town Bing had swung a dandy little trade for Dick Groat, and it was perhaps fortunate for him that Groat moved the Cardinals right up into contention and almost into the pennant.

Or maybe it wasn't. Bing had traded so well that Busch entered the 1964 season convinced that he had an excellent chance to finally win his first pennant. Instead, the Cardinals spent the first half of the season spluttering around in the second division—in part, my experience tells me, because the ball club had to adjust to a lineup that did not have Stan Musial as the wheelhorse around whom the rest of the hitters could rally. Never underestimate the psychological importance of the one big hitter in the lineup.

Rickey never did hide his dissatisfaction with Johnny Keane. Why should he? He was getting paid to advise Busch, wasn't he? If his criticism of Keane also happened to rub off on Devine, the man who had hired him and still defended him, that was scarcely Papa Branch's fault.

Keane was too mild, Rickey insisted, too soft. His players had little respect for him, they talked behind his back, they second-guessed his strategy. Well, of course they did. If U.S. Grant had been leading an army of baseball players, they'd have second-guessed him all the way to the doorknob of the Appomattox Courthouse.

Still, in fairness to Branch, the anti-Keane sentiment went considerably beyond the usual griping. There were 8 or 9 players who were not particularly reluctant to let it be known that the only thing wrong with the Cardinals was their manager. The most openly critical of the players was Dick Groat, a team leader.

With the Cardinals going so bad and the situation deteriorating so rapidly, Bing Devine decided to move in and do what he could to save his man's job. He called in Dick Groat and told him as forcefully as possible that he should apologize to Keane before the whole club.

"That sounds pretty silly to me," Groat told him. "If I'm going to apologize there ought to be eight or nine other guys lining up right behind me. But if you really think it will help the club, okay. Call your meeting and for whatever good it will do, I'll apologize."

Well, this may have been an effective way of shutting the players up but it obviously wasn't going to change anybody's opinion. What Devine was really doing was showing the players that he was standing solidly behind his manager. And whatever they thought of Keane, all the players did like Bing Devine.

And now, we come to one of those accidents of timing that are so frustrating to all of us who like to believe that there is an order to life which we can determine by the quickness of our minds and the strength of our resolve. Earlier in the week, a friend of Gussie's had bumped into Eddie Matthews out of town and begun to kid him about the "dissension" that was supposed to exist on the Milwaukee ball club.

"What are *you* laughing about?" Eddie said. "We may have some problems on our club, but we don't have any more than you people have on yours."

When he got back to St. Louis, Gussie's friend asked him, casually, whether there was anything to what Matthews had said. "Oh, he had to be kidding," Gussie said. "If there's any dissension on the club I'd know about it."

Within a short time after the clubhouse meeting, Devine and Keane were called to the brewery for a routine meeting with Busch to discuss the ball club before the Cards went on the road.

And right here we come to a second maddening accident of timing. The one man who has the ability to move easily between Busch and the hired hands is Dick Meyer, a brewery executive who helps out along the baseball front. Meyer is completely loyal to Busch, but he has such a fine diplomatic touch that it has become customary for all the baseball people to seek his advice before any meeting with Busch. Devine wanted to ask Meyer whether he and Keane should tell Gussie about Groat's apology and about the general sniping that had led up to it. Meyer, they were told, was tied up in a meeting of his own.

That left Bing and Johnny to come to some decision on their own as they were driving out to the brewery. Devine—still out to protect his manager—decided that if Gussie indicated he knew anything about it they'd tell him the full story, but that if Gussie didn't bring it up there was nothing to be gained by bringing it up themselves.

The conference turned out to be a short, routine affair. As they were going out the door, however, Gussie, remembering the Matthews gibe, called out almost as an afterthought, "Bing . . . there isn't any dissension or anything like that on the club, is there?"

Bing, taken by surprise, went the way he was mentally pitched to go. He answered that there wasn't. Busch then asked Keane the same question. Johnny hesitated for a moment and then he said, "No, there isn't."

Driving back to town, they both knew the fat was in the fire. No matter how they might rationalize it, they knew that they had deliberately misled Busch. When they arrived at the ball park they went right up to Meyer's office, and this time he was available.

Meyer had to tell them they had made a bad mistake. If Busch feels he is entitled to one thing above all else from his employees, it is absolute loyalty. The only possible way to salvage the situation, Meyer decided, was for him to tell Busch the true situation as quickly as possible. Either Meyer called Rickey in to support him, or Busch called Rickey in after he heard the story to advise him.

Predictably, Busch was furious. "What kind of games are they playing," he protested, "that they lie to me when I ask them point-blank and then go right down and tell you? I thought I was the owner of this team, but it seems that everybody down to the bat boy knows what's going on before I do. Well, I'm going to fire them both!"

Branch Rickey warned him that it would look very bad to fire both the general manager and manager in the middle of the year. Rickey's advice was to fire Keane but not Devine.

Busch could see the logic in not bouncing them together. His candidate for the outer darkness, however, was Devine. He could understand, he said, that Keane might believe that his primary loyalty was to his players. Yes, a manager did have to protect his players. But Devine, as general manager, was a company man. He was supposed to be Busch's eye in the organization. Devine's loyalty, he maintained, should have gone unquestionably to the owner, not to the manager.

Keane could stay on to the end of the season, Gussie decided, but Devine was through.

This may seem like a silly and trivial reason for firing the top man in your organization. Except for one thing. There are no silly or trivial reasons for firing a man you'd like to get rid of anyway. I think we are safe in saying that if Gussie's confidence in Bing had not already been undermined, Bing wouldn't have had to suffer through anything worse than a stiff lecture on the responsibilities of corporate management.

Rickey, a most unlikely advocate, continued to argue that Keane was the man who should be fired, not Devine. Guessing Rickey's motives is a game the baseball world has been playing, with indifferent success, for 50 years. Branch, being nobody's fool, would know how the press was going to handle the firing of Devine and he could guess what wise old octogenarian was going to be accused of having stabbed him in the back. Branch might be willing to risk that in order to get rid of Bing, but with Bing so completely out of favor, Branch would be in complete command, anyway.

Besides, Papa Branch's instinct for survival has always been very sharp. If they started firing general managers instead of managers, who knew who might be next? There is, of course, one other possibility we have to face up to manfully. Rickey may have been trying to do nothing more than give Busch the best possible advice.

The one time Gussie should have listened to Branch, he didn't. After he had cooled down a little, he did decide to follow Rickey's counsel to one small extent. He decided to delay Devine's execution for a few days so that he would be in a position to introduce his new general manager, preferably a well-known one, at the same time he was announcing the regrettable retirement of Devine.

How do I know this? Oh, come on now! You mean you can't guess what universally beloved and thoroughly unemployed operator eventually came into his mind?

I was reclining comfortably on my sofa watching the 11-o'clock news and dreaming my usual dreams of fame and fortune when I received a phone call from an old St. Louis friend. "I am authorized," he told me, "to offer you the job of running the Cardinals. You can pick your own title—general manager, president or whatever else you might want to call yourself—but you'll be in complete control and you can name your own figure. Wouldn't it be great to operate in St. Louis with all the money you need, Bill, instead of trying to make it on a short bankroll?"

Well, I've got my pride too. I reminded him that since I'd operated in Cleveland and Chicago with money pouring out of my tight little ears it would not really mark that unique a turn in my career.

"What about Devine?" I asked. "They're obviously getting ready to unload him. I wouldn't do that hastily if I were Gussie. He's got a good man there."

It was made clear to me that Bing was on the way out. Period. "The job is yours if you want it," he said. And then, quite unnecessarily, he emphasized, "I'm speaking for Mr. Busch, you understand."

"Look," I told him. "I'm very flattered. I'd be lying if I said I wasn't flattered. But I'll tell you something. You have to work just as hard operating a club for someone else as for yourself.

If I couldn't buy a substantial piece of the club I wouldn't be interested, and obviously, Mr. Busch isn't going to sell me any stock."

The following morning my friend called me again. "I want you to understand that I just wasn't out on the town last night," he said. "I'm authorized officially to offer you the job again now that you've had a chance to sleep on it."

"I can only tell you officially that I don't want it," I said. "I think you should keep Devine."

"That," he said, "has become impossible."

On August 17, three or four days later, Devine was fired. When I called Bing to express my regrets, he said, "Hey, you were offered the job, weren't you? I heard you turned it down."

With Bing out, Rickey brought in Bob Howsam, who had once run the Denver franchise in the American Association.

On August 28, the Los Angeles Dodgers came to town. Busch, listening to the game from his farm, heard Leo Durocher being interviewed after one of the games. Leo was saying what a great job Gene Mauch was doing in leading the Phillies to the pennant. Durocher was so impressed that he gave Mauch the highest praise within his power to confer; he said that Mauch managed a club just like Leo Durocher. In discussing his own fallen fortunes, however, Leo grew humble. During the days when he was being offered managerial jobs, he said, he had been too arrogant. He had either turned the jobs down flatly or demanded a piece of the ball club. Now that he was willing to manage on any terms, Leo said, there were no offers.

Busch had always liked the Durocher type of manager so much that he had hired two imitation Durochers, Eddie Stanky and Solly Hemus. When the original was called so forcefully to his mind, Busch immediately put in a call to the station and arranged for Leo to come to the farm secretly the following morning. What Gussie told Leo in effect was: "Look, it's no secret that we're thinking of making a change next year. If we do, and if you're available, I want you to manage for me."

While that isn't a definite commitment, it's just about as close as you can come. Busch knew he would be looking for a manager at the end of the year, and so did Durocher and everybody else. As for Leo, there was no doubt whatsoever that he could make himself available at a moment's notice.

Leo being Leo, the word soon went out along all communication media, including Radio Free Europe, that he was all set to become the next Cardinal manager.

But, as everyone knows, the Cardinals—sparked by Devine's last acquisition, Lou Brock—suddenly got hot. You could see a nicely developing situation where the Cards could finish as high as second place, leaving Gussie in the embarrassing position of having already fired the man who had put the team together and now having to bounce the manager who had brought them home with such a rush.

The pennant? Naw, there's no chance of winning the pennant. It's Magic Number time, Mac. What do you want the Phillies to do for you, collapse?

And then, it was as if Somebody Up There blew a whistle. The Cards couldn't lose, the Phillies couldn't do anything *except* lose, and Gussie Busch had become the first right-handed beer baron to make himself look utterly ridiculous while winning a pennant and world's championship.

It had become unthinkable, impossible and unpolitic to fire Keane. The manager who had been publicly humiliated was now sitting pretty. "Isn't it great?" everybody was saying. "Keane is in a position now to keep Gussie on the griddle and then write his own ticket."

That wasn't necessarily the true situation, though. The true situation was that Keane had two good reasons, both unknown to the public, to kiss the Cardinals good-by.

For if Busch had gone out and hired himself a manager for the upcoming season, Keane may very well have hustled himself up another spot. On September 5, within a week after the Busch-Durocher conference, Keane was visited by an emissary of the Yankees and offered Yogi Berra's job. The Cards were in Chicago, the Yankees were in Kansas City, so I think we can say, with some confidence, that the offer was carried by Bill Bergash, who was then the Yankees' traveling secretary. Bergash, a former St. Louis hand, is a close friend of Keane's. When Johnny was managing in Omaha, Bergash was his general manager.

It should be emphasized here that at that moment, the Yankees—like everyone else—were aware that Keane was a lame-duck manager. The Cardinals were 7½ games out of first place, the Yankees were 4 games out and neither side thought for one moment there was any chance that only one month later, they would be facing each other in the World Series.

A week after the original agreement, a Yankee official with the authority to hire—and there are never a great many of those—came to Chicago, where the Cardinals were playing, to seal the deal with a handshake.

Gussie Busch knew nothing about this. With 6 games to go and the Cards still a game and a half behind, the Cards returned to St. Louis for a 3-game series with the Phils. Gussie Busch came into the clubhouse before the first game and told Keane he wanted to rehire him. Keane answered that he had a lot on his mind and preferred to wait until the series was over.

Three days later, after the Cards had swept the series, Busch made his offer again. Keane again told him he preferred to wait.

After the Cards had won the pennant on the final day of the season, Busch came to the clubhouse and made his offer for a third time. At the victory party that same night, he told Keane, "If it's only money, that's no problem. We'll pay you what you want."

"Let's wait," Keane said, "until after the World Series."

At last, with the Series over and won, Busch came to Keane at the Series victory party and brought up the subject for the fifth time. "Look," Keane said, "we've got that press conference tomorrow. Let's wait until then."

Keane walked into the press conference and handed Gussie a letter, dated September 25 (three days *before* the Philadelphia series), informing him that he was quitting.

There was nothing, however, to have prevented Keane from tearing up that letter. The routine agreement between a manager who was out of a job and a ball club that had decided to fire its own manager had become an embarrassment to both sides. (So much so that both sides have stoutly maintained that no such agreement ever existed.) Through the freak of the Phillies' collapse in one league and the Yankees' resurgence in the other, the World Series opened with the manager in one dugout having agreed to manage the team in the opposing dugout.

The easiest way out for both Keane and Houk would have been for Keane to sign with the Cards again. He could have written his own ticket with the Cardinals for a couple of years, and then come on to New York with either Devine (who had signed on with the Mets) or with the Yankees.

The only trouble was that the obvious solution was unthinkable for Keane. He was in a position to write his own ticket, he knew, only because Bing Devine had lost his job trying to protect him. If Busch had managed to place himself in a position where the higher his team finished, the worse he had to look, then Keane was in a position where the better a deal he could make for himself the worse he would be selling himself out.

Forget the agreement with the Yankees. As a decent man, he had to quit.

The most interesting part of the whole affair, as far as I was concerned, was that it never seemed to occur to Busch, even in the face of Keane's stalling, that his manager wasn't merely maneuvering to make the best possible deal. Busch was perfectly aware that Keane understood that Devine had been fired for protecting him. But guys like Keane, he clearly understands, are purchasable. His whole life has led him to believe they are purchasable. Busch had only to make a quick inspection of any of his plants and he would find a couple of Johnny Keanes on every floor working—shall we say—at a supervisory level.

What is Johnny Keane? He's a baseball manager. In all the

world, there are only 20 jobs available in that MOS and Gussie Busch is the sole proprietor of one of them. Walk away? You've got to be kidding.

It all builds up, as we know, to the press conference at which the signing is to be officially announced and recorded. Now, let's be honest about this. The colorless if no longer anonymous Johnny Keane did display a most laudable sense of the dramatic and a sure instinct for the jugular. Keane set Busch up so that he would be waiting there with the blank contract, and then he slit his throat.

Keane's instincts were faultless. He and Devine had been treated shabbily, and the luck of the draw had put him in a position where he could make a statement for every working-man in the country.

For what Keane was saying was, "See here, Mr. Busch. Baseball doesn't really belong to you rich guys who buy ball clubs as advertising gimmicks or toys. It belongs to the guys like me and Bing who invest only the years of our lives. It is just about time that you were told that there are things that are purchasable in the relationship between men and things that are not. What is not purchasable is basic dignity and basic loyalty."

The blank contract sitting in Busch's hand became the perfect prop, because it let everyone know that Keane was telling him, "You do not have enough money, beer or bottle caps ever to hire me to work for you again."

Oh, he did it gently—just the kiss-off of the hops—but when it was over, Gussie knew that he had been told. Some of the writers who were there have told me that Gussie went into a state of shock. They told me that if Keane hadn't stayed around and drawn the questions to himself, the conference would have ended in total shambles.

Poor Gussie. After 13 years, he had finally won a championship and all he seemed to be getting out of it was abuse. For the first time in his life the St. Louis papers, which had always treated him with the utmost respect, ripped into him.

Well, let me tell you something. August A. Busch didn't buy

a ball club and win a World Championship in order to be criticized in the public prints. More to the point, August A. Busch is able to digest anything except the suspicion that he is being made to look ridiculous. August A. Busch has reached the time in his life where he has come to look upon himself as the patriarch of St. Louis, and to give him his due, he quite probably is. A scapegoat was urgently needed. A sacrificial lamb. And lo, August Busch looked all around and there was nobody in sight except the venerable Branch Rickey.

Busch suggested to Rickey that it would be far better for the organization from the public-relations standpoint if he were replaced. Rickey agreed. While Papa Branch was pushed a little, he really did resign.

But since "resignation" has come to be a four-syllable word meaning "fired," everybody assumed (as they were meant to assume) that it had really been Papa Branch's fault all along. There's no doubt about it, Mr. Rickey served Mr. Busch far better in the going than in the coming.

To me, the most remarkable part of this whole weird series of events is the complete reversal of form in everyone involved. Branch Rickey, a man who had spent his life leading sacrificial lambs to the slaughter, finds himself, at the age of eighty-three, in that most unaccustomed and uncomfortable role himself. He is out of a job. He is widely suspected of having talked Busch into firing Devine (although he actually tried to talk him out of it) and of having attempted to maneuver Busch into hiring Durocher to replace Keane (although the meeting between Busch and Durocher took place without his knowledge).

And look at Bing Devine. The general manager is, by definition, the man who fires the manager to take the heat off himself. This time, the general manager is fired for protecting the manager, a turnabout that could shake the whole general-manager dodge to its foundations.

Gussie Busch, the man who has grown accustomed to watching people jump at his command—and even in anticipation of his command—finds himself kicked in the groin by his manager and mugged by the press.

His performance through it all made you wince. At the end of the year, they threw a banquet for Bing Devine in St. Louis in honor of his selection as Baseball Executive of the Year which, come to think about it, is a pretty weird final scene itself. Every baseball man from the Midwest was in attendance. Everyone, that is, except Gussie Busch. Meyer and a couple of the other guys from the brewery were there—Gussie would have made sure of that. But Gussie had an appointment out of town—he would have made sure of that too. He should have attended, of course. He *knew* he should have attended. He should have made a self-deprecatory, wryly humorous speech. He should have said something like, "I feel like the man who is watching his mother-in-law go over the cliff in his new car. I come to you with mixed feeling." The moment screamed for him to show that he could accept defeat graciously. But, you know, he couldn't bring himself to go that far. I think Gussie was afraid that maybe, just maybe, he might be booed.

And yet, why shouldn't he be sore at Bing? Gussie deserved that award himself. Of course he did. No matter how you look at it, Busch started the Cards on their way to the pennant when he fired Bing Devine. We have all read how the St. Louis players, incensed beyond belief at learning that their beloved manager was about to be fired, banded together—a doughty crew—and vowed to go out there and show Gussie Busch and the whole wide world how greatly they respected him.

Well, that wasn't quite the way it happened. The thoughts that ran through most of their heads went more like this: "Holy smokes, we've lost Bing's job for him with all that sharpshooting and we're still stuck with Keane. How could anyone have figured that?" Having bowed their heads in brief memory of Bing, their thoughts then quite naturally turned to themselves and their own futures. Almost all of them were Bing's boys, and Bing was known to be a ballplayer's lamb. Branch Rickey was now in the saddle, they knew, and whatever else might be said for Branch he has never shown any inordinate affection, respect or loyalty to his players.

The Cardinals—that doughty crew—were overcome by an irresistible urge to protect their jobs. Complacency instantly disappeared. Lethargy was instantly overcome. The Cards became a running, hitting, fielding, fighting, hustling ball club.

For all the wrong reasons, Gussie Busch had pulled off the most brilliant front-office move of the generation. As a direct result of this move, the Cardinals became World Champions. Are you going to tell me that this didn't entitle him to a plaque worth maybe a couple of hundred dollars?

After Keane quit, Busch did what he had to do. He hired a local hero, Red Schoendienst. But Gussie is an honorable man. Before he hired Schoendienst, he called Leo Durocher. "I told you that you would be my manager if the job was open," he said. "But under the circumstances I can't hire you. I know I've gone back on my agreement. What do I owe you?"

Leo has never been famous for his charitable impulses, but where baseball is concerned he does have a code of his own. Leo has always said that if you didn't want him to work for you, he didn't want your money, a code which would have wrecked Rogers Hornsby's highly profitable career as a non-manager. Leo sticks to it. "If I can't work for you," he told Busch, "I don't want your money."

Besides, Leo is a riverboat gambler. He'd rather stay in the running for the big prize, just in case Gussie finds himself looking for a manager again in the near future. Money, Leo can always get.

What about Johnny Keane? Here is the most out-of-character figure of them all. Keane is normally the guy you see hanging around the lobby during any baseball meeting, hoping to catch on with somebody. That isn't meant to downgrade his abilities. Sure, he's a good baseball man, much traveled and widely experienced. Do you know how many good, solid baseball men —much traveled and widely experienced—are hanging around lobbies looking for jobs in today's shrinking market?

But Johnny Keane, the man who normally gets fired, wasn't hanging around any lobbies. Johnny Keane was sitting there with his choice between the two pennant winners. Johnny Keane, the man who gets fired, ended up as manager of the New York Yankees, the number-one job in baseball.

And the reversal of character holds even here. The Yankees, who are accustomed to standing back haughtily and letting the applicants come to them, hat in hand, needed him at the time of the official signing almost as badly as Busch did.

When the Yankees won the pennant, the most astonished person in the country was Ralph Houk. Houk, like Busch and Rickey, had quit on his team, and he had quit on them with far less reason. The Cardinals didn't really have any right to win the pennant, and when they did Busch had already taken steps that were irretrievable. Houk decided in August that 1) the Yankees were going to lose; 2) that it was all Berra's fault and 3) that Yogi would therefore have to go. When they fooled him and won, he went ahead with his plan just as if they hadn't. Ralph Houk's ability to adjust his thinking is so slight that he could not bring himself to admit that having been wrong in August, he might do well to draw up a new set of plans in October.

Houk shares two qualities with Busch: a firm sense of purpose and a too often nonexistent sense of humor, although they are qualities that stem from entirely different sources. Busch's is the rigidity of the aristocrat that tells him he can do no wrong. Houk's is the rigidity of the combat leader which tells him that the mission must be accomplished whatever the opposition, whatever the odds.

As a combat leader, Houk would study the terrain, absorb the intelligence reports, map out the battle plan and attack. If the battle plan called for him to take a machine-gun nest, you could be confident that he would either take it or go down moving toward it. You could be equally confident that his men would follow him every step of the way.

If it turned out that the intelligence report was wrong, that the terrain was rougher than he had been told, that there was a machine gun hitting them from an unknown angle, he would still follow the battle plan and he would still either take his objective or go down moving toward it.

Which makes him a whale of a combat leader and a disastrous general.

As a manager, Houk had an absolute horror of being accused of pushing the panic button (there's the military background again and maybe even the secret fear). By his definition any change in plans is a sign of panic. Houk, for instance, has usually been most reluctant to bring up any player during the season. As far as he was concerned, he had very carefully picked his squad during spring training, considering every angle, filling every hole, and to call up some other player to fill some spot that was not being adequately covered was an admission that he had been wrong.

It worked for him as a manager. Of course, it helps a little to have a squad with the ability of the Yankees, but it also helps if you have the ability, which Ralph Houk does have in abundance, to convince the players that they can do anything you tell them they can do.

Unfortunately for Houk, the promotion to the front office brought out his worst quality, that total inability to improvise, and negated his greatest virtue, his ability to lead men.

To adjust one's plans to changing conditions is not, of course, a sign of panic at all. It is a sign of balance, of intelligence, of real leadership. Freezing to an outdated situation, that *is* a sign of panic.

When Houk wrote off the Yankees as early as he did, he was pushing the panic button, plain and simple. When he went ahead with the plans that had been made in anticipation of losing, he was not only pushing the panic button again, he was indulging in the most obvious kind of self-justification.

The decision to make Yogi Berra, of all people, the manager of the Yankees was admittedly one of the more moonstruck episodes in baseball. So moonstruck that no one will ever be able to convince me that Yogi was ever anything more than a handy stopgap Houk latched onto in order to boost himself up in the front office.

Ralph has the kind of background and personality that makes it relatively easy for him to handle Dan Topping. Topping is a guy who once ran a football franchise with Shipwreck Kelly so that he could hang around with all those great football players. He is no longer that kind of a hero-worshiper. He has won all the pennants anybody needs, and he has grown cynical and weary. As a matter of fact, Topping wants out of baseball. He is hanging on, now that the Yankees have been sold to CBS, only because he wants to get Dan Topping Jr. established with the club. He is so fed up with it all that he may not even hang around long enough to do that. Still, Houk is the kind of man Dan always wanted to be, and it is most difficult to look into the mirror of your own secret self and fight back. As a millionaire sportsman you'd have to rank him about halfway between Busch, the aristocrat, and Jim Norris, the well-known collector of fight characters.

Houk has come a long way from the bullpen, and he did not make that trip because he has no capacity to learn. With that passion of his for detail—which is really, again, the platoon leader's concern about keeping his rear guarded—he had kept his hand very firmly in the farm system during his days as a manager. He was at least as aware as anybody else that the Yankee system, which had once been more fertile than the banks of the Nile, had dried up and turned to dust.

With Mantle's legs always chancy, and Ford fighting off new injuries year by year, Houk could see very plainly that the years of easy Yankee domination were coming to an end. Since the manager is, as we have said, always the fall guy, Houk's ambition became to move himself up to the front office so that he could be the man to assess the blame rather than the man who takes it.

While he has no capacity for public relations and even less interest in it, Ralph was also very well aware, if only from reading the papers, that he was no match for Stengel in the battle for newspaper space which everybody had become so concerned about. When the opportunity arose, Houk was there either to suggest or to quickly agree that Berra was just the man to compete with Stengel. Actually, Houk couldn't have cared less who became manager, just so long as there was a logical reason for removing himself from the line of fire.

Now, pitting Yogi against Stengel was the worst mismatch in history. No boxing commission would have allowed it. Yogi is a completely manufactured product. He is a case study of this countrys' unlimited ability to gull itself and be gulled. Yogi had become a figure of fun originally because with his corrugated face and squat body he looked as if he should be funny, and because when he turned out to be a great ballplayer in spite of his odd appearance a natural feeling of warmth went out to him, as to the ugly duckling who makes it big in a world of swans. It pleased the public to think that this odd-looking little man with the great natural ability had a knack for mouthing humorous truths with the sort of primitive peasant wisdom we rather expect of our sports heroes.

Besides, there was that marvelous nickname. You say "Yogi" at a banquet and everybody automatically laughs, something Joe Garagiola discovered to his profit many years ago.

Casey Stengel, an earlier prospector in those fields, had made this discovery long before Garagiola. Casey had always bounced his best lines off Yogi, and the newspapermen and magazine writers, picking it up, were happy enough to go along with the act, since it made their own jobs that much easier and also because, I suppose, enough of them eventually came to believe it themselves.

Not that Yogi had ever been heard to say anything funny. But by then he didn't have to. Every time Yogi hiccuped, he was answered by gales of laughter. Boy, you said to yourself, nobody can hiccup as funny as that Yogi.

I had first come to know Yogi during the time I was operating the St. Louis Browns, a charitable organization formed to provide work for the otherwise unemployable. Yogi was working in New York for a far more profitable organization, but he was still returning to St. Louis in those days to spend his World Series check in his native city.

I used to play cards with him regularly in the St. Louis firehouse, and although you didn't have to put a gun in his ribs to get him to talk, he had little enough to say. He certainly didn't deal in malaprops or basic peasant wisdom. He talked just about the way any guy would talk while he was involved in a friendly game of chance, like you or me or Adlai Stevenson. He was, to sum him up, a friendly guy, a regular guy, a neighborhood guy without sham or pretension.

His real talent was that he was a good audience, a natural enough legacy from a boyhood spent with Garagiola.

He would sit there, relaxed, until the phone rang and a call from his wife, Carmine, ended the game for the day. Carmine always saw something special in Yogi, she was always aware that he had it in him to go further than anyone else thought. She was ambitious for Yogi. And her ambitions didn't include a daily card game with the boys at the firehouse.

It wasn't until I hit the banquet circuit with Garagiola that I started to hear the Yogi gags. While I would be sitting there waiting to go to work myself, it would often cross my mind that I had heard the same stories credited to Babe Herman or Rube Waddell or some other athlete of rough-hewn reputation. I had even used a few of them myself to embellish my own banquet character, Satchel Paige.

The malaprops, witticisms and naïvetés attributed to the Yogi-man got the Yankees a lot of ink over the years. They were never malicious, never really unkind. It was more as if the writers were collaborating in a gigantic "bright sayings of clever children" contest, a department in which the quality of the contributions doesn't have to be very high because everybody knows that the children themselves are so endearing.

All right, you ask, if the newspapermen who covered him regularly knew he was neither a humorist nor a leader of men, then Houk and Topping must certainly have known it too. How then could they have gone ahead and named him manager?

That's what makes this such an illuminating little episode and illustrates so beautifully the way the business of baseball is conducted even on the club that is widely heralded to be the most efficiently run of them all.

Because the whole thing began as just another Yogi Berra joke.

It began in the major league meetings at the end of 1960 when three of the more pixieish sportswriters, disgusted by the increasingly ridiculous names that were being put forth as the new manager of the San Francisco Giants, decided to conduct an experiment to determine the speed of communication (rumor division) and the gullibility of the *genus* sportswriter in search of something—*anything*—to justify the expense account.

The three writers were Stan Isaacs of Long Island *Newsday,* Leonard Schechter of the New York *Post* and Larry Merchant of the Philadelphia *Inquirer,* all famed as twisters of the Establishment's tail. The concocted the evil little design of circulating the name of the unlikeliest prospect that it was within the powers of the human mind to conceive, and then sitting back over their drinks to clock the length of time it took for their own rumor to come floating back to them adorned by all sorts of authoritative, unimpeachable sponsors.

The unlikeliest candidate they could think of was Yogi Berra.

(Lou Boudreau became a manager the same way. A Cleveland writer, trying to brighten up an otherwise dull, workaday list of prospects, threw the twenty-four-year-old Boudreau's name in at the end, purely as an act of whimsy. Louie was so thrilled at the idea of being looked upon as managerial material that he went right up to the front office and sold himself as the new manager.)

The rumor bounced back to its parents so fast that it wasn't even fun. But since Yogi was now a bona fide candidate, reporters called him for his comment. No, Yogi told them, he hadn't been contacted yet but yes, he would most certainly welcome the challenge and the opportunity—which, I will wager, had never occurred to him before. Yogi, like Boudreau, was on his way.

The following year, the Red Sox found themselves looking for a manager too. The Red Sox were a magnificently run organization, as a quick glance at their lineup could have told you. With that left-field wall casting its foreboding shadow over the shortstop, the Red Sox had, by dint of long-range planning that staggers the imagination, come up with a lineup composed entirely of left-handed line-drive hitters. Because of that lineup the Red Sox found themselves looking for a manager. As might be expected, they remembered reading that Berra's name had been added to the managerial lists and decided that he was just the man they wanted—presumably on the grounds that he couldn't be a worse manager than Pinky Higgins and, since Yogi was still swinging his big bat, he could certainly outhit him.

The Yankees weren't about to give Yogi up, but he already had a legitimate offer under his belt.

A year later, Baltimore was in fairly desperate search for not only a manager but for a manager who might even create a little interest in the team. Lee MacPhail decided that Yogi was just the attraction they needed, and he went so far as to offer him a contract. That was Houk's chance to step in and suggest that Yogi might be the answer to New York's own problems.

Yogi did get the Yankees more space in the papers which was, when you come right down to it, what he was hired for, although he still didn't come close to the Grand Old Gnome of Shea Stadium. But then, Stengel had something going for him. Casey is a legitimately funny man.

There is, however, one point that should be added here, irrelevant though it might be. Yogi did do one thing that Stengel didn't. Yogi won the pennant, and Casey finished last. He cut it close, winning by only one game, but the pennant was really pretty much locked up through the entire final week. And whatever their protestations, a close race was exactly what the Yankees wanted.

Did he make mistakes? Of course he did. Stengel had spent a lifetime managing before he came to the Yankees. Houk had served a four-year apprenticeship in the minors and three more years coaching under Stengel. Berra had spent one year as a player-coach. When he was hired, it was obviously with the tacit understanding that he was going to be permitted to make his mistakes right out there in the open where everybody could see them. It didn't seem quite fair to tell him, at the end of the year, that he had been on probation all the time.

How much help did they give him? As a freshman manager he needed, above all else, a wise old head as pitching coach. Houk's first move as general manager was to dump his wise old head, Johnny Sain—although that seems to have been because Sain and Berra had never seen eye-to-eye. To replace him, Houk and Berra picked Whitey Ford, giving the freshman manager a freshman pitching coach, and a part-time one at that.

The pitching got messed up, no question about it. And Yogi was at least partly to blame. He was using his long relievers short and his short relievers long, and like all new managers he was waiting too long before he got his starting pitcher out of there.

Still, he was operating under a major handicap. The relief pitcher who can come in over the last two innings and get the other side out can cover up a multitude of sins. Yogi didn't have him. Except for one brief period early in the season when Steve Hamilton was stopping them, and the final month of the season when they had Pete Ramos, the Yankee bullpen was useless.

The Yankee relief pitching didn't stop the other team at the end of the game, and the Yankee hitters became lambs over the last couple of innings, a complete reversal of their history.

But then the hitting fell apart during the early part of the game too. For once, the Yankee long-ball was conspicuously absent. Mantle was out with injuries. Maris was a rally-killer until the last month of the season. Only Howard, among the big hitters, was consistent.

The first baseman ran hot and cold. The second baseman had a very mediocre year. The shortstop had a terrible year. The third baseman had an impossible year. The other outfielder, Tresh, was a major disappointment. Normally, you win a pennant when all your players have good years together. The Yankees won it with all their players having bad years together.

Admittedly, there are intangibles here. Maybe, under Houk, the pitching staff would have been better; probably it would have been. Possibly Richardson, Kubek and Boyer would have hit better under Houk. Possibly balls would have flown out of the park just like in the good old days. That we'll never know. All we do know is that they sure didn't hit any better for Ralph while they were losing those four straight games to the Dodgers in his farewell appearance.

I know something else, too. With all their difficulties, the Yankees did come on with that rush down the stretch. Unless I have been sadly misinformed by all those sensation-seeking columnists, the manager during that stretch run was Yogi Berra.

And now something else. Seldom in my experience has a manager of a pennant-contending team been more shabbily served by his general manager, during his time of trouble, than Berra was served by Houk. During the entire year, Houk made only one move. He brought up Mel Stottlemyre, who was widely acknowledged to be the best pitcher in the minor leagues.

Ramos, you say? Oh no. Ramos wasn't Houk's idea, although he has shown no particular reluctance to accept the credit. Ramos was *sold* to the Yankees by Gabe Paul, and even here he was sold to Dan Topping. When Houk was consulted he argued that they weren't close enough for Ramos to make that much difference. Houk's solution wasn't to go out and get a relief pitcher, it was to fire Berra. When CBS bought the club, Ralph told them that the Yankees weren't going to win the pennant because Berra had butchered the job, but that everything was going to be fine again next year when Yogi was gone. After all, if it wasn't Yogi's fault, somebody just might have gone home with the ridiculous idea that it was Ralph's.

Nor did Ralph stand by his manager, like an oak, when the players came to his office to cry that Yogi was a poor manager and notably lacking in the essential qualities of gentlemanly behavior and inspiring leadership as enunciated by the YMCA. It would seem far more probable that they departed with the distinct impression that they wouldn't have to put up with Yogi's crudities for another year since, as the season progressed, the players felt increasingly free to express their complaints to newspapermen.

To be fair about it, though, I could be doing both Houk and the players an injustice. These were players who had become accustomed over a period of years to bringing their troubles to Houk. Ralph himself is accustomed, by background and by nature, to listening to the troops and distrusting everyone else. It was natural enough, perhaps, that the players would influence him all out of proportion to their intent. It was perhaps inevitable that he would see massive indictment in what they only meant as mild complaint.

After that has been said, however, it is still clear enough that it was hardly any service to Berra to permit the players to come around behind the manager's back and weep on his ready shoulder.

When you sum up Berra's year as manager, then, you have to say that he was thrown into the job cold, that his team fell apart on him, that there was an absolute minimum of help from the front office and that he was being undercut by some of his players.

And still he won. I wouldn't award him a gold star for the year, but I wouldn't give him a failing mark either. Not by a long shot.

Berra is gone, and Houk remains to chart the future course. To me, this is ample cause for everybody in the American

League to take heart. I tell you that with Houk's rigid hand at the controls, the Yankees can be had. As they are.

In a time of swift change, the Yankees are in the hands of a man who cannot and will not change. Mantle, Ford and Howard, the superstars on this team, are all of an age where they can go overnight. The team is coming apart at the seams. They were able to squeak by in the American League, in a dogfight, for a couple of years only because they were the only team in the league which *knew how* to win a pennant. Even here, they looked so bad in two straight World Series that the other American League clubs could not help but get the message that the mighty Yankees are ready to be taken.

The Yankees can no longer trade minor-league averages for major-league players, because they don't have the minor-league averages to work with anymore. And that means they have to trade man for man. I haven't noticed Houk out there on the battle lines pitting himself and his judgment against his colleagues. If a trade can help you it can also hurt you, and Houk is not a man to leave himself that vulnerable to criticism. The Major still keeps his rear well protected.

I'll tell you something. I was sulking around the house for awhile, kicking the dogs and frightening the children, because with Del (The Yankee Clipper) gone; Ford (A Legend in His Own Time) Frick going, and George (What's So Funny?) Weiss on the brink of retirement, I was losing all of my targets.

No longer do I look upon myself as a hardship case. I have the wild and gladsome feeling that Ralph Houk is going to develop into a target worthy of his distinguished predecessors.

He's a natural target right out of the starting gate because he fancies himself a strong man, and like most self-anointed strong men, he has the habit of confusing strength with weakness. He met the challenge of his first serious holdout in the spring of 1964 by threatening Jim Bouton with a $100-a-day fine for every day he failed to sign. Now, this is out-and-out blackmail, and while it is perhaps not worthy of mention, it is also against the rules of baseball. Owners used to be able to indulge their instinct for this kind of petty tyranny back in the thirties before the players had any kind of representation, and you can just see little Ralphie Houk lapping it up in the hometown newspaper and dreaming of the day when he would grow up and be a feudal baron too.

This kind of thing demonstrates quite clearly that the Major still carries a shotgun where his sense of public relations is supposed to be. I tell you, Ralphie baby, you keep pulling that kind of rock and CBS is going to blow you right out of the chair with its own well-notched shotgun.

Sheer bookkeeping screams out that the Yankees must change their image in order to compete with the image of the bumbling, stumbling but lovable little Metsies. At bottom, all this "image" talk mystifies and bewilders Houk. His natural habitat is the field of action, not the executive suite and certainly not the marketplace. Sure, he will put on his gray suit and hold his press conferences and smile his broad empty smile, because he has been assured that this is all part of the job. But he doesn't believe a word of it. You take the hill, you smash the gun emplacement, you win the pennant, there's solid accomplishment! There's something you can plan and blueprint and come to grips with.

So Houk continued to go to the press conferences determined to put forth the warm and colorful image the bosses desire, and before he was halfway through, the old inflexibility would take hold and he would be saying, almost plaintively, "But we still win on the field and that's all that really counts, isn't it? Well, isn't it ... ? Isn't it ... ?"

Show me a man who operates on what his logic, his morality and all his nerve ends tell him *should* be true, instead of what *is* transparently true, and I'll show you a man who is not only going to fail miserably but who is going to wear his failure as proof of his own basic worth and integrity.

The Mets, who finished last, outdrew you in 1964 by almost half a million fans, Ralph. Why *can't* you remember?

Houk sets himself up as a natural target, too, because he is devoid of a sense of humor. Unlike Weiss, whose face clearly shows at all times that life is a grim business out of which only fools could take any pleasure, Houk usually has a big smile pasted on his face. It takes a little while before you see that the smile comes automatically whether you've said anything funny or not. He is going to smile at the suspicion of humor, just to make sure you don't catch on that he has none.

In one way you have to sympathize with him. Tough as he is, feared as he is, he is suddenly playing in a league he knows nothing about. He will find that these faceless CBS people who smile and cozen him, just like any other fawning, faceless fans, will have a ruthlessness such as he's never faced before. He is in there with the mechanical men of our time, with men who are activated solely by the figures being fed them from a machine. These are the combat soldiers of our time; we have achieved the age of the robot. If the ratings (i.e., the attendance) continue to go down they will chop him down, effortlessly, routinely, almost thoughtlessly. Just as they chopped down Judy Garland, Phil Silvers and others too numerous to remember.

And there won't even be anybody to hit back.

If Ralph does go, he will be replaced by about a dozen CBS vice-presidents. And won't *that* be fun! If there is anything more ridiculous than a corporate vice-president trying to run a ball club, it is a committee of corporate vice-presidents trying to run a ball club. Comedians, sportswriters and other opportunists should be able to have a field day with them.

The Yankee image was badly scarred and tarnished by the World Series and its aftermath. Where it had previously been cold, austere and chillingly efficient, it became cold, austere and clumsy. In the Series, they kicked all four losing games away, something not even the most visionary Yankee-haters ever expected to see.

In the managerial exodus that followed, the Yankees came off far worse than the Cardinals, image-wise. Keane, offered the world and all, won the admiration of the pure of heart by spurning Gussie Busch's gold. Berra, fired, signed on happily as a roving something or other, with duties so vague that you had to conclude that he was expected to earn his money by staying away. The best measure of Houk's sure sense of public relations is that the reaction to the firing of the old Yankee hero seemed to surprise him. To show their goodwill, the Yankees let it be known that they were giving Yogi a clause guaranteeing him severance pay of $25,000 above and beyond his salary, which only made it seem as if the Yankees would be only too happy to pay him the $25,000 to get him out of their hair. If it also seemed as if Yogi didn't care how badly he was treated just so long as he was well paid, that bitter lesson rubbed off on the Yankees in an odd way, too. The fans, grown accustomed to loving good old Yogi, didn't want to feel that way about him and so whatever feeling of distaste they may have felt was very quickly transferred to the Yankees.

The Mets were still to be heard from. This guy Grant, or whoever is calling the shots over there, is a really good operator. The hiring of Stengel and Weiss was originally nothing more than an easy way to integrate the club into the sports history of the city. With the hiring of Berra it was converted into a calculated plan to raid the Yankees, the easiest possible way of bringing the Yankee fans into Shea Stadium and, more fun still, of keeping the Yankees permanently embarrassed and permanently on the defensive.

With the Mets, Yogi will be the space-catcher the Yankees hoped he would be for them, because while Yogi can't play the comic lead, he makes an excellent second banana. With Stengel there to bounce his jokes off him, Yogi will seem to be funny again. And don't think the Old Man doesn't know how to do it. Casey could give public-relations lessons to B.B.D.&O.— and all the rest of the alphabet too. Casey's decade of unparalleled success with the Yankees seduced us all into forgetting where his real talents lie. Casey doesn't really care whether he wins or loses, just so long as the turnstiles keep moving.

For Berra, it might be a foolish move. Unless he had a sudden and highly unlikely feeling of revulsion at the way he had permitted the Yankees to treat him, he would have been far better off staying right where he was. The Yankees, to put it baldly, were stuck with him. Yogi could have sat there for ten or fifteen years, drawing down an annual $35,000 or so for playing golf.

Yogi apparently thought he had a chance to become the manager of the Mets after Stengel departs. His chances aren't that hot. He apparently thinks that with Weiss and Stengel around, he can draw on past associations and loyalties to take care of him. Unhappily for Yogi, Stengel and Weiss will both be gone very soon, and neither Grant nor Mrs. Payson nor Bing Devine owes Yogi Berra a thing. He was a public-relations coup for them, nothing more.

Notice, once again, the reversal of form that had become almost obligatory through this whole strange interlude. Yogi Berra, accustomed throughout his career to undeserved praise, is suddenly hit with undeserved criticism. The man whom everybody had always protected and coddled was the man who became the patsy.

3

⊖ ⊖ ⊖

Tippecanoe and CBS Too

IT never ceases to amaze me how many of baseball's wounds are self-inflicted.

Since I am known to deal in ball clubs, the way more worthy
men deal in antiques, I always seem to be made aware of what
clubs are available. If you are looking for a club right now, hire
an Indian guide for a canoe trip down the St. Lawrence, turn
left at Lake Michigan, get off at Detroit and ask the corner
cop to direct you to Briggs Stadium. One cautionary note:
Bring money.

I had heard perhaps two years ago that Frank Stanton, president of CBS, had evinced some slight interest in buying the
Yankees, and there was vague talk floating around, from time
to time, that the Yankees were among the teams that could be
had. Del Webb's participation in the affairs of the club had
been rather limited for years, and Dan Topping, who had once
thrilled to being part of the great sport scene, had found that
one championship was getting to be pretty much like another.
Besides, Webb and Topping had long since stopped seeing
eye-to-eye.

When I first heard the rumors, I called Roy Hamey, the
Yankee general manager, and Roy let me know that if a tax angle could be worked out the club could be had. The tax angle
loomed so prominently because Webb and Topping owned the
Yankees as a partnership rather than as a corporation, an over-
sight which made our real national pastime—how to make sure

profits can be claimed as a capital gain rather than as income—even more compelling than usual.

Over the next couple of years, the rumors kept popping up in rather unsubstantial and unsubstantiated forms just often enough to demonstrate to the true connoisseur that there was a little bit of fire still smoldering down below.

On Thursday, August 6, 1964, the smoke signals began to rise. I received a call from an old Chicago friend, Jerry Loebl, one of the country's top architects. Loebl is a close friend of Henry Crown, who is one of the nation's largest builders and also, in his spare time, the largest stockholder in General Dynamics. He and Connie Hilton—of the Hilton Hiltons—had been my backers in the foredoomed attempt to buy the old Athletics from the Mack family for immediate delivery to Los Angeles. Since those days, Crown and I have had a running project—conversational only—to buy the Cubs from Phil Wrigley and force-feed such comforts as night baseball and winning ball clubs to Chicago's underprivileged North Side.

Jerry Loebl was calling to tell me that Webb had just offered the Yankees to Henry Crown and his son Lester. Since they weren't interested, Jerry was passing the information on to me —I assume at the suggestion of Crown—for whatever it was worth. Well, the Yankees are a good club, a winning club, a bonnie club, but they are not the club for me. I want a club like the Washington Senators that I can build and promote and romance and have some sense of communion with, responsibility toward and accomplishment about. What are you going to do with the Yankees that hasn't already been done? Win another pennant?

What I really mean, as you undoubtedly sense, is that you've got to look great in Washington if you do anything and you can't look particularly good in New York no matter what you do.

I've got friends too, though, so I quickly called Hank Greenberg to pass the information on to him. Henry was not interested either. He felt that the economics of baseball were such that you could no longer handle that kind of deal by getting a syndicate together; you had to have some kind of corporate structure going for you to pick up the original sales price and absorb any operating losses.

There was one other consideration that had to give you pause, too. Whenever anybody is that anxious to sell something, it is well to examine the merchandise. When Topping and Webb run, the ship may not be sinking but the deck is awash. The word was out that Topping, with all his assets, was in need of cold cash, which is more than understandable when you consider what his annual alimony bill must come to. Still, you could not ignore the cold, heartwarming fact that Casey Stengel's little Metsies were in the process of outdrawing the Yankees by almost half a million fans. If the Yankee owners weren't frightened they had reason, at the very least, to be thinking long deep thoughts.

And then there was that ball park, the massive and legendary Yankee Stadium, complete with tradition and statuary. Well, the massive and legendary Yankee Stadium has been wrestling with a parking problem for years. The stands have reached the age where they are not only in need of a little fixing here and there but will soon require a complete overhauling and rehabilitation. The Yankees don't own Yankee Stadium—about three other organizations own various slices, depths and rights to the park—but the Yankees are responsible for the upkeep. At today's prices, as CBS will shortly discover, a complete overhauling will stick them for another million or two.

Most important of all, there was the ball club itself. Studying it objectively, you had to come to the conclusion that the team was falling apart even more rapidly than the park. Mantle's leg had become a day-to-day proposition. Whitey Ford's hip had been troubling him. Maris had never quite recovered from the shock of hitting 61 home runs. The Yankees were at that time, if you remember, dropping farther and farther out of the pennant race, and their minor-league system which had once provided the answer to all ills had coughed up one player and then subsided into a coma of its own.

There was little doubt that this was the kind of situation in which the seller would wake up far happier the next morning than the buyer.

The following Thursday—exactly one week later—I received an early-morning call from a New York man who has no connection whatsoever with baseball. He was calling to tip me off that the Yankees were in the process of being sold to CBS. Within half an hour, I received a second call, from a baseball man this time, passing on the same information.

To check it, I called Gabe Paul in Cleveland. Gabe confirmed that CBS had just bought 80 percent of the club and that the league office was asking for an immediate telegraphic vote to approve it. Gabe, in fact, had received a personal phone call from Joe Cronin buttonholing him electronically, an indication that Gabe was being looked upon as a possible security risk.

In my usual spirit of helpfulness I did what I could to undermine Cronin, but although Gabe was hardly delirious with joy, he felt that the Yankees were entitled to dispose of their property as they saw fit. He did promise, at my request, that he would call me back as soon as the deal was either approved or disapproved.

(To clear up one minor point here, I do not believe for one minute that Del Webb had been trying to use Henry Crown to set a price. Webb is a contractor—which is like saying Truman is a politician—and Crown is his best customer. If anything, the opposite would be true. Webb may have insisted that Crown be given a shot at the club before Topping closed with CBS. Webb would want to be very sure that Henry Crown didn't suffer from that depressed, left-out-of-it feeling. My own guess is that Webb was just giving Crown first crack. Despite the subsequent announcements that the CBS deal had been in the works for years and years, I suspect that it was made almost overnight.)

I was keeping abreast of the developments not only because I'm nosy—which I am—but because that original call from the non-baseball man had made it clear that the news of the sale was hardly restricted to the ten ball clubs. Bob Fishel, a close personal friend, is the publicity director of the Yankees, and it was perfectly apparent to me that unless he moved quickly the story was going to break over his head. It was also perfectly apparent to anybody of normal intelligence that the reaction was going to be brutal, even under the best of circumstances.

I kept calling Bob at his Yankee office, but I couldn't get him.

At about 10:30, Gabe Paul called back to let me know that the Yankees had the 8 votes they needed.

When Fishel still wasn't at his office, it finally dawned on me that he must have gone down to CBS, which was, at that time, only about five blocks away. I was right. Bob had been there all morning trying to get permission to give the story, in all its details, to the press while he still had some measure of control over the way it would be presented. Needless to say, Bob—who is one of the best publicity men in the business—was unable to convince anybody that buying the Yankees had to be handled any differently than announcing that CBS had just signed another girl singer.

I just missed him at CBS. I had put the call in to Stanton's office, though, and I could at least console myself with the thought that I had given the boys a thrill by making them aware that I knew what was going on. Because if I knew, who else?

Within the next few minutes, I received back-to-back calls from two other clubs. Having docilely given their assent they had decided to let good Ole Will in on the news and, just incidentally, to ask me what I thought the reaction was going to be.

"I think that you patsies are going to be clobbered," I told them both. "And you think so too or you wouldn't be all of a sudden asking me. Boy, it must have been like feeding time at the zoo. They throw the trained seals a fish, and you just stand there with your little mouths open wide and gulp it down.

What's the matter, have you finally figured out that you've swallowed a dead fish? Is the smell beginning to get to you?"

By the time Bob Fishel returned my call, I could tell him that I had heard about the sale from all around the country, which meant that it was just a matter of hours or maybe even minutes before one of the news services picked it up.

Bob knew it even better than I did but his hands were tied, which is the history of his career with the New York Yankees.

As it turned out, NBC had been handed the story very early in the day from a source who was mischievous enough to want to see NBC break CBS's own story. The newsbreak had been delayed only because the source had given them the story with the understanding that they had to find somebody else to attribute it to. (No, the source wasn't I. I'm holding back the name because I'd be breaking a confidence if I divulged it.)

In digging up an attributable source, NBC had apparently come to the conclusion that Charles O. Finley was the owner most likely to be opposed. Finley wasn't at his office but they were able to track him down, without too much difficulty, in Chicago. Which was quite interesting in that the American League office was somehow unable to find Finley, during this same time, in order to let him cast his vote. They still hadn't been able to find him, hours later, when they finally announced that the sale had been made.

Now, Cronin and the nine other owners in the American League may suffer Finley ungladly, but he is a member of the club nonetheless and entitled to the elementary courtesy of being permitted to cast his vote.

Still, I can understand how Cronin felt. He just couldn't wait to let Topping and CBS know that he had followed their instructions to the letter.

Eight votes were needed to approve the new owners. Art Allyn and Finley had voted against the sale. That meant that only one more vote had been needed to kill it. The key vote— the vote that failed—had been the Baltimore vote, for it was in Baltimore that the most involved maneuverings had taken place.

On the morning of August 13, Joe Iglehart awoke with an embarrassment of riches on his hands—another proof, students, that wealth, honor and position are to be avoided at all costs. Iglehart was not only the Chairman of the Board and the majority stockholder (46%) of the Baltimore baseball club; he was also the Chairman of the Finance Committee at CBS. He had been, that is, until 10 o'clock that morning when he thoughtfully handed in his resignation, a nimble piece of footwork that would have eliminated any possible accusation of conflict of interest if he didn't also happen to hold 40,000 shares of CBS stock worth $1,655,000.

Well, there *was* one other little problem too. In addition to being one of the largest single stockholders of CBS, Iglehart was a partner in W. E. Hutton Co., an investment banking house which is fortunate enough to number CBS among its clients.

The wise course of action for Iglehart to have followed under these somewhat restricting conditions would have been to withhold his vote. Since Iglehart hadn't filled up his safety deposit box with all that stock by following unwise courses, that was precisely what he seemed to do. Lee MacPhail, the general manager, cast the vote in favor of CBS without bothering to call a Board of Directors meeting. Since it is most unlikely that MacPhail had the authority to vote in league affairs without consulting the Chairman of the Board, it is hardly stretching credulity to arrive at the conclusion that MacPhail's vote was really Iglehart's vote. (Lee MacPhail not only works for the Orioles, his brother is the sports director of CBS.)

Three weeks later, when Cronin—acceding to Art Allyn's request—asked the other owners whether they wanted to hold a meeting and maybe talk things over a little, a Board of Directors meeting was finally called. Iglehart made it clear that he saw no reason for holding the meeting but again he didn't have to go on record with a vote. The other six directors split evenly, and since a tie vote was tantamount to a negative one as far as Baltimore was concerned, there would still be no meeting, no discussion.

Art Allyn had strode to the center of the stage, bellowing like an angered bull. The only defect in Cronin's telegraphic vote, Art said, was that it was clearly illegal. The league rules specifically stated, Art pointed out, that any action on the application of a new member was to be considered at a formal league meeting, upon receipt of a 10-day notice.

Cronin could claim—as he later did—that there were precedents for taking the vote by phone, but the fact of the matter was that the telephone voting had always come on sales where the acceptance of the new owners was routine and *unanimous*. Unanimous. Any organization from the U.S. Senate on down can suspend any rule it wants by unanimous vote, for the very sound and sensible reason that there's nobody to object to it.

Once it was established that there was going to be any opposition—yes, even if it had *only* come from Finley—it was incumbent upon Cronin to abide by the league rules.

Nor could anyone claim that the opposition was purely capricious. Art Allyn wasn't throwing down penalty flags because he is a fanatic on rules and technicalities; his real concern went to the underlying reason why the sale had been jammed through without notice and without debate.

And it had been jammed through. On August 10, only three days before the request for approval went out, the American League had gathered in Chicago to discuss a projected Monday night television package. Somehow, not a word had been breathed about any potential sale of the Yankees while all the owners were gathered together in one room!

The Yankees would seem to have had every reason for wanting to relieve the owners of the rigors of debate. Once the owners began to talk about welcoming CBS into the club, they would very quickly have recognized the antitrust problems they were sticking their heads into. Beyond that, if there had been any advance notice, the press outcry—which was 99 percent against the sale—could not have helped but make its presence felt inside the room.

The operational code, as Art Allyn told his colleagues when he finally did get Cronin to call a meeting, was VOTE NOW, THINK LATER.

The Yankees had done their best to unruffle Allyn's feathers. Del Webb stopped off at Chicago, between planes, to try to talk him into calling off the dogs. "I don't care one way or the other," Del told him, "but Topping wants the money."

Topping himself had been calling around to try to bring pressure to bear on Allyn. He even went so far as to ask Hank Greenberg to intercede on his behalf, Arthur having been our partner in Chicago before he bought Hank and me out. Arthur wasn't in the mood to be interceded with. It wasn't only that the sale to CBS was a mistake, he told Hank, but the arrogance with which the Yankees had bulled it through was more than he could stomach.

Arrogance is the Yankee trademark; it comes with the franchise. But the Yankees had shown more than mere arrogance this time. Topping and Webb had displayed a contempt for the rest of the league, to say nothing at all about an indifference to the greater welfare of baseball, that set a new high even by Yankee standards.

It is no secret that baseball had been engaged in a highly successful rearguard action against being placed under the restrictions of the antitrust law, ever since that delightful day in 1922 when the Supreme Court granted us an exemption on the grounds that baseball was "not a commercial enterprise."

Of course not. Baseball, like loan-sharking, is a humanitarian enterprise.

(When the Supreme Court says baseball isn't run like a business, everybody jumps up and down with joy. When I say the same thing, everybody throws pointy objects at me. Why is that, Doc?)

For those of you who have been wasting the best years of your life hanging around the 50-yard line, the foul line or the blue line (someday I wish somebody would tell me what the blue line is for), I had better explain that without the exemption baseball's reserve clause, which binds players to one club body and soul (their spikes are their own if they promise to take good care of them), would automatically be adjudged in restraint of trade. The baseball contract would become about as illegal as it is possible to get and the Justice Department would have to set about to spelling out new rules and regulations to get us back on the path of honest commercialism.

To keep the Justice Department from being overworked, baseball has enlivened the halls of Congress with its own lawyers (you may read lobbyists if you're a cynic) to keep the "friends of baseball" supplied with whatever encouragement—and maybe even information—was necessary to protect and preserve the time-honored privileges of the Grand Old Game.

Compared to what the oilmen spend to hold on to the exemption a grateful nation has accorded *them,* baseball has spent the merest pittance. By more modest standards, however, the figure would, I suspect, bring a soft, silent glow of appreciation into the eyes of all lovers of high finance.

While the exemption has never really come close to slipping away, there have been moments of quiet apprehension.

When, as an instance, the Supreme Court refused to grant boxing a similar exemption in 1955, Justice Frankfurter had the gall to write in his minority opinion, "It would baffle the subtlest ingenuity to find a single differentiating factor between other sporting exhibitions . . . and baseball."

Now, one of the troubles with discussing a subject like this is that nobody ever says what he means. No one really believes that baseball isn't a business; not you or me or Anna Maria Alberghetti. What we really believe is that baseball is entitled to its special exemption because of its special character and the special position it holds in the national life. I go along with that. I also believe we could exist very nicely without the reserve clause, but that's another story.

With the Supreme Court beginning to look as if it may cop

out on us at any time, baseball, which is no less alert to the Court's subversive tendencies than any hard-working Southern senator, has been pushing to get its exemption written into the law. And you can't blame us. After all, what faith can anyone have in a Supreme Court that doesn't know a business when it sees one?

On August 4, 1964, a grand day for baseball, Senator Phil Hart of Michigan (who is married to one of the daughters of William O. Briggs, the late owner of the Detroit Tigers) reported that long-sought-after bill out of the Senate Committee on the Judiciary.

The Hart Bill put all professional sports under antitrust but exempted all rules pertaining to player contracts and territorial rights, plus all rules and actions aimed at preserving public confidence in the honesty of the game.

Sports were going to be legislatively *exempted* from antitrust by a law which put them *under* antitrust, a marvelous exercise in opening and closing a door at the same time.

The vote from Hart's Senate committee was unanimous. Mannie Celler, the chairman of the House Judiciary Committee, was apparently ready to go along. A swift and automatic approval was assured.

This was the time the Yankees picked—nine days after Hart had reported his bill out of committee—to sell the club to the largest of all communications companies.

The first howls of protest had barely died down before the bill was back in Hart's subcommittee "for further study," a fine old legislative phrase which usually means "to be filed and forgotten."

Phil Hart, having shepherded the bill through his committee, might have been expected to be somewhat upset at finding himself standing in the national spotlight with egg all over his face.

However he may have grumbled privately, Hart has gritted his teeth and remained a true and faithful baseball man. The fact that John E. Fetzer, the Detroit president, also owns five

TV stations in Michigan (including a CBS affiliate) had not a thing to do with it. Since when have politicians been reluctant to offend their local TV moguls?

The subcommittee hearing did have a certain antic charm, especially for all of us loyalists who haven't felt Washington was quite the same since Ev and Charlie broke up.

As befitted his position, CBS president Frank Stanton was the principal witness. CBS had already shown how eager it was to cooperate with its new colleagues by turning down the opportunity to sign the Yankees with the Game of the Week package that had just been sold to ABC, an understandable enough corporate decision once you understand that CBS had the Yankees under contract for its own weekend package. There were those who felt the value of the package had been diminished considerably without the most glamorous of all teams in the fold, but Stanton quickly cleared up that misconception by explaining how the ABC program was really just as well off without the Yankees. I throw that in only to assure all CBS stockholders—including Iglehart—that there will never be a shortage of comedians while Stanton is running the show.

Frick, putting on his usual glittering performance, told the fascinated Senators how he had alertly consulted his own (that is, the Commissioner's) counsel, who had told him—you'll never guess!—that it was a league affair.

Ever vigilant, Frick had also consulted counsel to make sure there were no troublous antitrust implications in the sale. As near as we can make out, counsel told him they probably weren't violating any laws. I, for one, find it difficult to believe that was the extent of their reports.

Can't ask for a more objective opinion than that.

At the end of four fun-filled days, Hart announced that he believed the "opposition triggered by the acquisition was, to some extent, unjustified."

Which would seem to mean that it was also, to some extent, justified.

Lest anybody think he was caviling, however, Hart congratulated baseball for its willingness to submit itself to his bill, the rough equivalent of congratulating your five-year-old child for accepting a lollipop.

The only trouble with all this submission is that Mannie Celler, over in the House, no longer seemed willing to go along. Celler went so far as to meet with Milwaukee county officials and advise them to file an antitrust suit against baseball.

If I were CBS I would keep that Big Eye firmly focused upon the developing events in Milwaukee, because these two stirring examples of baseball's gross mismanagement are embarked, rather fittingly, upon a collision course.

If the Milwaukee suit ever reached the courts, the Justice Department, which has shown a peculiar lack of interest in the CBS affair, will be dragged into court, however reluctantly, to explain its position.

Will all due respect to Celler, his confrontations with baseball have never been among the more glorious moments of his long and meritorious service to his country. He kept his record intact, immediately after the CBS sale was announced, by saying, "There is a danger that professional team sports, like wrestling today, may degenerate into exhibitions rather than bona fide athletic contests."

The logic of the comparison escapes me, possibly because I have never run for public office, but he was making a very valid point. The Supreme Court exemption was based upon its considered opinion that baseball is a sport rather than an entertainment, which would indicate that the Justices had done their research at Griffith Stadium. Celler seemed to have grave doubts whether baseball was lending any particular aid and comfort to this legal illusion by bringing the world's greatest merchandiser of entertainment into the fold.

(Frank Stanton, obviously no Constitutional lawyer, wrote Cronin that CBS and the Yankees were a natural combination because "it has been the function of CBS to provide entertainment . . . directly to the public during the public's leisure time." No, no, Doctor, you haven't got the idea at all.)

You have to look hard these days to find a ball club that isn't a subsidiary of some corporation or other. Why should it matter so much if the Yankees happen to be a subsidiary of a television network instead of, say, a beer company? Especially since we have already agreed that the antitrust exemption is based upon one of those pleasant, useful fictions on which honorable men may agree.

One of the answers is that we should be trying to make it as easy as possible—not as difficult as possible—for the honorable men on the other side to keep agreeing. More directly and pointedly, the entry of CBS challenges that exemption in just about every area conceivable.

In the minority opinion mentioned above, Justice Frankfurter had seen fit to make the purely gratuitous observation that baseball was profiting far more than boxing from the mass communication media, and he had added balefully: "This opinion is concerned only with the sport as such, and not with the arrangements by which mass media show or report bouts. Such arrangements are beyond the scope of baseball's exemption."

If that meant anything, it meant that if baseball ever came before the Court again, it stood an excellent chance of losing its exemption on the grounds that even though it may be a sport on the field, it was, through its radio and television contracts, engaged in interstate commerce.

Baseball could make a case that technically speaking (which is the best way to speak when you are in trouble) it did not telecast its games itself, it merely sold the *rights* to permit its games to be telecast. And if you had a favorably disposed Court you might even get away with it.

But not with CBS in the lineup. With CBS in the lineup you had a communication network which by its nature could perform a miracle of interstate traffic, crossing all state lines at the same time.

The real sticking point to the CBS purchase, though—the overriding, irreducible problem—is that CBS was buying a ball club and joining an organization with which it was already doing business. The Yankees were, to all intents and purposes, the host team for CBS's Game of the Week show (which is now called Yankee Baseball of the Week) under a contract which paid them $550,000 for the year. The other teams picked up a game here and there only when the Yankees were on the road.

The Yankees kept all the money from that windfall themselves, just as if it were any TV contract for a local telecast. Last season, after many a false start, an anti-Yankee group got together to demand that the Yankees split the proceeds with the opposition.

Well, the history of the American League is rich with anti-Yankee cabals in which the rebels marched bravely and resolutely into the meeting and collapsed as soon as the first shot was fired. This time they had made their vows in blood, so the collapse wasn't complete. The Yankees, in an unaccustomed burst of good fellowship, agreed to keep only 75 percent of the money for themselves and permit the other nine clubs to split the remaining 25 percent. Not immediately, you understand, but in 1966. No sense letting the patsies get the smell of the loot in their nostrils too early.

Let's examine the CBS Game of the Week, with its attendant problems, in the narrowest possible sense; that is, only as it concerns baseball, not as it may very well concern the government. As things stand at the moment, CBS is getting those games for nothing because it is paying itself $550,000. Next year, CBS will be paying itself only $412,500 and the rest of the league will be cutting up $137,500. No matter how much CBS pays the Yankees, it is still getting them for nothing, a figure which the opposition would find very difficult to match. So much for fair competition.

When it pays the other teams (and, under a new arrangement, it apparently has five other clubs under contract), CBS, which owns the Yankees, is contributing to the financial support of another club. You can't do that. Rule 20, which deals with conflict of interest, prohibits it.

If the rule were enforced and CBS were ordered to abandon

the Game of the Week, baseball would lose a source of income. And not only from the Game of the Week. That's the least of the problems. To be consistent, CBS would be unable to bid on the World Series, the All-Star game or anything else. That means the bidding for those two fantastically lucrative sources would be restricted to the other two networks, NBC and ABC, with a corresponding loss of competition and, therefore, of income.

OK, you say, so why be a fanatic about it? Why not just wink at the rules under these special circumstances and let CBS stay in the ball game and build up the pot? Better to throw away all those years of scrupulous regard for public opinion than to throw away all that money. Let's be practical about it. The baseball fan has been so thoroughly disenchanted in these past few years that nothing would disenchant him further. Who really cares?

Well, a lot of people care. In his original press releases at the time of the purchase, William Paley, Chairman of the Board, said, "In negotiating . . . for rights to broadcast games, CBS will not be in any better position than any other network organization."

To which you are entitled to ask, "So why bring it up at all? Who asked?"

CBS also let it be known that its attorneys had provided a legal opinion that there was no conflict with antitrust. But when Arthur Allyn asked that CBS furnish copies of such legal memoranda and opinions to all league members, Dr. Stanton pleaded the privilege of the attorney-client relationship. In short, he had a legal opinion he wouldn't let his new partners see.

There's a great help.

Let's not worry about the baseball rules, though. It has been perfectly apparent from the beginning that baseball considers its own rules eminently collapsible where powerful interests such as CBS and the Yankees are concerned.

The only question at this point would seem to be whether the Justice Department cares. Three days after the sale had been consummated, the Justice Department leaked the story that it had studied the transaction over the weekend—what prodigies of legal scholarship must have gone into that—and decided that it would bring no suit.

After the Senate hearing, it leaked information again that it had dropped its investigation (*what* investigation?) but that it always could be reopened if developments warranted.

The Justice Department leak also made it clear, however, that it hadn't for one moment bought the baseball establishment's defense that CBS would have little influence since it only controlled one team out of twenty. "The Justice Department," it was said, "still maintains that the A. L. champs control most of the moneymaking machinery in the majors and hold the most power."

The leak is interesting on several accounts. Here is an authorized statement to which nobody wants to put his name. If I were a crank, I might point out that Paul Porter, baseball's eminent counsel, is a law partner of Abe Fortas, who happens to be one of President Johnson's closer friends and associates. I'll tell you something. If I were dealing with *anybody* in Washington these days, I'd be mighty proud to have Paul Porter representing me.

You will notice, too, that in walking away from the investigation the Justice Department was careful to leave the door wide open. If it is forced by circumstances to act, it will not be in the embarrassing position of having completely reversed itself.

It should be clear enough by now that in negotiating any contract with baseball—and certainly any contract with the Yankees—CBS is sitting on both sides of the table at the same time. It is both the buyer and the seller. The Justice Department in days gone by had taken the very stuffy position that under the capitalistic system the buyer and the seller must have interests that are not only different but which are in distinct opposition. The seller is supposed to be trying to get the highest possible price, and the buyer is supposed to be trying to get the lowest possible price. The name of that game, I believe, is competition.

The precedents would seem to have been there for everybody to see. Until a dozen years ago, the moving picture companies owned their own theatres; that is, they made moving pictures and then sold them to themselves (in the form of a distributing subsidiary). The Government told them they had to divest themselves of their theatres. The Justice Department took the position that it wasn't good enough to even let their distributors bid against other distributors, since the possibility of collusion was too great. Now that would seem, to a layman, to be a fairly exact parallel.

More recently, MCA, which had been the largest talent agency, went into the highly lucrative business of producing television shows. Uh-uh. The Government told MCA they had either to stop being agents or stop being producers because, again, they were in the position of selling their own clients (through the agency branch) to themselves (as the producing branch).

Make no mistake about this. The possibility still exists that sooner or later CBS will be given the alternative of divesting itself of the New York Yankees or foregoing the right to either broadcast or televise baseball games. If CBS takes the first option, the American League will have suffered its troubles for the sake of being confronted with a new crisis. If CBS takes the second option, baseball has lost CBS as a source of income.

It is entirely possible, of course, that if the owners had been given the time to consider all these potential booby traps—to debate them openly and to seek legal advice—they would have plunged ahead and welcomed CBS into the clan with open arms anyway. But they were certainly entitled to know what they might be getting themselves into. Which is precisely what Art Allyn told the owners in the September 9 meeting in Boston.

Allyn didn't force that meeting. Neither did the cries of pain from the press and public. The American League is fortunate in being governed by a president who is not swayed by predictions of disaster—possibly because he does not understand them—and a Commissioner who has become a legend in his own time.

But if Cronin and Frick were undismayed, CBS was beginning to wonder whether that kind of publicity was really doing them any good. William Paley wrote a letter to Dan Topping, which was promptly made public. "We are now greatly disturbed," he wrote, "that there appears to be some question about the Leagues' method of polling its members and by allegations that CBS has been a party to secretive and even high-handed manipulations."

Allyn and Finley could howl through the night in vain. CBS and Topping had only to ask. Through the magic of television the clock was turned back so that the sale could be voted upon in, of all things, the manner prescribed by the rules.

And this time, the sale came so close to being defeated—so much closer than the public ever learned—that it is still a mystery as to what finally happened.

The swing club here, once again, was Baltimore. A couple of days before the league was to meet in Boston, the Baltimore Board of Directors gathered together in secret conclave, studiously neglecting to inform Iglehart. This time around, they decided, Baltimore would pass its vote. Assuming that Finley was still with Allyn, that would be enough to defeat the proposition.

Iglehart had decided to disqualify himself from the voting, due to his somewhat ambiguous position, but when it came time to go to Boston he decided to make the trip anyway.

Allyn came to the meeting beautifully prepared. In a scrupulously documented appeal, he outlined all the problems baseball would be taking upon itself and, as the first order of business, proposed that the league hire a wholly independent expert on the antitrust laws to make a complete study, and that "consideration of the application for admission of CBS as a member of the American League be postponed" until the report came back.

When this resolution came to a vote, the Baltimore club did vote along with Allyn and Finley. Three votes were not enough to pass the resolution, of course, but the Baltimore vote stunned the meeting. It was obvious now that if the same lineup held on the substantive vote, CBS was dead.

As a result it was not brought to an immediate vote. Instead, the Yankees spent the day romancing Baltimore without, from all appearances, any success. Webb had to leave for the Coast to appear at a Boy Scout banquet, and when he walked out of the room he had no doubt that the deal was dead. (The Boy Scouts would seem to be an outfit worth keeping an eye on. In the old days they'd have had somebody like Raymond Massey make an inspirational speech. Not Del. Del will smarten those kids up in a hurry.)

Topping left the room twice, thinking he had lost. He even confided to a newspaper friend that he had another buyer ready to take over.

As I say, I just don't know what happened there at the end. Either Iglehart was able to bring the Baltimore people around, or the Yankees were able to con them again, or they just folded. At any rate, when the vote was finally taken, Baltimore voted aye.

The others all held to their previous votes so, in a way, I suppose you do have to say that the owners, apprised of the risks, went ahead anyway.

Some of the votes aren't too hard to understand. Fetzer and Autry are both in the radio TV business themselves, and they both have CBS outlets. They'd go along with the big network and worry about the problems later.

Gabe Paul wasn't too sure he wouldn't be going to the league himself at the end of the year for permission to move out of Cleveland, so he has to hold to the philosophical position that a club has the right to do anything it wants with its property. Johnston of Washington is in the brokerage business; he understands these kinds of deals. He's mesmerized by the glamour of the Yankees, anyway.

Boston surprised me. I thought Yawkey would be the man to step in and call a halt. But then, Yawkey and Cal Griffith will always go along with Joe Cronin, and Cronin was pushing hard for approval. As for Cronin, he follows in Frick's shadow . . . if Frick were substantial enough to cast a shadow. And Frick goes with the power.

At this point, Joe Iglehart's position—and Joe Cronin's tender concern for it—became the paramount issue in the meeting.

Rule 20 of Baseball's Constitution and Section 9 of the Reorganization Plan state flatly that no member of the league, no partner, no trustee, stockholder, official or employee of any member, directly or *indirectly*, "shall own stock or have any financial interest in any other member of this league. . . ."

It is further stated that anyone who found himself in violation of that rule would have to "dispose of his interest or stock" within thirty days after being notified.

Now that would seem to be about as clear as the English language is capable of getting.

It would therefore seem to have been self-evident that if the majority stockholder of the Baltimore club owned 40,000 shares of CBS, which now owned the New York Yankees, the only choice open to him was which block of stock he wanted to get rid of.

When Hank Greenberg and I bought controlling interest of the White Sox in 1959, Hank found himself peppered with letters from both Cronin and Frick warning him that he could not serve as an officer of our club until he got rid of his $200,000 worth of debentures in the Cleveland Indians. And debentures aren't even voting shares, they're nothing more than notes on a loan.

Rule 20 has been interpreted even more strictly than that. When Bill Bartholomay and his partners bought Chuck Comiskey's minority stock holdings in the White Sox two years later, the American League told him he would have to get rid of his *two shares* in the Chicago Cubs, for which he had paid $600.

Obviously, there was no way that Bartholomay, as a minority stockholder in an American League club—and his relationship with Art Allyn was such that his minority interest gave him nothing more than the right to belly up to the box office and buy his ticket—could do anything to help or harm a National League club. But that was never the point. The rule was put in there, again, to prevent even the whisper of suspicion.

As a matter of fact, neither a player nor a manager can hold a financial interest in the ownership or *earnings* of his *own* club without the approval of the Board of Directors. (This is primarily so that the league will be in a position to order an immediate divestment of the stock if he should be traded to another team.)

Let us see how Cronin treated Iglehart's dual interests. And let no man tell me that the ownership of 40,000 shares of stock doesn't give a man some glimmer of interest in the quarterly earnings report.

On the day after the original approval of the sale, Allyn, who was himself an owner (if only indirectly) of CBS stock, recognized that he had a conflict of interest and requested that the league take steps to make the entire CBS stock list available.

The telegram sent back to him on behalf of Cronin said, in effect, that Rule 20 didn't apply to CBS stockholders because the stock was so widely distributed. The telegram read:

TO OBTAIN A LIST OF COLUMBIA BROADCASTING SYSTEM STOCK-HOLDERS WOULD SERVE NO USEFUL PURPOSE AND WOULD NOT BE IN ACCORDANCE WITH THE PAST PRACTICES OF THE LEAGUE.

Well, it was certainly true enough that nobody had ever requested the stock list of a huge publicly owned corporation before, possibly because no publicly owned corporation of any size—medium, large or economy—had ever bought a ball club before.

Allyn wanted to know "what provisions of the Reorganization Agreement excepts publicly owned corporations from the safeguards imposed upon all corporations?"

On August 25, shortly after Cronin had called that September 9 meeting, Allyn had his own attorney deliver to Cronin, by hand, a letter which contained all the questions he wished to have distributed to the other owners before they came to Boston for the meeting.

Cronin and attorney John Hayes immediately called Allyn's attorneys in Chicago and assured them that everybody up in league headquarters was perfectly aware of the potential conflicts of interest and that all league members had already made voluntary disclosures of any ownership of CBS stock. Cronin therefore wanted Allyn to withdraw his request so that it would be clear that these disclosures had been made voluntarily and also so that it would not appear as if Cronin were himself acting only as a result of pressure from Allyn. (John Hayes is the attorney for the Boston Red Sox but he was acting as special counsel for the league in the Yankee-CBS matter.)

More specifically, Allyn's attorneys were told that Cronin deeply resented Allyn's implication that he, as president of the league, would not discharge his responsibilities as far as Joe Iglehart was concerned.

Iglehart had already informed league headquarters, they were told, that he and his New York lawyer were working on the best way, tax-wise, for Iglehart to dispose of one of his blocks of stock.

Hayes then "insisted" (Allyn's own word in a subsequent letter to Frick) that Allyn rewrite his letter to Cronin bearing these facts in mind.

Since Art had their word that his questions were going to be dealt with he did, in fact, have a new letter composed, considerably more moderate in tone than the first one.

One of the paragraphs Allyn revised at Cronin's specific request now read:

> I suggest that at the meeting full information be given as to whether any member, or any officer, director or stockholder of any member:
>
> a) owns any financial interest, directly or indirectly, in CBS or any of its affiliated stations;

   b) has any interest in any investment banking firm which par-
      ticipates in any financings for CBS;

   c) has any contract with CBS or any of its affiliated stations.

But Cronin didn't send Allyn's new letter out either. On September 3, Cronin sent out a letter of his own in which he
brought up the questions that had been asked by Allyn along
with Dr. Stanton's explanations. All except one. Noticeably missing from Cronin's letter was this vital point regarding full disclosure of any possible conflict of interest.

Full disclosure wasn't made at the meeting, either. Nor was
partial disclosure. To put it bluntly, Cronin never brought the
subject up at all.

That left Allyn to present his own assessment of these problems, after which he offered a resolution to the effect that consideration of CBS's application be postponed "until such time
as CBS is prepared to certify that no conflicts of interest exist
with respect to any of its stockholders. . . ."

Finley seconded the motion, and Cronin immediately ruled
it out of order. No explanation. No discussion. Just out of order.

It took no great perception by that time to see that not only
was Iglehart not going to be required to dispose of his stock, but
that he wasn't even going to be inconvenienced by having to
make any explanations. During one of the limitless recesses of
that long day, Allyn confronted Iglehart personally. Iglehart
informed him that he no longer had any intention of disposing
of his interest in either CBS or the Baltimore ball club. He also
told him that he was going to stay on as Chairman of the Board
of the Orioles and still serve as CBS's investment banker.

His new position was based on a legal opinion, dated September 3 (the same day Cronin wrote his own letter), *which had
been written for CBS by its own counsel.*

There may have been some lawyer somewhere who couldn't
come up with the legal opinion his clients wanted from him,
but I take it that he is now back at Aqueduct walking hots.

At this point, then, there was already a working relationship between Iglehart and CBS, not potentially but in fact. For Iglehart wasn't going to get rid of his CBS stock under any circumstances; if pushed to the wall, he was going to have to sell his Baltimore stock. CBS was providing him with a legal opinion to permit him to stay on as Chairman of the Board at Baltimore. CBS was telling him there was no conflict of interest, although the very act of telling it to him amounted to a conflict of interest in itself. Crazy!

The legal opinion was based upon the premise that CBS stockholders would not directly own stock in the Yankees because the ball club was being operated through a subsidiary corporation rather than as a division of the main corporation. OK, so what? Section 9, as has been stated time and again, forbids any financial interest in more than one team, directly or *indirectly*.

The CBS lawyer had offered Iglehart a second—and even more ridiculous—escape hatch on the somewhat less than ingenious grounds that in order to constitute a conflict of interest, his financial interest in a second ball club had to be "substantial" and "significant."

I don't know what the weekly budget is at your house, but at our house $1,655,000 takes on a significance that is not only financial but downright celestial.

In addition to which, that isn't what Section 9 says either. *Any* financial interest means *any* financial interest (like, say, Bartholomay's $600), just as *indirectly* means *indirectly*.

But not, it seemed, to Joe Cronin or Joe Iglehart.

Allyn, having been nicely had, wrote an angry report on the whole matter to Ford Frick, reminding him of his own responsibilities. "President Cronin," he wrote, "has displayed an unwillingness to shoulder the responsibility of purging the American League of the cancerous conflicts of interest which, if not probed and removed, could destroy baseball's reputation for integrity."

In appealing to the Commissioner, Allyn, ever mindful of Frick's own impressive record for doing the Old Soft Shoe around the more pressing issues, reminded him that one of the functions of his office was "to perpetuate baseball as the national game of America, and to surround it with such safeguards as may warrant absolute public confidence in its integrity, operations and methods."

He also called the Commissioner's attention to his power "to investigate . . . any act, transaction or practice charged, alleged or suspected to be detrimental to the best interests of the national game of baseball. . . ."

Perhaps the existence of these powers came as a surprise to Frick. At any rate, in the upset of the year Allyn seemed to be getting some action of him. There were well-authenticated stories around that Frick and Cronin had informed Iglehart that he would have to dispose of one of his interests before the season started. The rule, of course, says 30 days. Not Opening Day or May Day or Mother's Day. It says, quite clearly and legibly, "thirty days." Still, it is not the custom of baseball's hierarchy to enforce its rules where the power structure is involved, and Allyn was presumably content to allow them to break in slowly.

As a result, Art Allyn's testimony before the Hart subcommittee was surprisingly moderate, his passion strangely muted. Arthur felt that the power of the Yankees had been broken. He was, moreover, a member of a 6-man committee that had been appointed to work out the conflict-of-interest problems, and he was under the impression he had an agreement that Iglehart would be forced to sell one of his blocks of stock. With that gesture of good faith offered to the public, the committee was then going to modify and rewrite the rule so that it could accommodate the modern breed of owners with their highly diversified holdings.

Frick had told the Hart Committee, "If another owner has a big interest in CBS, of course he will have to get rid of it . . . we are working out ways of handling the situation and we take it very seriously." Allyn knew better than to think anybody paid any attention to Frick, of course. He thought he had an agreement because when the 6-man committee met at Bellaire, Florida, they signed a report accepting his guidelines.

Mr. Allyn was to discover that there was still one final scene to be played out before the final commercial. The five other members of the committee walked into the joint meeting of the two leagues at Clearwater and repudiated their signatures.

The owners were giving Iglehart a somewhat wider choice. In addition to the simple choice of 1) getting rid of his CBS stock or 2) getting rid of his Baltimore stock, he was given 3) the option of putting his CBS stock in trust.

This was tantamount to giving him the choice of cutting off his right arm, cutting off his left arm or clipping his fingernails.

After what were undoubtedly agonizing moments of soul-searching, Iglehart decided to go for the manicure. His decision wasn't really too surprising, though, since it was precisely the solution he himself had offered at the Boston meeting.

The assembled owners had simply voted to ignore their own rule.

All the trust meant was that he wouldn't be voting his stock. The dividends would still be piling up, and I presume he would still have been entitled to sneak a look at the morning quotations and even glance casually at the quarterly earning reports.

Arthur Allyn, who was flaming, contended that he had been double-crossed, an accusation which undoubtedly brought blushes of shame to every face in the room. He was so furious that he left the room and said that he was going to wire Senator Hart and demand that his testimony before the subcommittee be stricken from the record.

A few days later when I spoke with Arthur over the phone, he was still flaming. "I always thought you had gone overboard on what you said about these guys," he told me, "and I want to apologize. You didn't go far enough. These creeps are even worse than *you* ever said they were."

Postscript: A few days after an excerpt from this chapter appeared, in prepublication, in *Sports Illustrated* Magazine, Iglehart disposed of his stock in the Baltimore Orioles. I am sure that it was purely coincidental.

4

☻ ☻ ☻

The Lamb and the Fox

WHEN dealing with another operator—hustler or no—it is well to study your man with an eye to his strengths and his weaknesses, his vanities and his idiosyncrasies. Since hustling begins with a devout, unflagging faith in your own wits and your own cunning, it takes great willpower and even a small dash of humility (a quality that must be used sparingly since it is in permanently short supply) to admit you are overmatched. But much heartache will be saved him who, when the occasion demands, falls back to regroup for another day's battle against a less worthy foe.

The two men I least cared to match myself against during my days of freewheeling hustling were Branch Rickey and Horace Stoneham. Let us, students, consider Horace Stoneham. . . .

Horace Stoneham has only two occupations in life. He owns the Giants and he drinks. Horace is a sort of dumpy, chubby, apple-cheeked fellow who seems to be there for the sole purpose of being taken advantage of.

Some of the most wicked people I know have taken advantage of poor Horace.

In the middle of the 1948 season, Horace, having decided upon a new manager, paid a courtesy call upon Branch Rickey to request permission to negotiate with the Dodgers' all-purpose coach, Barney Shotton. Shotton had, after all, managed the Dodgers to the pennant only a year earlier while Leo Durocher was sitting out his mystery-suspension in California, deprived of all company except Laraine Day, Frank Sinatra and that ever-ready deck of cards.

"I'll give you your choice," said Rickey. "You can have Shotton or you can have Durocher."

"Well," said Stoneham, his chubby pink cheeks all innocent and aglow, "I'll take Durocher."

Branch Rickey had struck again. Papa Branch was anxious to dump Durocher with the least possible trouble to himself, and he had very neatly shunted him onto poor unsuspecting Horace.

In 1957, Walter O'Malley came to Horace Stoneham to confide that he had a little deal in the works whereby O'Malley would take the Dodgers to Los Angeles, Stoneham would take the Giants to San Francisco, and the Empire State Building, being somewhat difficult to crate, would remain in New York.

O'Malley, who has been immortalized in current literature under the name of Goldfinger, had a deal worked out for himself which, though still somewhat sketchy in my mind, went something like this: O'Malley was going to build a ball park, and in return, a grateful legislature was to grant him the divine right of kings. To make his move practicable to the rest of the league O'Malley needed a second team out on the West Coast. Oh, how he needed that second team! With troubles enough ahead of him in working his way out of Brooklyn it was of surpassing importance that there be smooth passage through the league.

Why not come along with me for the sake of fellowship? he asked Horace.

Why sure, said poor gullible Horace, beaming happily. Nothing like a cross-country trip to broaden a man's scope.

Life has a way of playing these nasty little tricks on Horace.

You may not believe this, but there was a time when I sank so low as to take advantage of poor amiable Horace myself.

When I bought the Cleveland Indians I was determined,

for reasons having to do with segregation, to move the spring training camp from Florida to Arizona. I had Tucson all set up for myself but since I also needed another team somewhere on the horizon to play against, I suggested to Jim Gallagher that he move the Cubs' training grounds from Catalina Island to Phoenix. Catalina was such a lousy place to train that I was confident Phil Wrigley would just jump at the chance. But no, Jim said, Wrigley wasn't quite ready to evacuate Catalina yet.

Gallagher suggested that I try Horace Stoneham, so I did. Was Horace interested? Sure, Horace was interested.

Together with Roy Drachman, a Tucson realtor, I worked Horace's deal out with the mayor of Phoenix. When the papers were ready to be signed, Horace flew down from New York. The following day, Roy and I drove over from Tucson for the ceremony.

As we entered Horace's suite at the Westward Ho Hotel we were greeted by the sound of his whisky baritone roaring insults into the telephone at the operators. With his full day's head start, he was already nicely loaded.

At lunch, Horace was still throwing those Scotches down, and I, being an amiable sort of fellow, had a few cans of beer just to keep him company. When the mayor finally arrived with the contract, Horace—ever mindful of his reputation as the perfect host—insisted that they have a couple of drinks together.

When the contract was finally placed in front of him, Horace put down the glass, picked up the pen and promptly dropped it. I handed it to him and he scribbled something that would pass as his signature.

With the press coming in for the story within the hour, we had a second contract prepared to permit us to fake a picture. Now, Horace has a simply amazing faculty of rallying himself when strangers are around. Once the press was on the scene, his eyes became unglazed, his shoulders squared and his speech unscrambled. He posed for the pictures nicely and went off and talked to the writers. If you didn't know Horace, there was no possible way to tell that he had been stoned ten minutes before they walked into the room.

Horace and I both had to go back up east that night, and we had reservations on the same American Airline flight to Chicago. The mayor insisted upon commemorating the occasion by taking us both out to dinner, however, and that was a mistake. When the time came to leave for the airport, Horace was stoned again. We had to pour him into a cab and then support him all the way out to the plane, the mayor on one side and I on the other.

Now, I wasn't too much help in that kind of an enterprise because my bad leg was in a heavy walking cast and I was on crutches. I was staggering under Horace's load, you might say, even more than Horace. Between trying to hold up my end of Horace and trying to keep myself balanced on the crutches, I must have looked like a particularly besotted cripple.

All the weight was therefore thrown upon the mayor, which meant that he, a rather short stubby guy to begin with, was staggering at least as badly as either of us. As luck would have it, the terminal was mobbed and you could just see all those registered voters glaring at us and saying, "Look at those three drunks. Disgraceful." All the poor mayor could do was duck his head, pray that his constituents wouldn't recognize him, and keep Horace moving toward the plane.

At last we got him up the stairs and dumped him into his seat. The stewardesses strapped him in, and immediately Horace dropped off to sleep.

I should have been as lucky. I was dead tired, the flight was about the roughest I have ever been on, but I couldn't get any sleep at all because Horace was snorting and snoring across the aisle from me.

The moment the plane hit the runway at Midway, he awoke—fresh and raring to go. "Hey, Bill," he said, straining against the straps, "let's get a drink."

A few years ago, I read a fascinating newspaper article detailing how Stoneham, through brilliant long-range planning and incredible hardship, had opened up Arizona to the big leagues, a feat which seemed to make the Lewis and Clark expedition look like a Sunday stroll through the park.

Oh yes, before I forget. Horace remained so furious at the telephone operators at the Westward Ho Hotel that he refused to quarter his players there. Instead, he put them in a motel and ultimately, either bought it or built a new one nearby. And a very profitable venture his motel is today.

What have I been trying to prove here with these tales of man's inhumanity to man? That Stoneham is a little lamb who somehow always comes up covered with roses? Not at all. I have not the slightest doubt that Stoneham was perfectly aware that Rickey was disenchanted with Durocher, especially since, when you think about it, Shotton was never Stoneham's type of manager at all. When you consider how Rickey likes to operate (and we shall consider it shortly), it becomes quite evident that anyone who was trying to encourage Rickey to turn loose of Durocher would have used precisely that approach, confident that Rickey would pull the old sleight-of-hand for which he is so famous and maneuver Horace into taking the man Horace had really wanted all along.

All Horace got in Durocher was the best manager of the day —given the proper tools and the proper setting. All Durocher did for him was win two pennants and one World Series.

As for the move to San Francisco, Horace was ready to get out of New York anyway. The Polo Grounds were falling down around his ears, the newspapermen, while fond of him in many ways, were fed up with his operation and his total unavailability and, the real crusher, Horace was deeply in hock to his concessionaire, Frank Stevens. O'Malley wasn't in any trouble at all; Stoneham was the man in trouble. So much trouble that the city fathers in Minneapolis had just finished building a stadium, confident that the Giants would soon be coming in to fill it.

O'Malley not only got him a better territory, he did all the preliminary work for him in San Francisco, thereby permitting Horace to slip out of New York without even a bad press.

With everybody so anxious to get in their blows at O'Malley, Horace even emerged with a modest amount of sympathy. As always, it pleased everybody to make Horace out as a poor, muddled but essentially decent fellow who had been fast-talked into leaving by that wily devil, O'Malley.

Poor, muddled Horace was fast-talked into moving into the fastest-growing area in the whole country, something—and you had better believe it—Horace had very carefully checked into. Since life's course always runs so smoothly for Stoneham there wasn't even the usual problem about the territorial rights. Tom Yawkey, his old pal, owned the San Francisco franchise. Yawkey is always so willing to help out a friend that he swapped the San Francisco territorial rights for the Minneapolis territorial rights, even up.

As for the Arizona deal, Horace undoubtedly considered my proposition, found that it suited his own purposes very nicely—since he was about to go into the Negro market too—and was quite content for me to go ahead and do legwork for him.

When the crystal ball clears you always seem to find that everybody sets out to take advantage of Horace, and by dint of great effort, manage to trick him into doing what he has already decided to do. Horace stays home and drinks, the other guy is sure he has outsmarted him, and it is hard to say which one is happier.

Stoneham and Cal Griffith are the last of that dying breed, the owner who has inherited the property, operates it himself and has nothing else going for him. Although the Giants would seem to be badly outgunned when it comes to money, organization and corporate backing, Stoneham manages to win a pennant every few years while other owners, having expended sums into the millions, are wondering why they can't get out of the second division. The Giants do start with Willie Mays, which is better than starting with a 10-day suspension. They also have their own country, the Dominican Republic, a small island populated entirely by people named Alou, plus an occasional 20-game winner named Marichal.

Where Horace really finesses the field, though, is in that rare ability to outdrink and outtrade the opposition simultaneously. The Giants won the pennant in 1951 when Horace got Alvin Dark and Eddie Stanky from the Boston Braves for Sid Gordon, Willard Marshall and Buddy Kerr, one of the best trades in history. As difficult as it may be to believe today, there was virtually unanimous agreement at the time that the Braves had got so much the best of that deal that they had put themselves right back into pennant contention. It turned out to be a trade that wrecked the Braves so completely that it led directly to their evacuation of Boston.

It is not completely illusory to say that if that trade hadn't been made, I'd have been able to move the Browns into Milwaukee and the history of baseball—to say nothing of the history of Bill Veeck—would have been materially changed, possibly even for the better.

Stoneham then won the 1954 pennant with another steal when he plucked John Antonelli from the Braves for Bobby Thomson. Antonelli was a strong young pitcher just coming to form. Thomson, his best years behind him, was a good ballplayer whose reputation had been enhanced all out of proportion to his true ability by the glamour of the homer of 1951. Perini, always Stoneham's lamb, had just finished his first glorious season in Milwaukee and he was eager to reward the fans and strengthen his team's pennant chances by bringing in the Hero of 1951.

Perini didn't want to give up Antonelli at all, but Stoneham kept throwing Antonelli's name into the conversation between drinks, while vowing that he would never give up Thomson. Whitey Lockman they could have, but Thomson? Never. The Hero of '51, he insisted, was part of the folklore of the big city, the idol of all Giant fans, a civic monument to whom the tourists came as to a shrine.

The more Perini couldn't get Thomson the more his mouth

watered. There was no longer any attempt to hold out on Antonelli but simply to get Thomson for him instead of Lockman. Which was precisely what Horace had in mind all along.

But it is the 1962 pennant, being most recent, that best illustrates Stoneham's technique.

It is an axiom in baseball—which only means that everybody keeps saying it—that the best trade is the trade that helps both sides. In the overall picture, it may even be true. Everybody says that he wants the player he has traded away to have the best possible season, a most noble and commendable sentiment. I recommend it highly to others. Lurking in the deep shoals of every trader's heart, however, lie dreams of pure larceny. The best trade is not the trade in which you give up something to get something, the best trade, if we will face up to this like men of the world, is the trade in which you give up nothing and get everything. At least, if I were given a choice that's the one I'd take.

Horace's great attraction to his colleagues is that he looks so innocent and vulnerable and is so well and favorably known for his drinking habits that he inspires them with an almost missionary zeal to get him drunk and steal him blind.

At every winter meeting, they come trooping into Horace's suite with the bottled goods in their hot little hands and a message of mutual gain on their lips.

Exuding fellowship and greed, they pour the drinks for Horace until they have him drunk enough to force upon him the players who are going to go on and win the Giants another pennant.

Because what they forget is that while they are pouring for Horace, Horace is also pouring for them. Full many an unwary voyager has foundered on Horace's Scotch-on-the-rocks. Liquor befuddles some and fortifies others. Stoneham's great virtue is that he appears to be most befuddled when he is most fortified. Horace, in short, can outdrink them all.

When Horace is going good, and there is nothing like trading talk to get the metabolism flowing, he can drink through a whole week, with small pause for either food or sleep. I take no stock in the beer-hall talk that Horace has a wooden leg; my own theory is that his giblets are made of sponge. When the time comes for them to snap the trap on their little red-cheeked lamb, they find a bushy red-tailed fox gleefully snapping the trap on them.

The building of the 1962 pennant-winner can serve as a textbook example of piecing a pitching staff together while giving up absolutely minimum in exchange. . . .

In December, 1958, Roy Hamey, a man of parts, tippy-toed into Horace's domain, ordered a few jeroboams and coolers, and talked his host out of Reuben Gomez in return for Jack Sanford, a strong-armed right-hander who was better known as a junior member of the Phillies' little band of night riders than for any exceptional pitching prowess.

Gomez had become one of those problems that will continue to vex baseball operators as long as we insist upon playing human beings instead of computers. Reuben was a good workmanlike number-three man on anybody's staff until he made the mistake of hitting big Joe Adcock with a pitch. When Adcock unexpectedly came after him with a bat, Gomez broke and ran. Pictures of him in full flight appeared in the papers all over the country—and probably back in his native Puerto Rico.

That one moment of his life had wrought its change in Rube Gomez. It was as if he felt that he had lost the respect of the other players and, having forfeited their respect, he seemed to lose all respect for himself. When you're out there in the big-league pressure cooker, a pitcher's attitude—his utter confidence that he has an advantage of will and luck and guts over the hitter—is almost as important as his stuff. Freddie Hutchinson won 95 games in the big leagues on little more than character and strength of purpose; Early Wynn won his first 275 games on stuff and his last 25 on memory and meanness. Usually, it's the other way around. Every team has its can't-miss pitcher who always manages to throw the home-run ball at the wrong time.

He throws it at the wrong time because he *knows* he's going to throw it at the wrong time.

Gomez, having broken and run—Lord Jim to the life—was never effective again. For Philadelphia, he was a total loss.

Sanford was a good pitcher for the Giants from the start; in their pennant year he won 24 games.

In November, 1959, Paul Rapier Richards, a cold professorial type, known in faultless sports-page prose as the Sage of Waxahachie, rode into town sitting tall in the saddle to trade livestock with Horace through the long night.

Paul is one of the great minds in baseball. He is so careful that he will pause for perhaps thirty seconds to find the precise word he is looking for. He is so cold that when he enters his clubhouse, with his rigid military bearing, the whole room goes silent.

Just as dawn was about to break over the ice-cooler, Paul convinced Horace that he should surrender a brawny outfielder, Jackie Brandt, for a frail, non-winning left-hander, Billy O'Dell. There are eyewitnesses who will swear that Paul, having stolen the center fielder he so badly needed, left the room chortling— although anyone who knows him must suspect gross exaggeration. When Paul is delirious with joy a small, scarcely perceptible smile plays across his lips.

It happened that Brandt had become a problem to Stoneham because Willie Mays had somehow got it into his head that the manager, Bill Rigney, thought Jackie was a better ballplayer. Willie, having just lost the great man of his early career, Leo Durocher, still had a great need to be shown that he was appreciated as a player and liked as a person.

Through no fault of his own, Brandt had become spectacularly expendable.

When the Giants won the pennant two years later, O'Dell won 19 games. The Orioles are still trying to solve their center-field problem.

In November, 1961, my good friend Ed Short, of the White Sox, arrived upon the scene to pit his youth, exuberance and staying power against Stoneham's experience. Short had a dream too. His dream was to talk Horace out of a couple of good young players in return for two aging pitchers, Billy Pierce and Don Larsen. Ed had to do his negotiating with Chub Feeney (an excellent baseball man himself), and Chub had to clear every move with Horace. Ed emerged, doing a slightly swoozled buck-and-wing, happy in the fond belief that he had swindled Horace out of four players.

You still haven't heard of three of those players. We would have been able to say that you haven't heard of any of them, except that the fourth man was Eddie Fisher who has developed into a great relief pitcher—under Al Lopez' magic touch—these past two years.

As for Pierce, he won 17 games for the Giants that year, while Larsen was giving them the middle relief man they had desperately needed. (Although the rumor that Horace really wanted Larsen as a drinking companion who could go the full distance is not to be wholly discredited either.)

That Horace, everybody said, he sure is lucky.

I was fortunate enough to have my initial experience in dealing with Horace from a somewhat different perspective. It came at the end of my first year of operating the old Milwaukee Brewers in the American Association, and I wasn't looking to outwit him, outdrink him or out anything him. I was trying to give him a bargain—not because I was anxious to help him but because it happened, under the circumstances I found myself in, to be the best way to help myself.

I had ended my first season the same way I had started it—deeply in debt. I was far better off at the end, however, because I had a couple of good young left-handed pitchers, Johnny Schmitz and Dave Koslo, who I knew were going to bail me out. Jim Gallagher, my old buddy, was the general manager of the Cubs, and he offered me $40,000 for Schmitz and $30,000 for Koslo.

I sold Schmitz to him but I had other plans for Koslo.

In those days, an independent like myself could still operate successfully in the minors by developing players and selling them to the majors. My grand design at Milwaukee was to set up an auction at which the majors could shop. Everything would be on display and everything would be for sale—to the highest bidder.

At the winter meeting, I called on Horace and told him he could have Koslo for $20,000.

"Oh no you don't," Horace said. "If he was any good you'd sell him to your friends in Chicago. You're not going to dump your second-liners on me."

I told Horace what the Cubs had already offered for Koslo, and of course he didn't believe me. I showed him Gallagher's telegram and he still didn't believe me. "If you can sell him for $30,000," he said, as if I were an idiot child for trying to put over something so raw, "why are you trying to talk me into buying him for $10,000 less?"

"Because," I told him, "I know that your attitude is precisely the attitude I'm going to have to overcome. I want to get you guys bidding against each other and I know that isn't going to happen as long as everybody thinks my best players are automatically going to the Cubs.

"You're right about one thing," I told him. "I *owed* the Cubs the first shot at my best player. All right, now I'm even with them. To get that point across I'm willing to sell a couple of players cheap. Marked down. But only a couple. If I were you I'd grab Koslo while the Get Acquainted Sale is still on."

I had started with Stoneham because it seemed to me that he, more than any other operator, had the kind of solid baseball background to understand that in order to make a success of the kind of free-wheeling minor-league operation I was running, it was logical for me to be doing precisely what I was telling him I was doing. I had leveled with him all the way, because the situation called for me to level with him. I didn't even try to tell him that I thought Koslo was a better pitcher than Schmitz.

He bought Koslo for $20,000, and it was a very good purchase for him. Over the long run, Koslo may have even been a better pitcher than Schmitz.

As an operator Stoneham has one blind spot; he has no interest whatsoever in promotion. It killed him in New York, and unless he gives Chub Feeney, a really bright young man, more freedom it will eventually catch up to him again in San Francisco.

When it came to probing for his weak spot in trading, I could come up with only one possibility. Horace has a highly developed case of the Irish-Catholic's clannishness. The names around him are predominantly the Feeneys and the Sheehans. One of the projects that was always simmering in the back of my mind at Milwaukee was to fatten up an Irish ballplayer for Stoneham, because I had no doubt at all that he would be willing to pay far more for him than he was worth.

Most of our players were signed right out of Wisconsin, though, and the woods of Wisconsin do not abound in Irishmen. I did have hopes for Merv Connors, a first baseman of severely limited talents. Merv did a bit of drinking himself when the opportunity arose—which on that club was always— and I had to get rid of him in a hurry before he flew all the way to New York by himself. Besides, I was faced with a perplexing ethical problem. Was it really fair to stick as congenial a drinker as Horace with as dark and moody a drinker as Connors. I didn't see anything basically unfair, understand, about ruining Horace's days with a lousy ballplayer, but I didn't think it quite fair to ruin his nights with a nasty drunk.

I'm sure I was right in my reading of Horace, though. Stoneham later fell in love with a non-hitting Irish shortstop named Buddy Kerr, who he insisted was one of the world's great fielders. Not even Leo Durocher—who knows a shortstop when he comes face to face with one—could convince him that Kerr was setting fielding records because he was covering so little ground.

Because his interests are so limited, Horace, more than most men his age, has remained an undiluted product of his background. Basically, he is little different from his father, Charles Stoneham, the original owner of the Giants. Charles Stoneham was a gambler, a bookie, a ticket scalper. The Stonehams, father and son, lived in the Broadway gambler's world of impulsive, compulsive and colorful characters, a world held together by a rigid code. Your word was good. You paid your debts. You didn't presume to judge the kind of life your friends and acquaintances lived, just so long as they observed the code too. Part of the code—never stated but always understood—was that you could depend upon a friend to be as consistent in his vices and follies as in his virtues so that everybody knew where they stood. A friend could be as much of a character as he wished, in other words, just so long as he wasn't a phony. He had to be, as they said on the West Side, "the gen-u-wine article, the real McCoy."

With Horace, the Irish-Catholic clannishness and the Broadway gambler's sense of loyalty came together to produce a man to whom friendship and loyalty are so much a way of life that disloyalty becomes an act of treason. A friend is a friend is a friend. If you cannot believe that, what is there left to believe?

Clancy Sheehan is a good example of the Stoneham loyalty to the clan. Horace went so far as to make Sheehan his manager after he let Rigney go in midseason, although the only logical grounds seemed to be that Sheehan was second-guessing Rigney so much that Horace felt he deserved a chance to do it himself. (The only other possible explanation is that maybe Horace didn't know what he was doing—maybe he was sober at the time.) Sheehan, who had no more chance of managing a club successfully than your little boy, took a club Rigney had always had in contention and guided it right into the second division.

Dutch Reuther, another old hand, comes out of the friendship slot too. It is Horace's good fortune that Reuther happens to be one of the better scouts around, because Dutch would remain with him forever even if he were one of the worst.

Stoneham has always been unusually loyal to his managers, too. He has given the manager's job, with the sole exception of

Durocher, to old Giants: Terry, Ott, Rigney and Dark, and even to Clancy Sheehan. Even after Sheehan made a laughing-stock of himself, Horace kept him in his old position as boon companion and chief wandering scout. Nobody would have expected anything else. Sheehan had performed, Stoneham would reflect, no differently than anyone should have expected Sheehan to perform. He had remained in character. His call upon Stoneham's friendship and support would therefore remain undimmed and undiminished.

His breaks with Leo Durocher and Alvin Dark, two entirely different loaves of bread, are perfect illustrations of the rockbound code by which Stoneham lives.

There has always been the story that the beginning of the end for Durocher came at a show-folk banquet when Leo laughed at a Danny Kaye burlesque of a drunken Stoneham slobbering all over himself while trying to make a speech.

Now, it is true enough that Horace would be sorely wounded to hear that Leo would be so disloyal, and he would be even more hurt that Danny Kaye, another close friend, would stoop to making fun of him. But Horace's anger at that sort of thing wouldn't last. Horace knows that Leo is a show-biz type, so if Leo travels with show-biz people and goes the show-biz route, that is to be expected. He would also know that if he himself wanted to hang around comedians he had to expect to become a foil for their humor, and that the humor would not necessarily be kind. After the original indignation had subsided, Horace would even accept the fact that he had opened himself up to that kind of ridicule by getting up at many a baseball banquet to make one of his rambling speeches.

Durocher was fired, in all probability, for reasons having to do with nothing more unique than his well-known habit of losing interest in a ball club once the club has dropped out of the pennant race.

Horace and Leo were still on good enough terms four years later so that Horace sought Leo out to inquire about his availability to take on the job again. And that's what brought on what now seems to be an unbridgeable gap between them. When Horace made the announcement that he had hired Alvin Dark without bothering to inform Durocher, Leo felt he had been kept on the hook and dangled, an attitude he made abundantly clear by blasting away at Stoneham in the press.

By Stoneham's code, that's unforgivable. You have a beef, come on up, I'll pour you a drink and we'll talk it over. You don't go shooting off your mouth for the whole world to hear.

Stoneham is not by nature a feuder. He has never, to my knowledge, ever attacked anyone in the press. On the other hand, he is not a man to forget. Horace just sits and waits. Sooner or later everybody in baseball figures to wander into the little corner of the baseball world he rules. An owner will come walking into his lair one night to try to out-bubbly him, and Horace will send him home no wiser but considerably poorer. With everybody else ... well, just by virtue of his ownership of the San Francisco franchise, he has the patronage rights, with all its attendant power, of a district leader. He controls his share of those few precious major-league jobs, and over the year he has been able to use them to reward his friends and punish his enemies.

He finally achieved that gratifying end with Leo Durocher in the fall of 1964. Let us all hope that revenge is its own reward because Stoneham could very well have hurt himself far more than he hurt Durocher.

From the time Stoneham made the big move to San Francisco, the Giants have been far richer in talent than in pennants. They do not win as often as they should because the San Francisco team is really three teams. A white team, a Negro team and a Spanish-speaking team. Bill Rigney was the first manager called upon to perform the acrobatic miracle of keeping those three teams in motion and, for a brief period, he came close to pulling it off. Alvin Dark managed to squeeze the one championship in there before his little juggling act inevitably collapsed.

There is only one man with free access to all three cliques, and that man is Willie Mays. Not because Willie is skilled in intrigue. On the contrary. He is acceptable to everybody on the team because he is essentially so guileless. Willie is Willie, and everybody admires him and likes him. A great part of Dark's initial success was due to Willie's willingness to assume the job of ambassador without portfolio for the man who had befriended him when Willie was a frightened rookie and Alvin was the captain of the Giants. Alvin's ultimate failure we will go into momentarily.

There is one man who could, even better than Dark, juggle those three teams for a while before the law of gravity caught up to him—Leo Durocher. First of all, Willie would go all out to help Leo, because Leo has always been the great man in his life.

(Although frankly, I suspect that Leo's influence over Willie may be overestimated by this time. People do not remain the same and neither do situations. Willie was always considerably more intelligent than he ever let on, and considerably more independent than the public was led to believe. Willie knows when he is being used, and he has reached the stage where he makes up his own mind how much he is going to let himself be used.)

Still, the situation does hold. Willie does love Leo, and while he is hardly going to be Leo's pet—or anybody's pet—ever again, there is no doubt whatever that each of them has played a big part—and a fondly remembered part—in the other's life. Leo could undoubtedly get more out of Willie, on and off the field, than anybody else.

Beyond that, Leo himself is without any racial consciousness —or even racial unconsciousness. Leo looks on each human being with the purest of motives; i.e., what can this guy do to make Leo Durocher's passage through life easier, more fun and more profitable? Leo doesn't care what your race, color or religion is. He just wants to know whether you can be of any use to him. Leo Durocher is a true hustler, and a hustler cannot fritter away his mind's time or effort on foolish prejudices.

Nor is Leo a man to let a bad situation run him. Leo would confront the San Francisco situation head on and, unless his hand has lost its touch, he would scheme, manipulate and maneuver to bring it under his control. It would blow up on him eventually, of course, just as it has blown up on everybody else, but he might be able to control it for a year or, with a great deal of luck, even for two.

At any rate, Leo would have a better chance than anyone else.

Nobody knows this better than Stoneham, because nobody has lived with the situation longer. But Stoneham was not going to give the job to Durocher, the logical man, if only because Stoneham knew how badly Durocher wanted it.

Instead, Stoneham hired Herman Franks, who was Durocher's coach, caddy and coat holder during the great days in New York. Horace obviously hopes that Willie will do for Leo's man what he would do for Leo. He won't, of course. Even with the best resolve in the world, he won't. He can't. These things stem from the interplay of personality, and personalities are not interchangeable.

If Stoneham wasn't perfectly aware that Franks was no Durocher, then Franks himself most certainly was. The more Franks thought about the problems confronting him in his first big-league managerial job, the more he began to sweat. When Durocher ended up without a job, in the wake of the Busch-Rickey-Keane fandango, Franks had the brilliant idea of asking Leo whether he'd be willing to come to San Francisco and work for *him* as a coach. (And, speaking of the interplay of personalities, what a fascinating situation that would have been.)

Surprisingly enough, Leo was willing. For Leo has come to the conclusion that he would rather dance in the chorus line than be out of action altogether. Or, to use a far better metaphor, that he would rather be a whale in a bathtub than a whale on the beach.

For Stoneham, this would seem to be the best of all possible solutions. He could have the benefits of Leo's influence without having to break his own code by hiring him again as manager. He could, if it pleased him, even comfort himself with the knowledge that he had brought a humbled Durocher to heel.

But no. Stoneham's code is far too rigid for that. He would not hire Leo Durocher. Period. During the drinking sessions with Stoneham over the winter months, Herman Franks would pick his spot to run over his coaching staff with him so that he could add at the end, "And you know the other guy I want."

And Horace would just grunt, "Yeah, I know. And you can't have him."

Horace feels that he cannot depend upon Durocher's loyalty, and in Stoneham's world that's the gravest of all sins.

Now we come to Alvin Dark. Let us begin by eliminating any lingering notion that Dark was fired because of anything arising out of that New York story in which Alvin either did or did not say that Spanish players were lazy and Negro players were dumb. Dark's mistake was that he generalized where he should have particularized. Horace would have been quite able to do the particularizing for him.

The break between the owner and the manager had come well before that. It had come for reasons that would be incomprehensible or, at best, comic, if you were not completely aware by now of the Stoneham code of acceptable behavior. In baseball, let me say again, you are dealing with human beings, and human beings are, as we all know too well, unpredictable, inconsistent and downright infuriating. Stoneham alone is consistent and predictable (possibly because there's nobody sitting up nights keeping score on him), and that makes him the most infuriating human being of all.

Horace Stoneham's relationship with Alvin Dark was altogether different than it had ever been with any other manager. Normally, Stoneham insists that his manager drink with him. It goes with the job. Horace is generous to a fault. When he drinks everybody drinks. Especially if he is paying their salaries.

Unfortunately, he does his drinking at night, which can make life difficult for a manager who requires more than a minimum amount of sleep.

Horace's familiar fraternal cry is "Sitsee." Always "Sitsee." He has been known to sit on the overcoat of a reluctant guest to hold him through the early morning hours. He once locked three weary writers into a hotel room with him, only to have them climb out through the transom when he thoughtlessly dozed off.

Fortunately for Stoneham, his employees seem to find his early-morning dissertations far more stimulating than those not tied to him by the healing bonds of a contract. Nowhere in the record book, at any rate, is there any indication that any Giant manager ever made a break for it. This is well for Horace, and even better for the manager. Horace's greatest pleasure is drinking with his manager. When he drinks with his manager they can talk baseball and when they talk baseball, Horace can second-guess him. The more Horace drinks, the more he second-guesses. The more he second-guesses, the happier he becomes. If he drinks enough—and the odds are that he will—he will become so overjoyed with it all that he will fire the manager for not knowing as much baseball as the owner. This is known as voting your stock. This also tends to be very unsettling to a manager until he learns that Horace knows himself well enough not to hold himself accountable to anything he says when he is drunk.

Alvin Dark is a rigid Southern Baptist, who lives by a code even more demanding than Stoneham's. Alvin does not drink or smoke or curse. He lives by the Bible. He tithes to the Church, speaks at religious gatherings, evangels among the heathen.

When Horace hired him, he was well aware that for once he was not getting a drinking partner in the bargain; that he was foregoing those long and pleasurable second-guessing sessions; that he was to some extent surrendering a certain amount of his normal control.

He hired him anyway, because Alvin was one of his old boys

and Horace believes in giving his old boys their chance. There was something else involved too. Alvin apparently had reason to believe he was going to be hired to manage the Giants when Durocher was through. Durocher left ahead of schedule though, Dark was still playing, and Bill Rigney, having just won the Little World Series at Minneapolis, was entitled to his chance.

Still, if Horace felt that he had sidestepped a promise to Alvin, however vague that promise may have been, Horace would want to make it up to him.

So the two men are not as far apart as they seem to be at first glance. Stoneham, like Dark, has his own highly moral precepts. It is only on definitions and values that they are at such odds.

Stoneham, as always, was willing to allow Alvin to be what he was, to accept him as he was and, I think we can say with some certainty, even to admire him for what he was. It may even have pleased him to have such a paragon working for him. The sensual man may not understand what makes the spiritual man tick, but he is usually quite willing to concede him the right to live his life as he sees fit, especially since the pleasures that he foreswears are his own. I have not, alas, observed that the spiritual man gives the sensual man the same break, and I have often wondered whether it is because he is concerned for his soul or envious of his pleasures.

Not to make Stoneham out to be a man of untoward tolerance, it should be added that he was willing to put up with all these spiritual values only because Dark also possessed the full complement of competitive virtues so admired in baseball. Alvin was always a rough, tough competitor, and a red-necked loser.

When Jackie Robinson, angered that several of his teammates had been knocked down by Sal Maglie, bowled little Davey Williams over at first base, it was Dark who gathered his teammates together in the dugout and informed them that somebody was to get Jackie. By coincidence, it was Alvin himself who immediately hit a routine double, kept right on running and, with Jackie dug in at third base, threw a jarring football block that not only flattened him but knocked the ball clean out of his hand.

Stoneham would not forget a thing like that. Stoneham would understand that Dark, like himself, is a man who will protect his own.

All things considered, Alvin was a good enough manager. He eked out the one pennant and if he never got the team together again, he was at least able to keep them in a respectable position. Stoneham and Dark lived their own lives by their own lights and met only to discuss the ball club. The owner's admiration for his manager remained undiminished.

And then the one thing happened that no one, in his wildest dreams, would have considered. If you had taken a pool to guess how a break between the owner and manager would finally come, nobody could possibly have come out a winner.

What happened? Not much really—just that Horace Stoneham came to believe that Alvin Dark had developed a flaw in that faultless character of his. Not on Stoneham's terms, but on Dark's own stern terms which prohibited all diversions, however innocuous, even a cigarette.

OK, big deal. You and I would have chuckled and thought, "Hmmmm, that's interesting. So Alvin's human too." Not Horace. Horace reacted as if it were a personal affront; yes, an act of disloyalty. It was as if Stoneham were saying, "I took you on your own terms and you were lying to me all along." At that moment, Alvin was no longer the gen-u-wine article, the real McCoy. When Alvin fell out of character, he fell from grace.

Human nature being what it is, the final act in the comedy was inevitable. Once Horace thought that there was a flaw, one single minor flaw, in Alvin's character, he was suddenly set free to judge not only the man but the manager. *The real flaw, after all, was that Alvin was not what he pretended to be.* All right, maybe he was not the manager he had seemed to be, either.

Where Horace had, for once in his life, refrained from second-guessing his manager, he now looked for flaws in everything

Dark did. And let me tell you, once you look for flaws in a manager, *any* manager, you are going to find them in abundance. Where previously Dark could do no wrong, he now could do nothing right.

The final step came when the special dispensation that had been given to Dark was canceled. If Clancy Sheehan was a crony, at least he pretended to be nothing else. And when the boss said, "Sitsee," Clancy sat and Clancy drank.

All right, if Clancy Sheehan and Alvin Dark were brothers under the skin, then Alvin Dark would sitsee and Alvin Dark would drink too.

Well, Alvin wasn't coming up to the boss's suite to drink. He was still not going to base a relationship on Stoneham's terms, and Stoneham was no longer willing to let it stand on Alvin's terms. Communication between the owner and manager practically ground to a stop. Win or lose, Alvin was through.

It got so chilly up there by San Francisco Bay that if it had not been for all the commotion kicked up by that New York interview, Horace would undoubtedly have fired Dark before the end of the season.

To anybody except Stoneham, of course, the interview would have provided the perfect out for firing Dark. It would even have made him a hero in some quarters. It is typical of Horace that given every logical reason to seize upon that excuse, he refused to take it.

For, as you know by now, Stoneham does not go that route. If he was going to fire Alvin, it was not going to be under false pretenses. He would stand by his manager loyally on that one issue and let him go as quietly as possible at the end of the season.

Say this about Horace Stoneham: he remains true to himself. He is what he is, and you can take him or leave him.

Just don't walk into his lair with a bottle of the bubbly and delude yourself that you're going to get any the best of it.

5

☻ ☻ ☻

Snake Oil for Sale

WITH the decline of the minors and the passage of the free-agent draft, the ability to deal players for your own good and profit has become increasingly important. It is through top-level trades that the operator must now, for the most part, fill his holes.

Interleague trading, which was finally put through in 1960, would seem to have made the big trade more comfortable for the weak of heart; it is far easier to let loose of one of your own starters when you know he won't be dedicating the rest of his playing career to make life miserable for you.

That's the theory anyway. But since practice and theory are so often at odds—one of the precepts the hustler must learn (it is to be hoped at minimum cost) and use (it is to be hoped to maximum profit)—the big trades, the ones that have influenced the pennant races in both leagues, have been made within the respective leagues.

So much for sheer logic.

The most important trade in the American League in recent history, since it moved both clubs into contention, was the one which sent Luis Aparicio, the premier shortstop in the league, to the Orioles for Pete Ward, a minor-league third baseman. Until the very end of 1964, it looked as if it were a trade which was going to win the pennant for one team or the other.

In the National League, the Pittsburgh Pirates traded themselves right into the second division by breaking up their infield and, in the process, the St. Louis Cardinals moved into contention and then up to the pennant with Dick Groat.

The Groat trade is well worth our attention. Groat, who was traded two years after he won the Most Valuable Player award, is the kind of player you give up at your peril. When you trade a Jim Gentile, you know exactly what you're giving up. It's all there in the home-run and RBI columns. There are a lot of guys who hit 30 home runs these days. Their value is usually less than meets the eye.

The value of a Dick Groat or an Eddie Stanky is not evident in the statistics, and not really evident on the field. Their value is in their knowledge, their opportunism, and their ability to make the right play at the right time. Most important of all, it is a fierce desire to win and an occult knowledge of *how to win*. You are trading intangibles and you tend not to get full value.

Eddie Stanky was on pennant-winning teams in Brooklyn, Boston and New York. Groat has now been on pennant-winning teams in Pittsburgh and St. Louis.

You trade such a player in haste and you repent in the second division. As Branch Rickey said about Eddie Stanky, "He can't hit, he can't field and he can't run. All he can do for you is *win*." When Papa Branch speaks, the wise man listens. Now that I think of it, Branch should have been listening to himself a little more closely, because he sold Stanky to Boston for—as it turned out in the end—$100,000. *Sold* him!

The master dealer and wheeler of them all was nonetheless Branch Rickey during his great days as master of the St. Louis Cardinals farm system.

Trading was an art with Rickey, and he approached it the way the master fakirs of old approached the Indian rope trick. It wasn't getting the rope to stand up that counted—any bush-league fakir could do that— it was getting his audience to sit up and take notice.

Branch, of course, held all the cards (no pun intended but I'll take it). He always had that bushy-tailed crop of good young players down on the farm and he'd let them develop until, as he liked to say in his paternal, humane way, they "turned to money."

The reserve strength down on the farm also allowed him to sell his name players while their market value was still at its peak but the players themselves were just beginning to slide down the backside of the mountain. All Branch ever wanted was more money than they were worth, plus a player or two who would turn out to be better than the "star" he had so generously handed over.

With all that merchandise, Branch was never a man to wait for the business to come to him. He was more like the old frontier snake-oil salesmen. He would load his wagon down with goodies and go from town to town, selling this shortstop as an all-purpose defensive nostrum and that pitcher as a specific for doubleheader blues. The artist in him demanded that he hypnotize the customer with his sales pitch and that when the time finally came to close the deal he pull the right card out of his sleeve—to undoubted internal applause.

The greatest proof of Rickey's genius was that you always knew what he was doing—except when he was doing it to you. Despite his reputation, he could get an operator into his room, mesmerize him with a three-hour smoke screen of verbiage, and send him home convinced the good old Branch had really been trying to help him out of his well-known philanthropic impulses.

The Rickey system was to drop in, unexpected, for a friendly visit, and once the talk had turned to his host's prospects offer a free consultation, as if he were some kindly old Dr. Christian unable to keep himself from looking down the kiddies' throats.

Branch would analyze your whole club for you, position by position, very subtly emphasizing your strengths rather than your weaknesses until you were convinced that you could win the pennant if you could only solve your one glaring weakness.

It was flattering to be told what a great job you had already done, of course, and since he would focus, in the end, on what was indubitably your weakest spot, you had to spend the first couple of hours agreeing with him.

Once there was agreement on where you needed help, Branch would swing into action. He possessed a mastery of the art of indirection that would have brought applause from Blackstone himself. (He had a little Houdini in him too. Branch could make your money disappear before your very eyes.)

It was agreed that you were weak at shortstop? "I can't help you there," Branch would say, sorrowfully. "But you see, if you would strengthen over here at third base, you are now permitting your shortstop to play a step closer to second base. Just by saving that step, your own shortstop has now become quite adequate and you haven't had to break up your second-base combination, the touchstone to success."

By some incredible stroke of luck, Branch had just the third baseman you needed and he was willing to let you have him relatively cheap.

Well, you're too smart for that. You aren't about to let him fob off a third baseman on you, especially when you're perfectly aware that he has a Triple-A shortstop who is supposed to be considerably more than adequate.

Rickey keeps downgrading the Triple-A shortstop, though, and keeps restating that fascinating thesis of strengthening your shortstop by changing third basemen. OK, you tell him slyly, you're willing to take your chances on the shortstop, inadequate though he may be, and considering Rickey's low opinion of him he should be willing to sell him cheap.

Ah. Now Rickey is trapped. Now he has to confess that the truth of the matter is that the Cardinals are counting upon the Triple-A shortstop to replace their own shortstop in a couple of years. But here's what he'll do for you. The Cards have a particularly bright shortstop down in the low minors who should be ready in about two more years. You take the third baseman to solve the pressing problem of the moment, and in two more years, when your shortstop will *really* have to be replaced, you can have first refusal rights on him.

You see the opening and jump in quickly. Since Branch doesn't need a shortstop at all for a couple of years and you need one badly now, then why doesn't he just sell you his Triple-A shortstop now, and in a couple of years, when the *Cards* need a replacement, the kid from the low minors will be ready to step in for *them*.

Well, Branch fights that tooth and nail for another hour or so, but the logic of your position is unassailable. You have him nailed with his own words. At length, there is nothing left for him to do except face up to it like a man and sell you the Triple-A shortstop at a suitably exorbitant price.

Question: Who has Rickey come down to sell you in the first place?

By making you coax him, Rickey has reversed the seller-buyer psychology. By letting you outwit him, he has put you in a frame of mind where you are so pleased with yourself that you are willing to entertain thoughts of large round sums of money. Branch has not only sold the player he has come to sell, he has quite probably got the maximum price he was shooting for.

Branch could pull this kind of shell game on the same club, over and over, because he was shrewd enough to study the front-office personnel as carefully as he studied the playing personnel. Like any practicing hypnotist, he was always looking for the perfect subject; i.e., the man who fell under his spell so easily that it was almost like posthypnotic suggestion.

In Chicago, he could absolutely mesmerize Clarence Rowland, the club vice-president, which was as good as mesmerizing Phil Wrigley since Rowland had Wrigley's ear. I saw him operate on Rowland very early in my career and it was not a sight to be lightly forgotten.

The Cubs had decided to break up their once great second-base combination, Billy Jurges and Billy Herman. Both of them seemed to have slowed up on the field, possibly because they teamed up so well and so vigorously off the field. At any rate,

Phil Wrigley had decided to take a leaf from the master's book and sell them while their market value was still high.

Almost before the echoes of that decision had faded away Rickey, who just happened to be in the neighborhood, dropped by the Cubs offices—936 Wrigley Building—to say hello to Pants Rowland. Within minutes—would you believe it?—they were sitting at one end of the big desk in the conference room discussing our problem.

I was a sort of general factotum in those days, and it was my habit to retire to the conference room in solitary poverty to eat my lunch. I caught the beginning of the conversation, lost them while they went downstairs to the restaurant, and picked them up again when they came back to complete the negotiations.

Young and impressionable though I was, I didn't think that Branch had picked our decision to dispose of Herman and Jurges out of the air (if only because radar hadn't been invented yet). The one thing I did know was that he was not interested in buying Herman or Jurges. Branch was always a seller in that kind of a market.

"You don't want to get rid of them both," Branch told Rowland. "It's too great a wrench on the fabric of the club. Your key player here is your second baseman because you can't afford to lose his bat." Since a second baseman could get by on know-how, Rickey told him, Herman would have years of value ahead of him if we teamed him with a fast young shortstop.

Well, that was all true enough if not particularly edifying. Herman's bat and know-how had made him the permanent National League All-Star second baseman. A case could be made right now that he is the best player still outside the Hall of Fame. Given any choice at all, there is nothing quite as effective as the flashy young shortstop playing alongside the wise old second baseman.

It was, of course, purely coincidental that the Cardinals' Triple-A clubs were top-heavy with flashy young shortstops like Bobby Sturgeon at Columbus and Marty Marion at Rochester.

One of the enduring myths of baseball is that Rickey gave the Cubs a choice between Marion and Sturgeon, and that the Cubs, in one of baseball's more horrendous miscalculations, chose Sturgeon. This is not really fair to Rowland, since Marion was the shortstop he was really interested in. Rickey had them both in the conversation at the beginning, but he was asking $85,000 for Sturgeon, and $125,000 for Marion—while giving the distinct impression that Sturgeon was the better buy.

It seemed, in fact, that Marion played an excessively deep shortstop and was being protected by his second baseman, Maurice Sturdy, a brilliant fielder who, just incidentally, had hit a robust .314. Branch wouldn't want to influence Pants—Judas Priest, no—and if Pants thought he'd be better off changing second baseman instead of shortstops, he just might do a lot worse than young Mr. Sturdy.

Finally, when the time was ripe, and Rowland's eyes had taken on a suitably glazed texture, Rickey said, "Here's what I'll do for you. You can have either one of them—Sturgeon or Sturdy—for $85,000. Take your pick."

The psychology of giving you a choice is just marvelous. In the first place it is an unequaled way of closing a sale. By making the choice, you are forced to the decision.

Psychologically Rickey has, in an odd way, added the values of the players together, even though he is only selling you one of them. You get a choice all right, but since few things are free in this competitive world, you are paying for it. Rickey didn't *give* you a choice, he *sold* you a choice. By the standards of the late 1930's, Sturgeon and Sturdy weren't worth $85,000 put together. Eighty-five thousand dollars was an enormous price in those days.

I was in and out of the conference room during the afternoon. I got back in time to hear Rowland take Bobby Sturgeon for the $85,000. While I was still wincing, Rickey was going into a song and dance about Rowland throwing in "that big awkward guy down at Moline. What's his name. . . ? The Russian outfielder?"

What's his name? At that point I threw up my hands, let out a wild, mad laugh and fled. The big guy down at Moline was Lou Novikoff, who had only led the league in hitting. Rickey not only knew his name, he knew his mother's name, his hobbies, his shoe size, his favorite brand of beer, his political party and his religious persuasion.

It was with some relief that I learned a short time afterward that Rowland had somehow resisted Rickey's final ploy and saved Novikoff for us.

With Sturgeon and Sturdy, Rickey couldn't have cared less whom we picked. Where he really played the shell game to perfection was when he gave the other team a choice, knowing in advance that they were going to take the lesser of the two players.

The classic case was when he stunned the Pittsburgh Pirates by giving them their choice between Johnny Rizzo and Enos Slaughter, who were not only the two most publicized outfielders in the minor leagues but were teammates at Columbus. Slaughter was by far the better of the two, as a hitter and as an all-around ballplayer. He had led the American Association in hitting (.382), runs scored, base hits and total bases. More than that, he was a Rickey-type player, fast, hustling, imaginative. He was also a left-handed hitter, and the St. Louis ball park is built for left-handed hitters.

But the figures were tricky. Columbus was a left-handed hitters' ball park. Right-handers had to hit the ball practically out of sight. With all that, Rizzo had hit a solid .358. He had hit almost as many home runs as Slaughter, 21 against 26. He had also hit 18 triples, which would indicate long drives to left center that would have been out of most parks. And he had 123 RBI's to Slaughter's 122.

All things considered, then, Rizzo undoubtedly had more power. More to the point, the *Pittsburgh* park was murder for a left-handed power hitter. The Pirates were already stocked with good left-handed hitters like the Waner brothers, Arkie

Vaughan, and Gus Suhr. What they needed, like bread, was a big right-handed bomb in the middle of their lineup.

Rickey knew that the Pirates had to go for Rizzo. By putting him in with Slaughter, he was upgrading Rizzo to Slaughter's potentialities. Well, he was doing even more than that. Since everyone knew that Rickey was close to infallible when it came to judging young ballplayers, the very fact that he appeared to be willing to give up the left-handed Slaughter and keep the right-handed Rizzo made it appear, on the surface, as if Rizzo must be the better of the two.

If it was known that Rickey was a great student of talent, it was also well known that he was a great judge of money. In return for such a gift, the Pirates could expect to pay. And pay they did.

You take risks when you play that game, of course. I know that Branch got caught early in the game when he offered my daddy the choice between Big Bill Lee, a right-hander, and Clarence Heise, a lefty. The Cubs were solid in right-handers with Lon Warneke, Guy Bush, Charlie Root and Pat Malone, and they had only one lefty, Larry French. They also had a scout named Jack Doyle who was an incomparable judge of minor-league talent. My daddy quickly took Lee, who went on to win 169 games. Heise won one game for the Cardinals.

Another of Rickey's favorite maneuvers with his rich crop of players was to present the prospective sucker . . . I mean, customer . . . with a most attractive list of players, most of whom he wouldn't have let him have at gunpoint. Branch would be asking wildly impracticable prices for most of them, which would not only serve to eliminate any possibility of a deal but also make the exorbitant price he was asking for the player he really wanted to sell look reasonable by comparison.

Frank Lane, who had been in a trading session or two himself, once caught him good during the time Branch was running the Brooklyn Dodgers. Branch had built himself another great farm system in Brooklyn, and this time he was getting a percentage of the income on all player sales.

Rickey dropped in on Lane in Chicago at the end of the season to commiserate with him on the sad state of his infield now that Luke Appling—who had been keeping the Chicago franchise afloat for years—was coming to the end of the road.

Fortunately, Rickey was loaded with shortstops again and, just as fortunately, he happened to have the usual shopping list on hand. The top item on the list was Bobby Morgan, the Montreal shortstop, and the price alongside his name read $250,000 and three players. Next in line was the Montreal second baseman Rocky Bridges, who some lucky buyer could have for a scant $150,000 and three players.

The infielders from the rest of the farm clubs were listed at similarly inflated figures, but down at the end, Frank's eyes lit upon Chico Carrasquel, who was finishing his first stateside season at Fort Worth, in the Texas League. Carrasquel could be had, apparently, for $50,000 plus the usual three players.

Knowing how Rickey operated, Lane bided his time until he was able to determine that the player Rickey was really there to unload on him wasn't an infielder at all. It was Sam Jethroe, a Negro outfielder of indeterminate age who was compiling a fat batting average at Montreal, mostly on sheer speed.

Rickey was willing to let Jethroe go for only $250,000 and three players. When you considered that you could have Jethroe for no more than it would cost you to buy Morgan, you can see that it was an absolute steal.

Frank professed to be interested, while making it clear the amount of money that had been allotted to him for the purchase of new players was limited. "First things first," he said. "Appling is about to collapse. I can't afford your top kids there, but if you give me a price on Carrasquel, I'll have an idea on what I can afford to pay for Jethroe."

Before they parted, they had agreed on a price of $25,000 and one player for Carrasquel with the understanding that they would meet again at Buffalo during the International League play-offs to close the deal.

In the intervening week or so, Frank made it a point to run

across Branch Rickey Jr. and ask for his assessment of Carrasquel, making it clear that a deal had been consummated with Papa Branch.

Papa Branch didn't show up in Buffalo, though, and so Lane, thinking fast, whipped off a telegram informing him he was about to announce the purchase of Carrasquel.

Rickey was on the phone immediately, protesting vehemently that he hadn't made a deal for Carrasquel but had only discussed him as part of a multiplayer transaction that was going to involve Jethroe.

Frank, needless to say, was bewildered. "Of course we completed it," he said. "You can check with Branch Jr."

Apparently Branch did check, because after a brief delay he was back on the line to say, "All right. I don't remember it that way but if I made an agreement I'll live up to it."

Frank announced the sale to the press immediately. A day or so later, Branch called back to get down to business on Jethroe.

"I'm not interested in Jethroe," Frank told him. "Whatever gave you that idea?"

Shed no tears for Branch Rickey, though. He unloaded Jethroe on the Boston Braves for $105,000.

You didn't outfox the Old Man often. What I remember most vividly was the sale of a sore-armed Dizzy Dean to the Cubs, easily the weirdest deal I have ever run across in my long and checkered career. It was no state secret, understand, that Dean had a bad arm. On the contrary, he had hurt his arm by getting back into action too early after his toe had been broken in the All-Star game, and you couldn't pick up a newspaper without finding sports columnists wondering whether it was wise for baseball clubs to risk such valuable property on a meaningless game.

Dean still had one thing left. His reputation. He was colorful, he drew fans and he was, after all, only twenty-seven years old. There is a saying in baseball that you can't get anybody out with your press clippings. Rickey set out to sell Dean's press clippings.

During spring training, word was passed around that Dean was available, a bit of news that moved nobody to any excesses of passion. Rowland went down to Florida to take a look at him, though, and a number of other clubs sent down their scouts too.

To show the assembled scouts how completely Dean had recovered, Rickey let him pitch exactly one inning through the entire spring. While Diz did get out of the inning alive, he made no effort to throw hard. That left Rowland to spend his afternoons watching Dean toss the ball along the sidelines, and his evenings listening to Rickey tell him how marvelously Diz was coming along.

When the clubs broke training camp, Rowland followed the Cardinals into St. Louis for their annual preseason game against the Browns. Back in Chicago, we were playing the White Sox.

I was charged with checking the ticket sellers at Wrigley Field, and our office was right next to the office Phil Wrigley used when he came to the park—which was as seldom as he could decently make it. Mr. Wrigley was in that day, though, to get the final report on Dean. I could hear him through the thinly partitioned wall as he talked over the phone with Pants Rowland.

Boots Weber, our general manager, was obviously listening in, because I could hear him wailing, "This is crazy . . . this is crazy."

The door finally opened and Boots called me in to lend him some moral support. All Rickey was asking, I was told, was $185,000 and five players, including George Tucker Stainback, Jr., a good-looking young outfielder, and Curt Davis, who was a very good pitcher at that moment and potentially a great one.

Rowland, who had not seen Dean throw a ball in anger all spring, was recommending most strenuously that we give it to him.

In return for all this largesse, Ricky was not only unwilling to give us a guarantee that Dean would be able to pitch, he wanted us—if you can conceive of such a thing—to give *him* a clause disclaiming any recourse against the Cardinals in the event Dean *couldn't* pitch.

Although Boots was never too outspoken where Mr. Wrigley was concerned, he was managing to get across his considered opinion that to buy Dean without a written guarantee was sheer lunacy.

But, it became apparent, Rowland was so mesmerized this time that he had been arguing all of Rickey's points for him. Rickey had promised him that Diz would pitch enough to win a pennant for us and that was good enough for Pants.

At last, Mr. Wrigley said, "What do you think, Bill?"

"Well," I said, "when you're paying a fortune for a guy who is supposed to have a bad arm and has only pitched one inning, you really ought to get the guarantee. If he can throw at all, there's no reason why Rickey wouldn't give it to you."

"No," Wrigley said, in a tone of finality. "We don't need a guarantee. Even if he can't perform very well, we'll get a lot of publicity from him. If he can pitch even a little bit, we'll get the money back at the box office. And if his arm ever comes back, we've got a bargain."

Poor Boots was grimacing and groaning like a man in pain. "You know, Mr. Wrigley," he said finally, "the expensive part of this is not really the money. We've got $185,000 and if you want to give it to Rickey, it's your ball club and your money. The players can't be replaced of course, but that isn't what bothers me the most either. What bothers me the most is that we're labeling ourselves the biggest patsies in the history of baseball. If we go ahead with this deal we're adding $50,000 to every deal we make from now on, because everybody is going to figure that if we're this easy a mark they're going to get their share too."

He looked to me for support again, which was not very bright in the light of Mr. Wrigley's reaction to my earlier advice. "Boots," I said, "you win some and you lose some. This one you've lost. He's going to do it."

"I sure am," Mr. Wrigley said.

While Boots looked on as if he were carrying a stiletto in his rib cage, Wrigley picked up the phone and told Rowland to go ahead. The best Boots could get out of it was Rickey's withdrawal of the really insulting proposal that we specifically waive any recourse.

That was pretty big of Branch, especially since it was perfectly understood that we did *not*, in fact, have any such recourse.

Diz did get the purchase money back at the gate, so Wrigley was right.

Diz pitched on a spot basis with a bad arm, with no speed, with nothing except brains and memory and colossal conceit, and finished with a 7-1 record. The Cubs came on with a tremendous winning streak at the end and slipped through to the pennant as the Pirates collapsed. So Rickey was right too; Dean did win a pennant for us.

Boots was more right than anybody else, though. It was years before the Cubs were able to enter into any kind of negotiation without the other club expecting to get all the best of it. Jim Gallagher, who succeeded Boots Weber, had to suffer the fallout from the Dean deal throughout his entire tenure.

I had, we might say, seen Mr. Rickey in full flight and I had reason to be impressed by his wingspan and his plumage.

Three years after the Dean deal, I went up to Milwaukee to begin my long and meritorious career as an operator. Having the world's worst ball club and no money, my sinister plan was to buy ballplayers on credit, putting a minimum amount of money down and promising to pay the rest at a conveniently distant date.

The major-league meeting that year was being held in Atlanta. Our plan was for Charlie Grimm, our manager, Rudie Schaffer, our business manager, and myself to sweep into town, in bedizened glory, and bedazzle the others with our charm, our confidence and our—ahem—wealth.

Charm and confidence we had aplenty. Money was another matter. Simply to raise our train fare and hotel money we had to hustle around town and sell season tickets for the upcoming year, the first time to my knowledge that season tickets had ever been sold to anybody except a few special boxholders.

There was also the problem of our wardrobes. Between the three of us we did not have a spare suit, and we did not think we would impress anyone unduly if we checked into the hotel carrying overnight bags. We overcame this problem quite neatly by filling our luggage with rocks. As we swept into the Piedmont Hotel behind the straining bellhops, Rudie was puffing on the biggest cigar he had been able to find, and Charlie and I were noisily flinging greetings at whatever familiar faces we could sight. While we were checking in, Charlie engaged the bellhops in conversation, entertaining them with humorous and even earthy tales about the good old days with the Cubs, while Rudie and I grabbed the bags and slipped into the elevators.

The two players I had my eye on to start with were a couple of Cardinal farmhands, Hy Vandenberg and Bill Norman. Vandenberg had pitched at Rochester in the International League. I felt he could help our club for a couple of years and then be sold to the majors at a good profit. Norman was an aging outfielder from the Texas league who had been touted to me not only as a good Triple-A player but as a shrewd baseball man who would be able to instruct our younger players.

I phoned Rickey, made an appointment, and went over to his hotel. And I tell you, as I walked into that lobby all my brashness oozed out of me. Visions of the Dean deal and the Sturgeon deal, and of the countless other Rickey triumphs, came floating through my head. For the first time, it occurred to me that if I let myself get trapped in a room with Rickey, there was a strong possibility that he would still have Vandenberg and Norman, as well as my promissory note, and I would end up with two guys I had never heard of. My master plan did not call for me to pay nothing for players I didn't want; it was to pay nothing for players I did want.

I picked up the house phone and called his room. "Come on up," he said expansively.

"No, Mr. Rickey," I said, completely deflated. "I'm going to send you up a note."

There was a message pad right alongside the phone. I wrote: *I will pay $5000 for pitcher Vandenberg and $3500 for outfielder Norman, a total of $8500 to be settled at a mutually agreed-upon date.*

I called over a bellboy, a fresh-faced young kid, handed him the note and told him to take it up to Mr. Rickey's suite. I fished into my pocket and, bleeding from all pores, handed him a dollar bill.

A few minutes later the bellboy came back down and handed back the note. "Mr. Rickey," he said, "says for you to come on up."

I took out another dollar bill and handed the note back to him. "Look," I said. "Take this back and tell Mr. Rickey I'd just as soon do this my way."

Down he came again. "Mr. Rickey still wants you to come up. He says I'm to tell you that he isn't used to dealing through messengers."

Well now, I could detect a slight note of resentment in his voice. The boy had obviously begun to enjoy his role as negotiator and was, I thought, justifiably disturbed at being downgraded. "I want you to do me a favor," I told him. "You take this note up one last time and tell him I'm going to leave if he sends it back again. Tell him I'm scared of him because I know if I go up there I'll end up buying two catchers I don't need for twice as much money as I've got to spend." Putting my arm around the boy's neck, I told him confidentially, "I *am* scared of him. This is one of the world's great con artists."

I reached into my pocket for the last of my dollar bills, but the kid put up his hand to stop me. "Don't worry, Bill," he said, "I'll handle it."

This time he came back beaming: "Mr. Rickey said to me, 'Does he look as if he's serious?' and I said to him, 'Mr. Rickey, he looks to me like he's already on his way!'"

"Well . . . ?"

"Bill," he said, "We just made ourselves a deal."

Rickey was the only man who could simply outtalk you, out-general you and outmaneuver you. Who could, in short, trau-matize and transfix you through the sheer force of language and personality.

The rest of us mere mortals have to do the best we can.

Before you can judge a trade or a trader, you have to appre-ciate that an operator's maneuverability is totally dependent upon the kind of a team he has. If you have a bad ball club, you are entitled to make trades just to confuse the issue. You are running a bargain counter, and remnants change hands in profusion. But if you are dealing in the kind of high-priced merchandise that is kept under glass, you can afford to put a carnation in your boutonniere, lower your voice and tread upon the high-tufted carpeting.

Any resemblance between George Weiss of the Yankees and George Weiss of the Mets exists entirely in the mind of George Weiss, a deplorably undemocratic condition which Weiss has never been quite able to absorb.

George Weiss of the Yankees used to sit in regal splendor during the winter meetings and let the world beat a path to his hotel suite. The outer room would be filled with employees from the Yankee organization, and even those you knew would greet you with restraint, almost as if they felt the eye of Big Brother on them. Weiss would always receive the supplicants in his bedroom. After a suitable wait, you would be ushered into his presence and permitted to propose whatever foolish transaction was on your mind. George Weiss would consider, and George Weiss would dispose.

I have mixed feelings about George's ability. He inherited a farm system that overflowed with players, and his formula was to trade three promising minor-league players for the established big-leaguer the Yankees needed to fill a weak spot. I can't argue too strenuously with that philosophy because I always operated the same way. Five-year plans are nice for economists, but the only pennant you can win is the one coming up.

At the end of his career with the Yankees, Weiss was suffering from the deaths of his three great scouts—Paul Kritchell, Bill Essick and Joe Devine (the men who really built the Yankees' farm system)—and without them the flow of young ballplayers was stopped at the source. As Branch Rickey once said, "When it comes to judging ballplayers, Weiss can't tell the difference between a bull and a cow." By the time Roy Hamey took over, the minor-league system had been stripped bare at the top and was empty at the bottom.

Confronted in his old age with the task of building the Mets from the bottom up, Weiss has done—giving him all the best of it—an atrocious job. He stocked the team, predictably, with every glamour name he could find. The only trouble was that the glamour names on the list were old and worn out. Then he sat back and waited, as was his custom, for the other clubs to come to him. He could not seem to understand that he was dependent at this stage of his life upon the charity of others. Even King Farouk was able to adjust to his reduced station more realistically than Weiss.

The Dodgers have been the team with the rich farm system in recent years, and Buzzie Bavasi—O'Malley's dancing master —has become the best operator. Bavasi broke in under Rickey and he still uses some of Rickey's approaches. Like Papa Branch he seeks you out, hits you fast and dazzles you with his riches.

Buzzie will greet you by handing you a long list with perhaps a dozen names on it, almost as routinely as if he were handing you his calling card. Before he gives you the slightest indication of what he wants from you he will say, "You can have any three of them."

What he has going for him, of course, is the same thing Rickey and the Yankees used to have going for them: their reputation for having the best scouts in the business. There is the feeling, impossible to put down, that since the Dodgers were interested enough in these players to sign them and bring them up through their great farm system, there have to be a few golden nuggets in there somewhere among a dozen names.

If you can forget that they belong to the Dodgers, though, and if you are at all realistic, you see that he is offering you only the players who have been unable to break into the Dodgers' lineup or the minor-league players the Dodgers are ready to write off.

"Oh come on," you say. "You don't expect us to trade a decent ballplayer for anything you got here, do you?"

"But you can take any *three* of them," Buzzie says, as if junk, piled high enough, takes on all the characteristics of the more precious metals.

Once he sees you are not interested, Buzzie will get down to the hard business of pitting value against value. But you can never escape that opening gambit. Buzzie proffers that list of his by now much like a runner doing his deep-knee bends before taking off his warm-up suit.

Oddly enough, he has worked it best on George Weiss, even though his is only a slight variation of Weiss's own technique with the Yankees. Bavasi plucked Bob Miller, a serviceable right-hander he needed very badly, from the Mets by giving them Tim Harkness and Larry Burright, whose only noticeable accomplishment was that they had worn the Los Angeles uniform and even, on occasion, gotten their names in a Los Angeles box score. Weiss seemed to have some difficulty understanding that Harkness had played a little first base for them only because the Dodgers were still searching for a replacement for Gil Hodges, and Burright had played a little second base for them because they had no second baseman at all. Both of them had been found wanting in open positions, hardly a recommendation. Neither of them, it developed, could help the Mets, which meant that neither of them was a big-league ballplayer. Gee, what a surprise that was to Bavasi.

This year, Bavasi's list was adorned and made resplendent by the name of Frank Howard. The Dodgers had obviously come to a top-level decision that Howard was hurting them in ways that his occasional outbursts of power could hardly overcome.

Those other names, clustered around big Frank's, took on such an added luster that Buzzie could have swung deals all over the American League. Because of the connection with Gil Hodges, though, Washington has become a Los Angeles farm club (you may read dumping grounds if you wish). Being among the more trusting souls on this universe, I am sure the thought never crossed either Bavasi's or O'Malley's mind that if friends were indeed friends and if one good turn did indeed deserve another they were establishing proprietary rights to anybody of exceptional talent whom the Senators might one day come up with. Friends *are* friends, nevertheless, and Bavasi was able to make a deal for Claude Osteen when he had reason to worry that Koufax might be finished.

In addition to Howard, Washington got a carload of Bavasi specials, hot off the list. Having worn Los Angeles uniforms, they all have the glamour of Los Angeles players. In Washington uniforms, they haven't done at all badly. Howard has been everything Washington had a right to expect. Pitcher Pete Richert has been more. Third-baseman Ken McMullen has been serviceable.

The weird part of the deal is that Washington threw in $50,000. I just haven't been able to figure out that part of it. In the old days the strong club always threw in some money to help the weak club pay off the mortgage, but in today's market, money doesn't mean anything. Finley may still sell a player to raise cash—as he sold Jim Gentile to Houston—and Gabe Paul will still sell a player under the proper financial pressures, as he sold Pete Ramos to the Yankees. But in this case the money went the other way, from the weak to the strong. I don't recommend turning $50,000 away from the door on any kind of a night, but Walter O'Malley does not seem to be in any inordinate need of $50,000.

In the old days, money was the means by which you could

balance the scales. AND CASH became part of the footnotes of the record blocks of almost any player who was traded. I had Norm Cash briefly at Chicago, and I toyed with the idea of getting him involved in a trade with a slightly superior player so that I could add the notation FOR CASH AND CASH to the literature of baseball. The only trouble was that it meant *I* would be giving up the money, which seemed a bit drastic even for so worthy a cause. I also felt it would be nice to get Andy Carey from the Yanks so that I could then make a trade for CASH AND CAREY. Andy and I both retired before our time, alas, and baseball history suffered another blow.

Norm Cash was, ironically, a throw-in in lieu of hard cash in the trade, whereby I gave catcher John Romano to Cleveland to get Minnie Minoso. Unfortunately for Frank Lane, he lost all crowing privileges by passing Cash on to Detroit for somebody named Steve Demeter in what was nothing more than a cat-and-dog trade; that is, a trade that is made for the sole purpose of getting newspaper space. This entitled Bill DeWitt to claim occult powers when Cash, in flat defiance of my edict, won himself a batting title two years later by hitting (gasp) .361, with (sigh) 41 home runs and (ohmigosh) 132 runs batted in. In subsequent years, Cash has shown that he can't hit big-league pitching.

This brings us to the fascinating subject of how a player can have one full year so far above and beyond his natural talents. As a man who has spent his entire life in baseball I can tell you, without fear of contradiction, that I don't have the slightest idea.

Other baseball men will look wise and say "Momentum!" That means they don't have the slightest idea either.

These days, with money in such ill-repute, you have to balance off a trade by throwing players of various ability onto the scales until they seem to be in balance.

While throw-ins may be more important now than ever before, they have always been irresistible to the compulsive trader. You always feel a little safer if you can con the other guy into throwing in one more player, because every throw-in gives you another possible saver in case the real deal goes sour.

If the throw-in does come through for you, it is obligatory to adopt a jaunty, self-satisfied air so that everyone will understand that he was the guy you were really after all the time. In my experience, to be perfectly honest, a throw-in has never been more than an afterthought. We won the pennant in Cleveland in 1948 because Larry MacPhail had given me, as a final throw-in in a less than earth-shattering deal, my choice from a list of six minor-league pitchers. I took Gene Beardon, mostly because he was the only one on the list who had not played for a Yankee farm and therefore figured to be the one they knew the least about. (See how I'm making myself look smart even while I'm denying it.) The truth is that he had been playing for Casey Stengel out in Oakland, and Stengel advised me to grab him. I didn't know a thing about Beardon, and his one year of incredible success was as big a surprise to me as it was to MacPhail, Stengel and everyone else.

The hot hand at the moment is undoubtedly being held by Bing Devine, who traded the Cards into the pennant. Bing is young, bright and imaginative. Like Bavasi, he had the good fortune to come up through the minor leagues, where he was able to pick up the solid background that so many of the businessmen or ex-ballplayers in so many of the other front offices lack. With the Mets, where he will be building from the dungeon on up, he has a chance to do some real operating—as soon as Weiss gets off his back.

Devine's first great trade at St. Louis, hindsight tells us, was getting Curt Flood from Cincinnati. This is a trade which is interesting because it illustrates an important point. Every major-league club scouts every other club's players almost as thoroughly as it scouts its own. If you get interested enough to send out a top scout like Mayo Smith or Charlie Metro, for a full-scale appraisal, you'll end up knowing just about as much about the player as the team that owns him.

Devine knew that Cincinnati had another center fielder in

their system, Vada Pinson, who looked as if he was one of the great prospects of all time. Pinson had everything Flood had, plus even more speed and considerably more power. When Cincinnati had Flood fooling around in the infield, that was the signal for Bing to make his move. Gabe Paul has never been famous for undervaluing his players. In this case, Cincinnati needed some relief pitching badly, and Devine was able to pry the twenty-year-old Flood away from him for three minor-league relief pitchers of exceedingly limited ability.

Flood remained a good fielding, no-hit outfielder for the Cards for three years before he suddenly developed into a top big-league hitter. So the question remains: Just what would the Reds have done with him during those three years?

Bing will gamble, much in the way that a Lane or a MacPhail would gamble. Gambling, as any preacher will attest, can become a weakness. This is particularly true in player trades. Dealing in the slave mart can be heady stuff. You are controlling the fate of other human beings—celebrated human beings, at that—and it is not unnatural to find yourself being carried away by the power and the glory of it all. One of the tests of the good dealer is that he knows his weaknesses and, within reasonable limits, protects himself against himself.

When I was with the White Sox, we were in need of a first baseman. (When I left the White Sox we were still in need of a first baseman.) The Cardinals not only had a first baseman on first base, they had one of the best first basemen in baseball, Bill White, playing in the outfield. I saw no reason why I shouldn't make both Bill and myself happy by putting him back on first base where he belonged.

The Cardinals needed a catcher as badly as we needed a first baseman and I had an excellent young third-string catcher, Earl Battey, who was seeing very little action. I drove to Bing's home outside St. Louis on a Sunday morning and we worked out a trade in which I was going to give him Battey plus Ken McBride, who had just finished a good year at Indianapolis. The deal was coming along nicely when into our lives walked

Eddie Stanky, director of player personnel. And when Eddie walked in the door, I knew the deal was dead.

Driving back, I could commiserate with myself on my tough luck in having Stanky walk into that room at just the wrong time—except that I could be fairly certain that it had not been accidental.

So here is a man who recognizes the dangers and protects himself as much as humanly possible.

Bill DeWitt has been able to adjust much more readily than Weiss to his changing circumstances. William O. is one of the patient men, and patience has carried him a long way. In St. Louis, where he stayed alive by auctioning off his best players to the contenders, DeWitt was remarkable in that he always got the top price, and then a little extra. Year after year he would sit patiently by the telephone, making no move himself, and always, within the final 48 hours before the trading deadline, the pennant contenders would rush to the phone. He once got $100,000 from George Weiss for a pitcher named Fred Sanford, who may well have been the worst pitcher ever to become part of the Yankee starting rotation. In addition to the $100,000, Weiss gave him a couple of pitchers and Sherman Lollar, who was to become an All-Star catcher.

Bill always did favor that figure. Just before I bought the Browns from DeWitt, he had sold catcher Les Moss to the Red Sox for $100,000 and a player to be delivered later. When I came in, we still had the player coming. I took Jack McDonald, a pitcher, but Cronin and I also arranged to get together at the winter meetings so that we could shuffle up a few players and make it look as if we were doing something. The deal was made on schedule, and whom did we get back as part of the package but Les Moss.

As soon as Bill got a good club of his own, he showed he could operate the other way too. At Detroit, he really did some wheeling and dealing, even to trading managers with Frank Lane. Within a couple of years he brought Detroit up from the second division and right into the pennant race.

From Detroit, he went to Cincinnati and traded the Reds right into the pennant. But then something happened that you very rarely see. Once he had established a contending team he deliberately reverted to type and became again much closer to the patient man he had been at St. Louis.

William O. will still ask high prices for his players, but he does not become unreasonable.

Fans are always writing in with suggested deals, and more often than not their deals are wildly out of touch with reality. You may not believe this, but there are many operators who overvalue their own players as badly as any fan. Gabe Paul and Ed Short, two of my closest friends among the operators, both think they're offering great deals if they're committing anything less than grand larceny. Gabe and Hank Greenberg were once very good friends, but the deals Gabe offered Hank at Cleveland, in all seriousness, were always so ridiculous that Henry came to believe Gabe was insulting him.

Gabe has done a remarkable job of building an interesting, and even a contending, team over the winter, climaxed by the triumph of bringing Rocky Colavito, the people's choice, back to Cleveland.

Gabe had a chance to bid on Rocky a year previously, though, just before Detroit sent Rocky to Kansas City. Gabe felt that Detroit was unpatriotic or something for not trading him to Cleveland when everyone knew how important Colavito could be to his operation. It never seemed to occur to Gabe that if Detroit traded him to Kansas City instead of Cleveland it just might be because Finley had made a better offer. It never seemed to occur to him that if Colavito was that valuable to the Cleveland franchise then Detroit had a right to expect him to outbid the opposition.

Ed Short is also willing to give you a pound of hamburger for a pound of steak any old time, and he gets rather annoyed when you don't look upon it as a great deal. Having started out as a publicity man, Ed is highly conscious of the publicity value of a trade, especially during the winter meetings when all the writers are there breathing on him for news. He was terribly upset last fall when Los Angeles made the Osteen deal. Having made one of his great offers for Howard himself, he was laboring under what may have been a misconception that Bavasi had agreed to contact him before he dealt Howard anywhere else. It didn't help his digestion either when the Twins traded Arrigo, another of the pitchers he wanted, at approximately the same time.

Ed will face his own problems realistically, though, and he has the courage to do what has to be done. He had seen Chico Carrasquel grow fat and lazy, and when his countryman, Luis Aparicio, seemed to be going the same route, Ed went ahead and made the big trade with Baltimore. He was perfectly well aware that the trade would probably shake Luis up so much that he'd whip himself back in shape and play the type of ball, offensively and defensively, that he was capable of. And it did. But if it was a good trade for Baltimore it was an even better one for the White Sox. Pete Ward turned out to be a hitter, Hoyt Wilhelm has been a strong relief pitcher, and Ron Hansen has given them an excellent replacement at shortstop.

The other trader who has been looking good these past few years is Cal Griffith up in Minneapolis, the upset of the generation. Cal was under his uncle's shadow for so long that there is still a tendency to look upon him as a lamb. It is difficult to forget the pleasant days, not too far gone, when the Griffith family was prepared to sell you anybody on the club if you waved enough money in front of them. Besides, you think of that silly operation of theirs, with all the relatives on the payroll for performing duties just barely visible to the naked eye, and it is hard to take Calvin seriously.

And if we are going to be honest about these guys, Calvin always seemed so stupid that you almost felt sorry for him.

If there is anything more costly in a trade than underestimating the opposition, it is impatience. And it is when you underestimate a man that you are most apt to become impatient to get the shearing over and done with. I was the guy who really helped to get Cal's club moving. We had won the pennant in Chicago in 1959 without any hitting at all, and I felt we needed some power if we were going to repeat. I wanted Roy Sievers, and I kept waving money at Cal—$150,000, to be exact—never doubting for a moment that he would succumb to such sweet music. Cal just sat there, tapping his feet and asking for another throw-in. I gave him a good prospect in Don Mincher and finally, I started him on his way to fame, fortune and Minneapolis by tracking him to his lair and forcing Earl Battey upon him as the final player in the package.

If I didn't know better, I'd almost be tempted to ask who was the stupid one, Cal or me?

In Minneapolis, he's finally got some money to work with. You've also got to say that, one way or another, he's been coming up with a real good player every year—Killibrew, Allison, Versalles, Rollins, Hall, Oliva.

Calvin can no longer sit back and wait for people to come to him. He's a contender. He has to trade to one particular category, and that's the toughest trading of all. Cal has to give up offense, which he has in abundance, to improve his defense. He has to decide what he needs, where he can get it and what he is willing to give up for it. We are not talking about value-for-value anymore, we are talking about giving up what you can afford to give up in order to get what you need.

This is a little different from deciding whether you want to take somebody else's money, and Calvin has shown no indication that he has the stomach for it or the ability to pull it off.

The possibility also exists that I've underestimated Calvin all along. I'd have sworn that Cal would blow the whole deal in Minneapolis because I didn't think he was bright enough to take advantage of the original enthusiasm and momentum.

Calvin has fooled me. Looking back on that Sievers deal I can see that it was not for the first time.

The legitimately stupid office over the years has been up in Boston. Generally, Boston has been reluctant to trade with anybody except the Griffiths, where there was the family relationship through Cronin and a good fighting chance that they would be outfumbled.

Boston is the only club where I prefer to conduct the negotiations over the telephone. In the first place, I have a feeling that you'd terrify the current business manager, Dick O'Connell, if you hit him head on. More important still, it isn't easy to make the kind of deal you were able to make with the Red Sox over the years without laughing in their face.

Boston was always easy to deal with because you could deal to their left-field fence. Right-hand hitters who could barely make the team anywhere else looked great in Fenway Park, where the game was to hit the ball in the air and hope for a friendly breeze to come along and waft it over the wall.

When I took over at Chicago, I inherited the contract of a big right-handed first baseman, Ron Jackson, who could hit a ball a long way when he hit it—which was never.

We had him down in the minors somewhere, but his options were running out and we had to decide what to do about him. Suddenly I thought of Boston and put in a call to Bucky Harris, who was running things for Tom Yawkey in the time-honored Boston tradition. The Red Sox had a pitcher, Frank Baumann, whom I had known as a high school kid in St. Louis and had always been very fond of. He'd had some arm trouble, but he had told me it was in pretty good shape and I was confident he would be a big help to us in relief.

Harris jumped at the deal. In person, it would have been impossible to hide the triumphant gleam in my eye. Just so he wouldn't have second thoughts, I hastily said, "Well, that isn't even up really. I think I should get a second-line pitcher."

All I was trying to do was to keep him in a happy enough frame of mind so that he wouldn't ask *me* for a throw-in, but Stanley was so pleased to get a big right-handed hitter that he obligingly threw in a minor-league pitcher himself.

Baumann was just great for us the next year. In fact, he led the American League in Earned Run Average.

Normally though, you prefer to face your opponent eyeball

to eyeball, because if you flatter yourself that you are a hustler —or even a salesman—you feel you can outsmart the other guy or outdrink him or, one way or another, dominate the negotiations through the force of your charm, intellect and personality.

I was always an aggressive trader myself, probably too aggressive. Rudie Schaffer and I always came to the meetings with dozens of possible deals worked out, and Rudie would go out and scout the lobby for unwary travelers. When he'd come across one of the operators on our list, he'd engage him in casual conversation and either listen to his plans or throw out a suggestion himself, all with the aim of steering him into our suite.

We grabbed John Quinn in the Florida meetings at the end of 1959, and by dint of beautiful teamwork trapped him into one of the best deals he ever made. We were looking for power for the White Sox, as you will remember, and one of the places we needed it most was at third base, where we had been alternating about five utility infielders. We knew Gene Freese of the Phillies was available, and we also knew that the Phillies were embarked on one of their periodic 5-Year Plans.

Our own One-Year Plan was to get Freese for Johnny Callison, a twenty-year-old outfielder of undoubted promise. Callison had hit a big .173 for us, and he certainly didn't look as if he was going to be of any particular help to us for the next couple of years.

Rudie found Quinn down by the newsstand, engaged him in conversation and found he was talking a Freese deal with somebody else. "Gee," Rudie said, "you might be able to get an offer from Bill. He's kind of discouraged with Callison, you know. We know he's going to be a good ballplayer, but when? We think that with some hitting in the infield we might have a chance to win it again this year. I'm not promising anything but why not give it a try?"

So in Rudie comes with Quinn. We make the deal just as we had planned, and if the Phillies hadn't folded so completely in 1964 Callison would have undoubtedly been the MVP of the National League.

Before you can judge a deal, though, you have to know what each side is looking for. A player trade is not a karate match. You don't have to end up with a winner and a loser. I spent the past winter publicly berating myself for letting Callison get away because the public likes to know that you make as many mistakes as they do, a point on which I am particularly equipped to oblige. Actually, it wasn't a bad deal for the White Sox at all. Freese was a good hitter for the White Sox in the one year he was with us (while Callison was still doing nothing at Philadelphia). Freese was not Al Lopez' cup of tea, though. The following year, we passed him along to Cincinnati (via Milwaukee) in a 3-way deal which brought us Juan Pizzaro.

Freese did for Cincinnati precisely what we hoped he would do for us. He provided the extra power they needed to win the pennant.

There have been an infinite number of deals in which Rudie steered the lamb in, and if sometimes we turned out to be the fox and sometimes we were the lamb, we could at least tell ourselves that we were in action.

Although trading is too much of an art to be bound by rules, there is one rule I think it's always wise to observe. Don't be too smart. Don't jump to conclusions before you have made a personal check of all the facts.

One of the worst trades in history, I think, was the one in which Art Ehlers, the Baltimore general manager, passed Roy Sievers on to the Senators for Gil Coan. It was a trade that bewildered everybody at the time, because although nobody thought Ehlers was much of a baseball man, nobody thought he was *that* bad. I knew why he had got rid of Sievers, though. I knew he was sitting back, chortling to himself at how cleverly he had swindled Clark Griffith. I was chortling rather nastily myself because I knew that the man he had outsmarted was himself.

Roy Sievers had a chronic shoulder dislocation. In the spring of 1952, he had picked up the first ground ball hit to him at third base and dislocated it again while—of all things—throwing the ball to first. Roy came back to St. Louis so disheartened that he was ready to quit. "Do something for me first," I told him. "Go down and let Dr. Bennett look at it, because if you were my son this is where I'd send you."

Dr. George Bennett was the unchallenged expert in anything pertaining to sore or broken arms. After examining Sievers he sent me back a letter saying that nothing could be done in that kind of a case and that if Roy continued to play ball he would always be subject to instantaneous injury.

I got Dr. Bennett on the phone and said, "Gee whiz, I didn't have to send him to you to find out he's got a bad shoulder. Any doctor in the country could have told me that. I sent him to you because nobody else can do anything. You're supposed to be the greatest. If you're the greatest, that means that you either know something nobody else knows or you can invent something nobody else can. We can't just tell this guy that his arm is gone; you might as well cut it off as tell him that."

Dr. Bennett agreed to look at the X-rays again. Since Sievers had a pinched nerve in the arm, he told me, nothing could be done for three or four weeks, anyway.

During the ensuing month, Dr. Bennett went to work and devised a completely new operation. After it had been completed, he told me that Sievers could get back into action before the year was over, and that the shoulder would not only heal but would increase in strength through the years.

All communication about the operation was conducted over the phone, however. The files Ehlers inherited when the Browns went to Baltimore contained only the original letter in which Dr. Bennett had written Sievers off.

If Ehlers had *called* me to ask what the letter was all about, I'd have told him. I'd have also told him that in the winter following the operation, we had paid Roy to come to the park every afternoon so that he could work out at first base where the demands upon his arm would be at a minimum. Not only was the arm all right, but Roy had developed into a pretty fair first baseman.

But Ehlers preferred to be smart.

The only other rule I have—and it is a rule I commend to all new operators—is to get the man out of uniform the moment he has been traded. During my first year at Milwaukee, I made a deal with Buffalo for big "Shovels" Kobesky, the International League's home-run champion. Kobesky came to Milwaukee fully prepared to lose balls over our friendly right-field fence, and we were fully prepared to let him. In my dreams, I could see all kinds of new home-run records being set by the gigantic, incomparable Kobesky. A couple of months into the season, the gigantic incomparable Kobesky was hitting about .160 for us and he had a total of no (0) home runs.

At the same time, by sheer coincidence, our head scout, Dutch Reuther (he was also our only one), came down with the gout in New York. The Dutchman was recovering, in excruciating pain and unbelievable luxury, at the Commodore Hotel. We couldn't really afford any hotel bills, let alone the Commodore's, but we figured that a friend with a rich man's disease deserves a rich man's hotel. An even more compelling philosophical argument was that there wasn't anything we could do about it.

While Dutch was laid up, Charlie Stoneham, who was running the Jersey City ball club for his brother Horace, came by to visit him. They got to talking about baseball, naturally, and about that all-time International League favorite, the storied Shovels Kobesky. When Charlie departed, Dutch called me in great excitement to tell me he had unloaded Kobesky on Jersey City for $7500, a most satisfactory sum for a minor-league transaction. Both clubs, Dutch said, were to announce the sale simultaneously the following morning.

Our club was playing in St. Paul that night, and I saw nothing wrong with letting Shovels play.

Play he did. Like the Shovels Kobesky of old. The following morning, Milwaukee fans were able to read, in adjoining columns, that Kobesky had hit three tremendous home runs and that he had been sold to Jersey City.

He did very little for Jersey City the rest of the year, though. Poor Shovels was just over the hill.

It was years before Charlie Stoneham could run into the Dutchman without saying, "What a pal. You've got one friend in all the world who comes to visit you on your sickbed and you stiff him for seventy-five C-notes."

The moral of the story is, need I say, that you have no pals along the slave mart.

6

☻ ☻ ☻

Where Are the Drunks of Yesteryear?

IN the entertainment business, there is only one surefire merchandise. Personality. Lovers of Shakespeare came out of hiding not long ago to make Richard Burton's *Hamlet* the longest-running *Hamlet* in the history of the American theatre. I am sure that some of them (three guys in the balcony) came to see the play. Ted Williams was such an overpowering personality that he kept the Red Sox franchise in the black for years. And not only the Red Sox. Nobody fully appreciated Ted's value to the entire league until people began to survey the attendance figures after he retired.

With competition for the entertainment dollar reaching the bare-knuckle stage, personality has become more important than ever. We are in an age, students, in which Dick Nixon running for President appears on Jack Paar's show and asks him for his autograph. Show business and politics, being run by practical, cigar-smoking businessmen, manufacture personalities on an assembly line. Baseball, fighting for its life, has been stifling them as fast as they appear.

What makes it so sad is that the athlete has a role in our society that reaches even beyond showmanship. The athlete is one of the last symbols of that superfluity of our society, the physical man. The average man finds that although the instincts of his primitive forebears may beat a tomtom in his blood, his own daily conflict has been reduced to the drive downtown, the paper work in the office, the return trip. The conflict is undefined, the enemy is indistinct, the battle remains permanently unsettled. He doesn't really know whether he has won or lost; there is only the vague feeling that he is somehow losing.

There is in all men who work with the brain some sense of guilt toward the man who does what our instinct tells us is the work of the male animal—to live by your sweat and your muscle and your animal reflexes. The ballplayer wins and loses day by day, as the primitive man won or lost day by day. It is all illusion, of course, and the illusion collapses if the ballplayer turns out to be just another company man who gets up in the morning, drives to the job, puts in his hours and goes home. The athlete who catches the imagination is the individualist, the free soul who challenges not only the opposition but the generally accepted rules of behavior. Essentially, he should be uncivilized. Untamed.

The wonderful world of sports is not only losing its wonder, it's losing its sportiveness. I wouldn't argue for one moment that today's athletes don't perform with a skill and finesse that staggers the imagination. The 4-minute mile, which used to be considered a physical impossibility, is now a rather disappointing jaunt. Today's infielders can make plays on the cannonball that is shot toward them that the old-timers couldn't make with the beanbag they used to play with.

We have precision athletes playing a precision game. And precision can get to be pretty dull stuff, even under the arc lights. What is missing is the sense of enjoyment. Of *fun*. Come on, fellows, SMILE once in a while, will you?

What baseball needs more than anything else is the simple courage to be disreputable.

Babe Ruth did not provide a noble example for the youth of the nation, which is undoubtedly why the youth of the nation loved him. He was a drunk, a spendthrift, a braggart, a brawler, a gambler, and a few other things not usually recommended by your friendly neighborhood marriage counselor. He was, they tell me, also crude of speech. I mean he was known to use the indicative mood where the subjunctive was clearly called for.

But when you gazed upon the Babe, you knew you were looking upon no ordinary human being. He was an odd-looking man, oddly featured and oddly shaped. A man from Mars, upon seeing the spindly-legged, potbellied earthling drag his club to the plate, would know that whatever the Babe was doing up there he could do it better than anybody else in the world. He would know that he was looking upon a giant of a man, one of the wonders of the strange new world.

Today's players all seem to be in training to become Herbert Hoover.

Conformity is the villain. Everyone must fit the mold, march in lockstep, bow low to the public-relations man. Conformity in education, conformity in dress and conformity in thought has led, rather naturally, to conformity of behavior. What we have are good gray ballplayers, playing a good gray game and reading the good gray Wall Street Journal. They have been brainwashed, dry-cleaned and dehydrated! They have been homogenized, orientated and indoctrinated! Their mouths have been washed out, their appetites stunted, their personalities bleached! They say all the right things at all the right times, which means that they say nothing.

Ruth was not unique. Wake up the echoes at the Hall of Fame and you will find that baseball's immortals were a rowdy and raucous group of men who would climb down off their plaques and go rampaging through Cooperstown, taking spoils, like the Third Army busting through Germany.

Deplore it if you will, but Grover Cleveland Alexander drunk was a better pitcher than Grover Cleveland Alexander sober. Ellis Kinder of more recent vintage was another drinker of note. Kinder's reputation was so illustrious that it managed to keep him in the minors until he was in his mid-thirties.

In 1949, the Red Sox came to New York needing to win only one of the final two games to win the pennant. The Yankees beat Mel Parnell, a 25-game winner, in the first game. That left it up to Kinder, who had already won 23 games.

Old Eli (short for Old Granddad) toured with Artie Richman of the now defunct *Daily Mirror*, a friendship going back to the days when Kinder pitched for the St. Louis Browns and Artie covered the Browns' training camp with his brother Milt Richman (UPI), who had once been a Brownie farmhand. Artie had fallen into the habit of covering whatever team Ellie was pitching for over the last week of the season, so they could take off for a long, leisurely, liquid trip back to Old Eli's home in North Carolina.

After the first game, the players came to Artie in the Red Sox locker room, one by one, to plead, "For God's sake take him out tonight, Artie, and get him drunk. Get him drunk and keep him drunk. We can't afford to have him go out there sober tomorrow."

They wrote the next day that Old Eli had ice water in his veins. Branch water would have been more like it. Kinder took the mound stoned. He allowed one run in the first inning, on a sliced triple by DiMaggio. After that, Kinder pitched one of the great games of his life before he went out for a pinchhitter in the eighth, with the score still 1–0.

Joe McCarthy, the Red Sox manager, was criticized by the second-guessers for taking him out, which was ridiculous. When you're behind in the eighth inning you don't really have any choice. Besides, Kinder seemed to be in imminent danger of sobering up.

Paul Waner, one of our better Hall-of-Famers, was another who was known to wobble into the ball park from a night on the town. P. Waner was always tough up there at the plate, but never tougher than when he was playing off a drunk. When Paul blossomed out in glasses in the last days of his career he was astonished to discover that the ball could be seen so clearly. He liked it much better when the ball was blurry, he said, because it had seemed so much bigger. Paul had never really objected to seeing two or three of them at the same time.

I know that I once saw Paul line a sure triple into the right-center-field gap at Wrigley Field, take a wide turn around second base and go sliding into the bullpen mound in the left-field foul grounds, no more than 60 feet away from his destination.

This gave us assembled fans some hint that Paul was feeling poorly. When he won the game in the tenth inning by lining a home run into the right-field bleachers, we all felt rather poorly ourselves.

Lloyd Waner, another excellent hitter, was always over-shadowed by his big brother. Paul and Lloyd once went hunting in a rowboat, with Paul bringing along an adequate supply of the liquid that warms and refreshes. Paul, normally a good shot, kept missing the overflying birds, which annoyed and puzzled him. Since he could hit a little round baseball when he was drunk, he saw no reason why he couldn't hit a great big bird. Finally, he muttered, "Something must be wrong with this gun." He pointed it downward, sighted and fired, putting a hole through the bottom of the boat. Lloyd and Paul thereupon looked at each other sorrowfully while slowly, ever slowly, the rowboat filled up and went down . . . down . . . down.

It is customary for physical culturists, health-food addicts and sportswriters to say that if the Kinders and the P. Waners had only "taken better care of themselves," there was no telling how great they would have been, thereby completely missing the meaning of their lives. There are players who are, by nature, self-effacing, modest, home-loving. Push them into the limelight, force them into situations that conflict with their natural retiring personalities and their performance will suffer. The same thing is true with the drunks, the swingers and the screwballs. When you turn them into dull, conforming, sober citizens they lose the very thing that makes them great. You cannot perform a frontal lobotomy on the personality and expect the patient to function.

I learned that lesson, long after I should have known it, with Pat Seerey, a roly-poly, beer-drinking outfielder who could hit the ball a mile and a half—but not very often.

I decided finally that Pat's trouble was his weight. I brought him down to our ranch in Tucson over the winter, put him on a supervised diet and had him receive batting instructions from Rogers Hornsby. The project began to fall apart from the very beginning. In order to curb his appetite we had to feed him Benzedrine pills. The Benzedrine kept him awake at night, we found, and so we had to give him sleeping pills.

In between taking pills and batting instruction, Pat kept sneaking off into town for a beaker or two of brew. At the end, however, we had him pretty well slimmed down. We also had him dull, listless and hitless. Without his beer and his belly, he simply wasn't the same Pat Seerey we all knew and loved. As the season began, we hastily had to put him on a beer and malted-milk diet to get the good fat back on his belly and the happy gleam back in his eye.

Pat played his best when he was living the way Pat wanted to live. What I had failed to understand was that his best just didn't happen to be good enough.

Jim Brosnan is the most recent example of baseball's resistance to anybody who refuses to prostrate himself before the shrine. Brosnan wasn't a drunk. He was something far worse. Brosnan was a practicing literate. The truth of the matter is that Brosnan wrote even better than he pitched. He had the true writer's gift for the recognizable truth and the true writer's sense of rebellion. You read Jim Brosnan's book and, knowing nothing about baseball, you had to say to yourself, "Yes, this is the way it is."

Brosnan wrote that ballplayers drink hard liquor and have more than a cursory interest in sex. He even led his more gullible readers to believe that some managers and maybe even some baseball operators are neither lovable nor competent.

So Bill DeWitt pulled paragraph 3 (c) of the uniform players' contract on him. He not only silenced Brosnan but he revealed to the public that there is a quaint little LOYALTY section in which the player not only agrees to be diligent, faithful and obedient but in which he surrenders his right to say or write anything "without the written consent of the club"—a clause which is not only patently unconstitutional but which is, far worse, stupid. What William O. and the rest of the herd do not seem to understand is that the public-relations pap that is forever "reaffirming the grand tradition of baseball as the National Pastime" by picturing the players as somewhat retarded devotees of bubble gum and comic books does not really attract anybody except a few retarded devotees of bubble gum and comic books.

Brosnan should have been a gift from heaven. Here is a character no one could possibly make up, a big-league ballplayer who writes a best-selling book. Here you have a character who writes better than most of the writers and knows what he is writing about. If I had him I'd not only permit him to go around making speeches blasting me and baseball, I'd pay him to do it. I'd challenge him to a public debate (wouldn't it be a shame if we swindled some free TV time?) and I'd pen angry broadsides to answer his angry broadsides. (Wouldn't it be a shame if customers came into the park to boo or cheer him—or me—in person?)

I have had a mild disagreement or two with Walter O'Malley, but you can say for him that he is one operator who knows that controversy is not a dirty word, unless money is a dirty word too. As for me, the only dirty word I can think of, offhand, is "conformity," because it is a word which tells a man that he has no mind, no opinion, no name of his own.

As a man with some experience as a promoter, I would doubt whether anybody reaching the age of consent still believes that young athletes lead a monkish existence and that baseball operators—your humble host included—are sportsmen, benefactors or philanthropists. If you put the current Russian leaders (whatever their names are) into a room with Del Webb to negotiate the latest crisis, I would guarantee that the Kremlin would have a gleaming new paint job this summer.

So Jim Brosnan went to the White Sox, where Ed Short, a onetime publicity man, shut him up too.

The most interesting thing about Brosnan was that he was a very mediocre pitcher through the great part of his career. It was only during the year he was writing his book that he achieved some little stature, and it was during the year that the book was on the best-seller lists that he blossomed forth into the best relief pitcher in the league and helped carry the Reds to the pennant. Once he had blossomed forth as a writer—his real view of himself—he operated far more effectively as a pitcher. Once he had been silenced, he became nothing.

Could somebody be trying to tell us something?

I never had a best-selling author but I did have an actor, Johnny Berardino, for whom I had great hopes. A ballplayer who turned himself into a famous actor in the off-season would obviously be a great attraction. I mean, can you imagine what John Barrymore would have drawn to a ball park on Wednesday afternoons if only he had been able to hit the curve?

Unfortunately, Johnny had more ambition than talent in those days. (Even more unfortunately, he couldn't hit the curve ball either.) He was given a featured role in *The Kid from Cleveland,* the movie we made after we won the pennant—and which they still persist in playing on TV in the face of Newton Minow's sternest warnings. John played the villain while the rest of us played ourselves. Between you and me, it was hard to tell the difference.

John was very serious about his acting, though, and he has improved mightily. Housewives who turn on their television sets in the early afternoon when they should be yelling at the kids, or out buying beer for the old man, see him these days in a long-playing bedpan opera entitled *General Hospital,* a program of undoubted moral uplift and intellectual stimulation.

Without having seen the program, I am sure that John's doctor is tough but tender, stern but fair; a credit to himself, his community and his noble calling. I know this because television, being an industry which can be reduced to a quivering heap by two letters from Omaha, is not about to take on the AMA.

John's help was negligible in winning the championship and World Series. His finest hour came during our triumphant trip back to Cleveland. To make the long ride less hazardous, we had piled cases of champagne and sparkling Burgundy on board. The wine and bubbly flowed freely; it was also squirted, thrown, bathed in and, most of all, drunk.

Some of the players broke into song, others broke into battle and some battle-tested warriors even drifted off to sleep, an innocent and happy smile upon their lips.

Not Honest John Berardino. John clambered onto a table (and anybody who could *clamber* in John's condition was obviously made of superior stuff), struck a suitable dramatic stance and, stopping only occasionally to quaff from the bottle in his hand, proceeded to declaim from the works of Shakespeare.

He ran the gamut from *Othello* to *Henry V* to *Romeo and Juliet,* playing all parts himself, a virtuoso performance which definitely anticipated Alec Guinness and Peter Sellers. At times, roving bands of revelers would gather around to lend him their ears; at other times he shouted his immortal lines to the moist, if otherwise empty air.

In the morning, as the ragged group of celebrants wiped the sleep out of their eyes, there was John the Actor, hollow of eye, black of beard, a little hoarse, more than a little disheveled and still stinking drunk. His clothes hung stiff and spotted from the assorted layers of drying wine. Remembering him as he stood there, in the morning light, weaving gently on that table—poor, mad Lear on his dark and windswept heath—there is not the slightest doubt in my mind that John was the true founder of the Theatre of the Absurd. Let it be carved upon his Emmie: Good Lear, No Hit.

A city holiday having been declared, we were greeted at the railroad station by the victory-maddened citizenry. John, still pursuing his endurance record for nonstop declamation, made the wrong turn down the parlor car. Instead of finding himself in front of a cheering and appreciative throng, he found himself on the rear platform, performing before a small group of baffled but obliging freight-yard laborers.

We finally got him straightened away, though, and he traversed the victory route, fighting sleep gamely and still breaking into occasional snatches of *As You Like It, The Tempest* and such other Shakespearian works as came fleetingly to mind.

So you can understand, friends, why I have never been able to bring myself to watch John Beradino (apparently he dropped the second "r" when they picked up his option), the star of *General Hospital.*

I have, never let us forget, seen this man play Lear.

My nostalgia for the drunks probably goes back to the Chicago Cubs, with whom I was raised. The Cubs never did get the publicity of the St. Louis Gas House Gang, who succeeded them as the National League power, probably because—again—nobody ever brought the personality of the club to life with one apt and catchy phrase.

But, oh, what times and, ah, what characters. We had no scholars on that club, no junior executives. We had ballplayers in whom the blood ran red. Three of my Cubs are in the Hall of Fame. Two of them, Alexander and Maranville, were drunks. The third, Gabby Hartnett, can be found standing along the coaching line at Kansas City this year, so you can ask him about those card games with the lucky rookie of the year. If he doesn't seem to recall offhand, remind him about the Pullman seats with the long, horizontal mirrors along the side wall.

Hartnett was one of the greatest actors the game has ever known. Don't tell me about Jimmy Cagney, holding his gut as he crawls through a rain-filled gutter. You never saw a real death scene, cinema fans, unless you were fortunate enough to be in a ball park when a foul tip caromed off any part of Gabby's sensitive body. Down he would go, rolling in the dirt, writhing in pain. Out would rush the trainer to examine the wound. All at once, Gabby would grow limp. His body would cease its contortions. He would stiffen and lie still. A hush would fall over the park, as the fans observed the silent tableau of the white-

clad trainer huddled over the all but lifeless body. And then!
And then . . . fans, up would jump Hartnett, restored by some
miracle to active life and useful duty. And how they'd cheer as
he courageously shook off all aid and limped to the plate to test
his injured wrist, shoulder or finger with a couple of warm-up
pitches. And how the park would rock as he indicated that,
suffer though he might, he would continue.

In a good week, Gabby would return from the dead three or
four times.

The first drunk I ever saw, I suppose, was on my first trip to
the Cubs' training camp at Catalina Island, when I was perhaps ten years old. Arriving at almost the same time as my
daddy and me was Vic Aldridge, one of our starting pitchers.
Vic came into the hotel with one huge suitcase, so heavy that
it took two redcaps to lug it to his room. Minutes later, he was
asking me to pick him up some socks and underwear.

In his bag was a toothbrush and maybe 100 bottles of Pinaud's
hair tonic, which was most favorably known along the water-
front for its generous alcoholic content. The bottles had a sort of
cap from which you could shake only a few drops at a time, a
great aid to hair grooming and an even greater aid to Vic's life
expectancy. Even when he was drinking with the rest of the
boys, Vic would eschew the regular liquor and drink his hair
tonic. "I've tried that *good* whisky," he'd say, almost with pride,
"and it makes me sick."

A year later, Vic went to Pittsburgh in the trade that brought
us Rabbit Maranville and Charlie Grimm. (Vic immediately
helped the Pirates to the pennant and won two World Series
games.) We had a terrible club at that time, and in order to
loosen the players up a little, my father decided to make Maranville the manager. He may not have done much for the rest of
the team, but he sure loosened up the Rabbit. With nobody to
be responsible to but himself, the Rabbit did not draw a sober
breath—literally—for the rest of the year.

Maranville was a very cute little guy, fun-loving and mischievous. The tiny size and the nickname made him a colorful figure.

In addition, he had his own personal trademarks. His vest-pocket catch (he caught all fly balls down at his belt buckle) always brought anticipation and applause. He invariably disdained to swing at the first pitch—which meant the pitcher invariably tried to throw it right down the pipe—putting himself at a wholly unnecessary disadvantage since he really wasn't much of a hitter.

He loved to put on a show, though. If he hit a triple, which was seldom enough, he'd show his pleasure by turning handsprings, cartwheels and backflips at third base. I can remember seeing Rabbit turn a gleeful handspring, land nimbly on his feet, bow to the wildly cheering audience and turn back to find the umpire calling him out. The Rabbit had neglected to call time, and the third baseman had put the ball on him somewhere in midair.

It was an honest enough mistake, and Rabbit saw no reason to fine himself. He was not, to put it mildly, an iron disciplinarian.

It was as a drinking man that Rabbit always went for the long ball. The first time my daddy ever took me to New York was during Maranville's tenure as manager, and the Rabbit made it a memorable trip. Normally, as should be evident by now, he was a friendly little fellow, without a care or an enemy. He must have been drinking "fighting whisky" in New York, however, because when his cab pulled up to the Commodore Hotel he was arguing furiously with the driver. "I guess I'll just have to give you a licking," he said, hopping out of the cab and putting up his fists. The cabbie watched him bounce around, bobbing and weaving, for a few moments, then hit him with a shot that knocked him flat on his back.

Rabbit brushed himself off, surveyed the situation calmly and said, "All right, I can't lick you. *That* we've established."

He walked up to the first cab on the line, stuck out his jaw and told the driver, "I'm going to lick a New York cabbie tonight, and since I can't lick that other fellow, it's going to have to be you."

Rabbit took a wild swing, and the cabbie flattened him.

Rabbit bounced up again and went on to try his luck on the next cabbie. He went right down the line, through maybe half a dozen cabbies, getting flattened with one punch each time before some of his players came running out to rescue him.

"Somewhere in this city," Rabbit was explaining patiently as they carted him into the hotel, "there is a cabbie I can lick, and as soon as you guys let loose of me I'm gonna find him."

That was our manager.

By the time we had a championship club, our shortstop was Billy Jurges who, being handsome, single and carefree, could go pretty good. The action joint in Chicago was the Carlos Hotel, and many of the players were thoughtful enough to keep private rooms there. One of the group had a girl friend who was very jealous, which seemed rather unreasonable of her since her hero was married. This doll came to the Carlos one evening looking for the poor overburdened fellow and was told that he could be found in Jurges' room. She came bursting through the door and by way of rebuking him for some new infidelity, real or imagined, pulled a gun out of her purse.

Jurges stepped in between them like a good host, smiling benignly, his hand upraised in sweet reason. The young lady said something unladylike to her boyfriend and pulled the trigger—putting a bullet right through Jurges' hand.

Turmoil! Sirens! Police! Doctors! Newspapermen! Scandal!

Shootings were part of the local color in Chicago those days. Witnesses, informers, honest cops, innocent bystanders . . . sometimes even gangsters . . . were shot up every day. But you didn't go around shooting shortstops in the middle of a pennant race. That kind of thing was most disturbing to local industry because it played havoc with the betting odds.

Billy, being single, kept the intended victim's name out of it, leaving everybody to believe that he had got shot on his own merits. I hate to blow the whistle on Billy, but he's been traveling under false colors for years.

My own idol was always Hack Wilson, and since nobody ever again is entitled to the pure adulation that a boy gives to his first hero, nobody will ever be quite as noble and majestic a figure to me as Hack.

Having said that, I now have to admit that if any player of exceptional ability ever did drink himself out of baseball long before his time, it was my boyhood idol. This is a terrible indictment to lay on any athlete, of course, and it is with great regret that I have to inform the members of Troop #5 that Hack stayed around long enough so that he still holds the National League record for home runs in a single season and the major-league record for runs batted in. And I'm warning you right now: if anybody breaks those records during my lifetime, I'm going to stand up and fight for my man. If the new record-breaker does it sober, he gets an asterisk alongside his name.

Hack was a man who commanded your attention from the moment he stepped onto the field. He stood only 5'6" and weighed something over 200 lbs. He was a heavyweight above the waist, with tremendous shoulders, a barrel chest and a watermelon gut. Below the waist he was a lightweight, tapering down to tiny child-size feet.

Like Maranville, he had his copyrighted plays. Contrary to current opinion, Hack was a very good outfielder. He played center field for us when he first came up, and everybody would wait for him to come racing in to make one of his diving, sliding catches, bouncing along on his belly which, as I believe I have indicated, provided ample protection.

He was the only ballplayer I ever knew who could get three uniforms dirty in a single game. It was as if there was something about a clean white uniform that offended everything he held dear. Everybody in the park would be watching as he stepped into the batting cage for the first time, because he would always pick up a handful of dirt and wipe the sides of his pants. A great cheer would go up (Let's hear it for the dirty uniform, folks!), for there seemed to be a general understanding that Hack had, once again, established himself as a member in good standing of the working class.

By the time the game started, Hack would always look as if

he had just delivered a ton of coal. (Will somebody explain to the kiddies what a ton of coal is?)

It wasn't fair, really, for Hack to have had to play in Chicago during the Roaring Twenties. Nobody should have been forced to enjoy himself that much. Poor Hack, he never had time to go to bed. I saw him being sobered up in a tub of ice water the day he went out and hit three home runs. I mean, how did they expect the guy to be able to play ball under those conditions?

There was about Hack the simple innocence of the man who takes the world exactly as he finds it. He once got himself into a dandy spot with Judge Landis by going over to Al Capone's box before a game to have his picture taken. When Landis summoned him to his office to bawl him out, Hack was sorely perplexed. "Gee, what's wrong with that?" he asked the Judge. "I go to his joints all the time and he's always nice to me, so why shouldn't I be nice to him when he comes to ours?"

The Judge just observed Hack for a while, shook his head, and decided that explanation would not really be very fruitful. "Just don't do it anymore," the Judge told him.

Despite his sweet and trusting nature, Hack was always willing to get into a fight for a worthy cause. In those days, almost every city had one loudmouthed fan who achieved a certain parochial fame for riding the players. In Chicago, it was Young, the Milk Driver. One tremendously hot day Hack, being particularly hung over, was oozing sweat out of all his pores and having a terrible time at bat. Young, seizing upon the opportunity to add to his woes, got on him viciously. "Wilson, you drunken bum," he'd scream, "you can't hit nuttin'!"

Hack would have been the last man on earth to have denied the accuracy of both indictments but, in his condition, Young's voice was wearing on the nerves. Seated in the dugout, somewhere around mid-game, Hack began to think out loud. His thinking went something like this: "I have grown weary of today's game. It is hot and my head aches and that so-and-so Young, the Milk Driver, won't let up on me. I think I shall hop up into the stands and belt Young, the Milk Driver, on top of the head with a baseball bat. This will serve three very worthwhile purposes. It will prove to Young, the Milk Driver, that I can indeed hit something; it will get me thrown out of the game so that I can go home and rest up for my rounds tonight; and it might even shut Young, the Milk Driver, up."

Hack went up into the stands with a baseball bat and belted Young, the Milk Driver, quite solidly over the head. Hack was soon on his way home as planned and, as soon as he regained consciousness, Young, the Milk Driver, was on his way to consult his attorney.

While it would not be fair to accuse Hack of being oversensitive to criticism, it would not be inaccurate, I think, to say that he knew when he was being insulted. Hack's buddy and roommate was Pat Malone, a friendship which was bonded in bourbon and bottled in rye. Pat could easily keep up with Hack, which was not too surprising in that Pat had spent a good number of years down in the minors because of his reputation for being an unmanageable drunk. When my daddy, encouraged by Jack Doyle, decided to take a chance on him, he was able to pick him up quite cheap. Hack had been picked up in the minor-league draft himself two years earlier, when the Giants neglected to protect him.

The two of them rollicked all over Chicago together, putting their glasses down only long enough to go out to the park and lead the Cubs to the pennant.

Ray Culp, a Cincinnati pitcher who was probably the most wicked bench jockey of all time, liked to get on Hack. Hack took it in good spirit. Once, however, after the Cubs had finished a series in Cincinnati, he and Pat were hurrying through the railroad station to catch the train, having dallied overlong at a friendly bar. The Reds were leaving town themselves. Hurrying across the terminal from the opposite direction were Culp and his own roommate. "Have we got a minute?" Hack asked Pat. Pat squinted at his watch and decided they might be able to spare one minute but precious little more.

Hack skidded to a stop, dropped his bag and belted Culp out

with a right hook. Pat, who had nothing against anybody particularly, dropped his own bag and belted out Culp's roommate just to show whose side he was on. They then presumably sang two choruses of "Friendship" and shuffled off to catch the train.

Pat Malone, as you can see, was always ready for action. Rain, shine or hurricane. Hurricane? You're darn right, hurricane.

When the Los Angeles Hurricane of 1932 hit, the Cubs, who played their exhibition games in L.A., were quartered at the Biltmore Hotel. At the first tremor, everybody went running out of the hotel and down into Pershing Park, directly across the street. Pat was heading for the exit with the others, thoughtfully carrying a bottle in each hand to treat the seriously wounded. He and a young lady reached the door together. Pat, being a gentleman, deferred to her. She, quite obviously impressed by such thoughtful behavior under such trying conditions, thanked him. A conversation was struck up, quite possibly about his foresight in carrying sustenance with him in the event the city's entire food supply should be destroyed. Pat, not wanting to hoard his supply in this emergency, suggested that the conversation—to say nothing of the bottles—could be carried further. She being agreeable, they went off to batten themselves down and wait out the storm.

They apparently had a great deal in common, because when the players were rounded up the following morning, Pat was listed among the missing. As time went on, my poor father became increasingly fearful that poor Pat had become baseball's first hurricane victim.

Three days later, Pat showed up, smiling quietly.

For a while, our second-string catcher, behind Hartnett, was Rollie Hemsley. Hemsley was known to sports lovers everywhere as "Rollicking Rollie," and if there was a Rollicking Rollie anywhere in baseball, it was inevitable that he would end up with us. In later years, he became one of the very first members of Alcoholics Anonymous and, by talking about his experiences, he probably did as much as anybody else to spread the word. But he was no member when he was with the Cubs and, unfortunately, he wasn't anonymous.

After I became an employee of the Cubs, I made one of my rare trips to New York with our traveling secretary, Bob Lewis.

When we got back to the room from dinner the first night, there was a call waiting for us. Hemsley, we were told, was in the can in Manhattan. We rushed down to the jail, squared things with the cops, brought Hemsley back to the hotel, put him to bed and locked the door behind him.

At 11:30, we got a call from a jail in the Bronx. They had a ballplayer of ours, Rollie Hemsley. "How'd he get out of the room?" I asked Bob.

"Probably called the bell captain . . ."

We went to the Bronx, got him out, brought him up to the room, locked the door and ordered him not to call the bell captain.

At 3 in the morning, the phone woke us up. This time, Rollie was in a jail in Brooklyn. Three different jails in three different boroughs and the night was still young. Evidently, Rollie was out for the record.

"Give me one good reason why we should get out of bed, get dressed and go to Brooklyn," Bob said, "and I'm on my way."

I gave it a great deal of thought.

"Me neither," Bob said. "Let's give Queens a break and leave him right where he is."

In the morning we picked him up. Rollie wasn't sore. It was the first good night's sleep he'd had in weeks.

I had gone to Milwaukee directly from Chicago and put together a group of voyagers and floaters that defied description. Anybody without a price tag and a vestigial tail was welcome to our jolly little group, and we never really had to come to grips with the question of the vestigial tail.

Bill Norman, who was an elder statesman among the players, would get together with me at the beginning of the season to split up the town so that I wouldn't embarrass the players by stumbling across them while they were at play. When it came to the better joints, we broke it down to a time schedule so that we could all have the benefit of the superior service and atmosphere.

Boy, what a great group that was. They were of uncertain habits, destination, pursuits and abilities, but they always got themselves to the ball park on time and in condition to play. Almost always, anyway.

Bill Norman did call me from the Wisconsin Hotel one night with the thrilling news that Merv Connors, our first baseman, was about to jump out the window.

Now frankly, that seemed rather unlikely to me. Connors was a solitary drinker—he would drink only out of a jug—but he had never struck me as a troublemaker. I wanted to know how Bill had ever got such a ridiculous idea.

"Because," Bill said, "he's standing on the window ledge right in front of me and he says he's going to."

After weighing the evidence carefully, it seemed to me that Bill had reasonable grounds for suspicion. He had somehow talked Merv into waiting, he said, until I could get there to speed him on his way, a sentimental gesture that touched me deeply.

Sure enough, when I came into the room Connors was poised in the window, surveying the sidewalk below.

"Merv," I said, allowing a slight note of reproach to creep into my voice, "have I ever done anything unfair to you?"

"There's one thing I got to say for you, Bill," he said, staring straight down. "You've treated me very well. Just beautifully."

"Then I'm entitled to ask you for one small favor, right?"

He glared at me suspiciously, certain that I was going to try to talk him out of his scheduled flight.

"No," I said, "I'd be the last guy in the world to stop you from doing whatever you want. Our boys are in the far-flung battlefields of the world fighting for human dignity and the right of individual determination. But don't you think you owe it to me to wait until I can call the photographers so they can get a picture of you hitting the sidewalk? You'd make every front page in the country, Merv, and the way things are going we could sure use the publicity. Maybe," I added hopefully, "you could change into your uniform while we're waiting."

Connors emitted a short, appreciative laugh—the only time I ever saw him laugh in my life—climbed down off the ledge and, without a word to either Norman or me, lay down on the bed fully clothed and dropped off to sleep.

I went home and started making calls. Because if Connors got a notion to jump again I didn't want him to be a total loss. Ballplayers were awfully hard to get in those days, and I traded him away within 24 hours.

Charlie Grimm was a barrel of laughs but only a social drinker. The social drinker, when put to the test, makes a very unsatisfactory drunk. We were so confident we were going to win the American Association play-offs at Toledo that first season that I had the champagne and wine cooling and the banquet room already rented. When instead we were defeated, I gave the players the option of going ahead with the original plans or heading right home to Milwaukee. The players decided it would be nice to head for home and hold the party on the train.

This was during the war when trains were rather hard to come by. We got ourselves a day coach, though, and in no time at all everybody was stiff. When you're celebrating losing, the mood is harsh and businesslike. What I remember most clearly—before everything began to blur, Judge—was Heinz Becker, our big first baseman, taking a swing at somebody, missing, and hitting a passing player so hard that he almost ripped his ear right off. That was all right, though. A victory party wouldn't be a victory party (even though this wasn't technically a victory party) if there wasn't at least one fight. The ear? Oh, we got that sewed back on as soon as we got back to Milwaukee.

At the height of the celebration the players marched through the Pullman trains, liberating all the pillows for a giant pillow fight. The feathers were so thick around us during the peak of the battle that it was as if you were standing inside one of those paperweight snowstorms. When the storm finally subsided, we had waves of feathers breaking over us like the turf.

When we pulled into Anderson, Indiana, we found that the local detective force was waiting for us. Their plan was to drop our car off at a siding and let us continue our celebration in splendid isolation.

That wasn't what we had in mind at all. Charles, incensed, went out to argue with them. He was standing on the platform between trains, where they normally would have had some portable steps to let us debark.

Charles pulled himself up to a sort of stiff attention and inquired what the trouble could possibly be.

"For one thing," the detective said, "you're covered with feathers. For another, you are as drunk as a lord."

"I never drink," Charlie said, blowing an errant feather from beneath his nose. "I am perfectly sober...."

And with those words, he just stiffened up and toppled straight off the platform. Like a log he fell, and like a log he lay there.

It turned out to be the best argument Charles could have made. The Anderson detective force apparently decided that if we were that far gone they didn't want us on their hands. A guard was placed on either end of our car to make sure we didn't kill ourselves and to keep us from bothering the other passengers. The party rolled on right into Milwaukee.

Three days later, Bill Norman and half a dozen other celebrants were still around town, going strong.

It was a wonderful party.

Which reminds me of another wonderful party we had in Boston after we had beaten the Red Sox in the 1948 play-off game. That party came to an end with the sun beginning to show through the window and nobody left in the Kenmore Hotel ballroom except Joe Gordon and myself. Joe was playing the piano, and we were both shouting out our songs of victory and joy.

Into this simple, heartwarming setting wandered a wayward drunk intent—unnecessarily intent it seemed to us—on letting us know that he didn't care for our voices. Joe pushed the piano stool back, walked across the ballroom and flattened him.

Looking down at the guy, Joe brushed off his hands and with a nicely balanced mixture of satisfaction and weariness, he said, "That gives us a clean sweep of Boston. Now I can go to bed."

I think I'll have one more can of beer and go to bed myself.

7

☺ ☺ ☺

Mention My Name
in St. Paul

I DON'T mean to shake you out of your lethargy,
shatter your complacency or disturb your sleep but the minor-
league meetings are being held this year in Florida. OK, now
that the class is awake I want someone to tell me who the
president of the National Association is . . . Nobody? None of
you ever heard of Phil Piton? No, Piton. P-i-t-o-n.

A minor-league meeting can be best compared to one of those
noble attempts to resurrect burlesque in order to show what it
was like in its great days. It isn't really a performance, it's a re-
production of a performance. It has no life of its own, no relevancy. Minor-league meetings have been irrelevant for about
twenty years.

The agenda of any minor-league meeting revolves, therefore,
around the latest last-ditch plan to save the minors. If all the
plans to save the minors were laid end to end they would just
about pave the way to the cemetery. Now that I think of it,
they just about have.

A couple of years ago there was a great deal of excitement
about a new plan—supported, echoed and endorsed by the
Commissioner—which called for the major leagues to subsidize
one hundred minor-league clubs, most of them nonexistent, the
neatest trick in resurrection since Lazarus was last seen, heading due north, over the plains of Palestine.

More recently, everybody's hopes have been lifted by the promise of the new free-agent draft, even though it is such a limited draft that it will be of extraordinarily little help to the minors.

The only thing that can be said in its favor is that it is not a hallucination. The free-agent draft has a future because it was not designed to help the minors at all. It was designed to help the major leagues by discouraging the reckless distribution of bonuses. A fully implemented free-agent draft, which I proposed in 1952, would have helped to keep the minors going. My fellow operators, led by George Weiss, not only killed my plan, they had most unkind things to say about me.

This thing now is far too little, far too late.

While Piton will gavel the meeting to order, the keynote address should really be delivered by good old Mark Antony, who has a very good track record at this sort of thing. The boys are long past the point of praising the minors, they gather together annually these days only to say a few kind words over the body.

It was Branch Rickey who, quite unconsciously, started the victim on his way when, because of the necessity of finding playing talent for the cash-poor St. Louis Cardinals, he reached into his fertile brain and pulled out the farm system. (Ready cash and St. Louis have never been synonymous. I give illustrated lectures on that subject every Wednesday afternoon.)

As other clubs rushed to develop their own chains, organization men were hired to run the minor-league teams. The independent operator was cut out, taking with him all the elements of free enterprise—initiative, imagination and brigandry—that had made the minors great.

Without an equal chance to make a living commensurate with their abilities, the bright young hustlers either headed for the exit or never bothered to enter. Bright young hustlers, you see, will not put their minds and energies to work that does not hold out some promise of a quick fortune. Not when the world is beckoning with opportunities where the take is unlimited. What might have been a slow decline turned into a complete collapse because there was nobody left down there to put up a fight.

The death blow came when the major-league operators, with their accustomed foresight, televised their own games into minor-league towns, giving the local fans the choice between seeing the best baseball for nothing or paying good money for an inferior product. I tried to salvage what was still salvageable in 1952 by introducing legislation which would have reimbursed every minor league whose territory was being invaded. My fellow operators, led by George Weiss, killed that one too.

In fact, if Mark Antony is unavailable for this year's assignment due to a more pressing engagement, his place on the podium could very easily be taken by George Weiss. Weiss, the noblest Roman of them all, fought every suggestion that might have saved the minors because with the Yankees' great scouting system, money and prestige, and Weiss' own considerable gifts for organization, the Yankees were able to operate the best of the farm systems and parcel out their overflow talent so as to control the other clubs in the American League.

Times do change, though, and George would now be able to preside over the obsequies as the bewildered operator of the talentless Mets. Weiss now has the job of stocking his club with young players, and with the minors dead there are few enough young players to go around. While George has plenty of Mrs. Payson's money to throw about, he has found that the high school kids prefer to take their $100,000 or so from more glamorous teams—like the New York Yankees used to be.

My own early lessons were learned in the minors, and usually taught to me by willing teachers.

The great figure in minor-league baseball in those days was Mike Kelly. Mike was an independent operator at Minneapolis when I came to Milwaukee, and while I was the last of the minor-league freebooters, catching on to the last caboose, Mike had spent his entire life at that kind of operation.

I don't know how to describe Mike Kelly except to say he was just a big, bluff, jovial, red-faced Irishman whom everybody loved. In the play *Death of a Salesman,* Willie Loman talks with awe about the old salesman who had only to check into a hotel room, put on his slippers, pick up the phone and call the buyers. And without leaving the room, Willie says, he made his living. Mike had it even better. Mike could call any of the 16 big-league owners and they would literally jump to help him out. Horace Stoneham was his particular friend, and if Mike ever came up short, Horace or one of the others would always send him a good ballplayer. When he wanted to sell a player, they would be happy to give him an extra good price.

Whenever there was a lull at a baseball meeting, you'd say, "Let's go up to Mike's." Mike would only have a simple room amidst all the ornate suites of the big-league clubs, but there was always a steady flow of visitors, there was always good talk, and if you stayed through the night, everybody in baseball was sure to come floating through.

I can see Mike now, sitting in the middle of the room holding court, a drink always balanced on his knee. Looking back, I can see that I spent some of the best nights of my life waiting for that glass to fall. No matter how much he drank, though, or how much that knee jiggled, the glass never lost a drop.

He dominated all discussion, and what an education it was to listen to him. He would sit there, balancing that drink on his knee, and just to listen to him was to receive a priceless education in operations, trading, larceny and such other of the applied sciences as came to his nimble mind.

Since we both operated in the American Association, I was sometimes fortunate enough to get my lessons direct. Mike had a spotted Dalmatian hound, named Jitterbug, who was with him wherever he went. The hound had a seat of honor alongside Mike's desk in the office and he examined all visitors critically. During the game, Jitterbug had his own special seat alongside Mike in the front row of the right-field corner so that he could watch the game with Mike and snarl at anybody in a gray uniform.

There was one game where we were leading by one run in the last of the ninth with men on first and second and two men out. A line drive was hit down the right-field line. Hal Peck, our right fielder, came flying over to pick it up and Jitterbug came flying over the railing to bite Peck right in the leg. The ball lay there at Peck's feet. Every time Peck would reach for it, Jitterbug would snap at his hand. While Peck was reaching and Jitterbug was snapping, the tying and the winning runs crossed the plate. Mike whistled sharply, and Jitterbug trotted dutifully back, wagging his tail happily in the manner of a good dog who knows he has earned his night's lodgings.

I protested bitterly to league president George Trautman that the hound had undoubtedly been carefully trained to bite in the clutch. Mike didn't deign to so much as acknowledge the protest, but Trautman ruled it was an act of God, leaving me to decide whether I wanted to fight it out on theological grounds.

Every dog has his day, though, and I once had my chance to get back at Mike. I was always trying to make some kind of a deal with him, since we were the only two independents in the league, but with the kind of setup he had with the majors he hardly found it necessary to deal with a fresh kid from Milwaukee. Especially since we were both in the business of looking for young players whom we could develop for sale.

I had bought a last-place team in the middle of 1941. At the end of the year, by judicious use of the system of deficit spending that was becoming so popular in economic circles, I was buying up a lot of good new players. I was getting pretty good information, of course. Jack Doyle, the great Cub scout, had recommended three players from the Sally League: Eddie Stanky; Frank Marino, a pitcher; and Hughie Todd, an outfielder-first baseman. I was in action within 48 hours, but I found that Mike had already beaten me to Todd. I offered to take Todd off his hands at a quick profit, and he just laughed and laughed and laughed.

Mike was initiating me in other ways too. He had a park that sat maybe 15,000. He had always had a good strong team, and when we shot right up into contention in our second year, we filled the place up pretty well. We'd look around the stands and estimate a crowd of maybe 9,000 to 10,000 and when the turnstile count was checked it would come to maybe 6,000.

The visiting team runs a check on the attendance, I should explain, by sending its own man around with the home team's ticket manager when the gates are first opened in the morning so that both clubs can jot down the turnstile count. In our case it would usually be Red Smith, our coach. After the fifth inning, when the game has become official, both teams assign a representative to make the tour again and take the final turnstile count.

It's funny. Something can go on and on and you think nothing much about it, and then one day, out of the blue, it clicks in your head. One day out of the blue, the thought suddenly occurred to me that we couldn't be *that* wrong *every* time out. Sure. Mike Kelly would be testing to find out whether the new boy in town really had anything on the ball or had just got himself a team together through blind luck.

OK, Mike. The next time we went to Minneapolis, I hired a couple of private detectives to wander around among the ticket windows and just casually keep an eye on everything. I was careful *not* to hire the Pinkertons; Mike would undoubtedly have had occasion to use them himself through the years and if my suspicions were correct I had a surprise in store for Mike so sweet that I wanted to make sure I would be springing it on him personally.

The detectives checked two days in a row, to make sure they had a pattern. They found that Mike was opening two extra turnstiles just as the fans began to arrive in force, and closing them up again as soon as the game got underway.

Wasn't that great? Mike had gone into business himself. His private gates were two of the best ones, too—a grandstand gate and a gate along the right-field line. What initiative! What enterprise! What a shock he was in for!

I had the detectives write out affidavits complete with times, gate numbers and all other pertinent information. Then I tucked the affidavits into my pocket and went up to pay my respects to Mike and Jitterbug.

Seating myself across the desk from Mike, I casually moved the conversation toward the struggle we independent operators were engaged in against the massive might of the major-league farm systems, and what a thrill it was for a young man like me to sit at the feet of the master and watch him his wonders to perform. Before very long, I was talking about the difference between a major-league operation where you had all the money you needed (I hadn't heard of St. Louis yet) and a minor-league operation where you were always skimping a little here, saving a little there.

"It's a funny thing," I said. "Even the crowds look different. I used to pride myself on how close I could estimate a crowd at Wrigley Field and down here—at your park, for instance—I always seem to be way off. Would you believe it, I'd have sworn we had a crowd of nine to ten thousand yesterday."

Mike was looking at me quizzically now, a slight smile playing around his lips. Jitterbug, who was always perfectly attuned to him, was sitting straight up on his chair, looking ... well, looking quizzical too.

"Young man," Mike said, putting on his most virtuous air, "you have to be around a long time before you can estimate the size of a crowd accurately." Jitterbug, looking equally virtuous, scowled at me rather nastily.

"You sure do," I said brightly. "Because I certainly could never have estimated the size of your crowds from what I've been getting paid off on."

"Young man," he said, as if the thought, hitherto unthinkable, had just occurred to him. "Are you suggesting that I might be manipulating my turnstiles?"

"Noooo," I said, deciding to stick the needle in a little deeper than I had originally intended. "But if it weren't that my daddy always told me you were one of the few men in baseball that he could trust, I just might think that you mislaid a turnstile or two every now and then."

"Now how," he said, "could I possibly do that?"

"If it weren't for what my daddy told me," I said, looking at him flush, "I'd say you were opening up a couple of gates after the original morning check."

He leaned back, grinning at me, and it was as if he were patting a good student on the head. "Now that would be the most despicable thing I ever heard of," he said. "I'm sorry I didn't think of it myself."

I took out the affidavits and placed them in front of him. "Do you know something, Mike," I said, grinning back, "I'm sorry *I* didn't think of it myself."

Mike looked them over, still amused. "Now who'd have thought any of my turnstile men would have held out on me like that," he said. "What do you think I should do? Conduct a thorough investigation?"

"Oh, I've got a better idea than that. I've just thought of something that might get us both off the hook. You know, breach the misunderstanding. Heal the wounds. Let bygones be bygones."

"I try to get along with the competition," Mike said. "We're all just poor boys down here in the minors trying to scratch out a living."

"I'll tell you what I'm willing to do," I said. "Just so there'll be no hard feeling, I'll give you five hundred dollars for Hughie Todd."

"Five hundred dollars!" he screamed. He had been waiting to see how tough I was going to be, and I could see that I had surpassed his fondest expectations. For one moment, I was going to relent and up the price to ... well, maybe a thousand. But then, it is never a good idea to throw away an advantage.

"Look at it this way, Mike. I could have asked for somebody a lot better than Todd."

"You could have asked for somebody a lot worse, too," he muttered.

What you have to understand here is that Mike knew very well that I was never going to blow the whistle on him. If he had told me to drop dead that would have been the end of it. He had played his little game with me, though, and I had found him out. By his code, that meant he had to pay off.

Since it was well known that Mike didn't sell players to other minor-league clubs, especially in his own league, he asked only that I dig up some worthless player so that it could be announced as a straight player-for-player transaction.

As I was leaving, he called out, "Bill. . . ."

I turned back. The smile that had been playing around his lips throughout the entire session finally broke out. "Welcome to the American Association, laddie boy," he said. "I think we're going to have some fun."

Fun I had.

By the time we had built a pennant-winning club in Milwaukee, St. Paul was deep in the cellar and suffering badly at the box office. Naturally, I wanted to help them. Put in a slightly different, and possibly more accurate way, I also wanted to help myself. We were riding on top of the league, and we couldn't even make expenses in St. Paul.

Promotionally, St. Paul had only one asset that I could see, the blood rivalry with Minneapolis. According to the official rules of vendetta, I had no right whatsoever to declare myself in on such a long and honorable feud. And if I could have thought of anything else to do, I wouldn't have.

To attack St. Paul, I had to violate one of my basic promotional precepts. The best promotion of all, I have always believed, is a rerun of that well-reported encounter between David and Goliath. (In those days, by golly, they had writers who could *write*.) For best effect, I had always looked upon myself as David, and it pained me to have to cast myself as Goliath.

But facts are facts. If I were being pushed by hard necessity into the armor of Goliath, I would be the loudest, most obnoxious Goliath anyone could wish for. There is nothing more sickening, students, than a mewling, apologetic Goliath. Goliath must pound upon his breastplates and rattle the mountaintops. His imprecations should bellow forth like thunder and from his fangs should drip pure venom. I mean, I don't care whether the kids in the neighborhood had made fun of him in his youth because he was so big and awkward. I don't even care whether he came from a broken home. A Goliath looking for love and understanding is no good to anybody, including himself.

Goliath is there for only one reason. To make the other side want to throw rocks at him.

I went on the radio in Minneapolis and blasted the city of St. Paul. I blasted their fans and their park and their bridges and their hotels and I expressed grave misgivings about their sewer system. I would never again, I announced—working myself up into a fury—submit my fine, upstanding young players to the atmosphere of such a backward, jerkwater town. Instead, I was going to have them stay at the Nicollet Hotel in the fine, progressive metropolis of Minneapolis and take them in and out of St. Paul by streetcar, preferably under cover of darkness. "I have no intention," I said, "of forcing my players to remain in St. Paul for one minute longer than is absolutely necessary for us to meet our legal obligations. And understand this: it doesn't matter to me whether anybody comes to the park or not, because the less I have to do with the people of St. Paul the happier I will be. I want nothing to do with them except to go in, knock their brains out and get out of town as fast as humanly possible."

St. Paul, frightfully oversensitive, took offense. The paper attacked me. The radio commentators attacked me. Little boys playing in those cholera-ridden streets abandoned their hoops and marbles in order to attack me. Needless to say, the mayor, sniffing a stray vote or two in the air, attacked me most bitterly of all, as prologue to a stirring speech about the glory and the beauty of St. Paul.

Normally, I made only one trip a year with the club. This time, it seemed to me that the least I could do would be to go into St. Paul on our next visit and give the paying customers a chance to hiss the villain. We came in for a Sunday double-header, and for some reason I have never been able to understand the place was almost completely sold out. I sat in a box alongside our dugout, as I normally do on the road, exchanging pleasantries with the natives.

In the first game, we came from behind to beat the Saints by something like 14–9, and a certain restlessness could be observed running through the grandstand. In the second game, the Saints scored 7 runs in the first inning to relieve the tension. We came back in the top of the second with 9 runs. As the final run was crossing the plate, I turned my head toward the dugout to shout a few words of encouragement and cheer to one of our players. At the same moment, a Coke bottle came flying past, just ticking my cheek before it splintered into tiny fragments against the top of the dugout.

Well, fun is fun and a crowd is a crowd but a Coke bottle is a lethal weapon. This was carrying the Goliath-David imagery a bit too far for our effete times.

Some of my players were on the top of the dugout stairs pointing excitedly to a young fellow seated in the front row of the grandstand seats. I vaulted the little fence that separated the boxes from the grandstand and shouted, "Get up, you bum." When he showed no inclination to oblige me, I slapped him back and forth across the face, first with the palm of my hand and then with the back.

Holy smoke! The fans came rushing at me from everywhere and, within seconds, the Milwaukee players were racing up from the dugout, bats in hand. Fights broke out all around me, and the sound of falling bodies filled the air. Attorneys were racing up and down the aisles, briefcases swinging and pens at the ready, to bring legal aid and succor to any citizen with a cut, a bruise or a vivid imagination. That was all right. I had had my shot at free enterprise, and now they were entitled to theirs.

It would be remiss of me, I think, not to mention that we had very good crowds in St. Paul on every one of our subsequent visits that year, even though the citizenry remained curiously unfriendly.

And, oh yes, it might be of some slight documentary interest to note that we also increased attendance to most satisfactory levels when St. Paul came to play in our own modest little wooden ball park in Milwaukee.

It was at Milwaukee that I also learned the invaluable lesson that there are more things in heaven, on earth and on the ball field than one lone man could expect to control.

In beefing up my club for my first full year, I was negotiating with George and Julius Shepps of Dallas for Grey Clarke, a third baseman who was leading the Texas League in hitting, and Heinz Becker, a powerful first baseman.

Clarke was somewhere around thirty years of age, and Becker had bad feet, which made them both poor prospects for a profitable resale to the majors. Both of them, however, figured to be the good solid minor-league players who form the backbone of a Triple-A club. Becker had another great asset. He had also had the foresight to be born in Germany, which assured him of an enthusiastic reception by the good burghers of Milwaukee.

In negotiating over the telephone, I had agreed to pay $15,-000 for the two of them, a very large sum for a minor-league deal in those wonderful pre-bonus days. I was moved to be so generous with the Shepps brothers because, in the course of those telephone conversations, I had grown very fond of them. I had grown so fond of them because they had agreed to take nothing down and wait a full year for settlement.

As our season came to an end, Dallas was playing Tulsa, a

Chicago Cubs farm, in the Texas League play-offs, so I went down with Jim Gallagher, the Cubs general manager, to close the deal. We arrived in Dallas in the morning, and I immediately called George Shepps. We had lunch together, Shepps showed himself to be a fine Southern gentleman (which means he still wasn't asking for anything down) and we closed the deal.

The ball game was being played at night. Jim and I went up to the press box, which was high on top of the open stands. Just before the game was about to start, Shepps joined us. "By the way," he said, "your player is in the hospital."

"My *what* is *where?*"

"Clarke. You know, the third baseman you bought this afternoon. He was rushed to the hospital at about five o'clock with an acute attack of appendicitis. I understand he's on the operating table right now."

I'm a trusting soul, of course. "Oh," I said. "You knew about it in advance, huh?"

Shepps tried to explain that it wasn't quite that easy to get advance information about acute attacks of appendicitis. He also tried to explain that since I didn't have to worry about Clarke's condition until next spring, Dallas was the only club that was going to suffer. Dallas, after all, was losing him for the rest of the play-offs.

Somehow I remained unconvinced. Or, at any rate, unmollified. "What if he dies on the operating table?" I asked, looking on the bright side of things.

Shepps shrugged. "That would be too bad," he said. "You'd be stuck."

Gallagher, who knew how high my hopes had been, commiserated with me through the first couple of innings of the game. Shepps was feeding me the latest medical bulletins on *my* ballplayer, and I was feeling increasingly sorry for myself.

Heinz Becker made my world a little brighter in the third inning by stepping up and belting a long drive into left center.

For all his bulk and his heaviness of foot, Heinz had a very colorful way of diving into a base headfirst. He went chugging around first, as I cheered him on, but at the last minute he apparently decided he was going to show me he had a little gazelle blood in him. Instead of diving, he hit second base with what was supposed to be a fadeaway slide. He looked more like a rhinoceros falling into a pool. He lay there, out of breath. He lay there, and he continued to lay there. People were running out onto the field. A stretcher was not far behind. A *stretcher?* They were carrying *my* player off in a stretcher?

Alongside me, Shepps was hastily excusing himself so that he could go down to the clubhouse to check the damage. A few minutes later, a message was brought to me: "Mr. Shepps says to tell you that it isn't a *serious* fracture."

Oh boy. I've just spent $15,000 which I don't have for two players who have suddenly been converted into hospital patients. One of them has just been cut open and the other has just broken his leg before my very eyes. I couldn't believe it. By all the laws of probability, we had hit a million-to-one shot.

Boy, I was flaming. I leaped up, fully intending to run down to the clubhouse. Gallagher grabbed me by the arm. "Bill," he said, "where do you think you're going?"

"I'm going down to see Shepps," I said grimly. "Maybe he'll be willing to sell me a second baseman with smallpox."

I had been planning on making a tremendous splash back in Milwaukee by calling a press conference to announce this astute deal I had made. What could I possibly tell my admiring public now?

Jim Gallagher came back to the Adolphus Hotel with me to try to cheer me up. Hotels being somewhat more stuffy than ball clubs about settling up bills, I had taken the smallest possible room. One of the luxuries I was foregoing was air conditioning and, as we sat there, the room quickly filled up with heat and gloom. "Why did I have to rush right in and close the deal today?" I'd ask Jim over and over. "Anybody with any brains would have come to the hotel, taken in the ball game, looked over the players, and *then* closed the deal. In a day or two. At his leisure. But me? Oh no. I had to come barging into town like Billy the Kid and show how fast I am with a buck."

Jim, who really felt bad for me, was saying all the usual things about how it was the kind of luck that could have happened to anybody.

"Yeah," I said, almost enjoying my self-abasement. "Anybody who's a complete *idiot*."

Things would look different, he assured me, once I was back in Milwaukee.

That would give me plenty of time to brood about it, I told him, because I had no intention of telling everybody I had just paid $15,000 for the two leading hitters in the Dallas hospital. "I'm not going back to Milwaukee," I told him, "until at least one of them is back on his feet."

I headed due east to Miami, made a leisurely journey up the East Coast and by the time I finally did get back to Milwaukee, two weeks later, Clarke was out of the hospital and I had assurances that Becker's leg was going to be all right.

A couple of months later, the Japanese bombed Pearl Harbor. All of a sudden, I had made a great deal. In Clarke, I had an overage third baseman; in Becker, I had a first baseman with the flattest feet in baseball. Both of them were safe from the draft, and both of them had some great years for us. I sold Clarke to the White Sox and Becker to the Cubs at an excellent profit.

Still, it *could* have been a double disaster. In baseball, I discovered, you cannot always judge the kind of a deal you have made until all the precincts have been heard from.

There is the business side too. You can get lucky or unlucky, depending upon the time, the place, the wind, the war and a few other windfalls or catastrophes, small or large.

When we arrived in Milwaukee, the broadcasts of the games

were being sponsored by Pabst Beer for about a buck and a half—which was about 25 cents more than they were worth. As per custom, Pabst also had the exclusive right to sell their beer in the park.

Late in the summer, after we had begun to draw crowds ranging all the way up into the 2,000s, Pabst scheduled a free boxing exhibition at Lakefront, with Jack Dempsey coming in as referee.

Now, good luck to them and all that, but I did feel that as our sponsor, they should have at least let me know ahead of time so that I'd be able to reschedule our own night game. Bucking Dempsey and a free fight with our little club was like bucking a free showing of *My Fair Lady* with your local high school drama group.

We were fairly well aware that Pabst didn't look upon us as the advertising medium off which they were going to live or die, but I didn't think it was really necessary for them to go that far out of their way to show us how unimportant we were.

The only decent thing for me to do was to cancel the contract and throw them and their beer out of my little ball park. This proved most salutary for the free and untrammeled flow of my digestive juices but rather disastrous for our income.

To hustle up another sponsor and another beer, I called on Schlitz and Blatz. The other beer in town was Miller's Hi-Life, which was well below the Big Three in sales and had shown no interest at all in sports. Still, to cover all bases, I wrote them a letter.

Blatz and Schlitz showed less than no interest, and now I really began to worry. Just as my worrying was reaching Olympic proportions, the general manager of the Miller brewery phoned to ask if I could come down and discuss my proposition.

"Let's see," I said. "You're less than seven miles from here. The next screech you hear should be me pulling up to the front door."

"You sound rather anxious," he said.

"If you think I *sound* anxious," I said, "wait until you *see* me, face to face."

At the brewery, I explained why I thought it would be a great deal for Miller's and a passably good deal for us. We worked out a formula in which the broadcasting rights would be on a sliding scale based upon where we finished, and our concession percentage would be on a rising scale based upon the amount of beer that was actually sold at the park. They couldn't get stuck if we failed to excite the fans and we wouldn't be locked in if we began to prosper. As a necessary adjunct to that kind of formula they, of course, had to guarantee to supply all the beer we ordered.

The actual signing was deferred until the following day when Fred Miller, the owner of the company, would be in to preside at the ceremonies for the benefit of the press, the cameramen and any interested bystanders.

As I was walking out, I bumped into a dark-haired fellow I had been playing handball with at the firehouse, three noons a week. He was a young guy like me, a lefty like me, and a real good handball player unlike me. "Hey, Fritz," I said, "what are you doing here?"

He looked at me, rather oddly, and mumbled something about dropping in from time to time to see his friends at the brewery.

The next day, I came in to meet Fred Miller and sign the contracts. There, waiting behind the desk, was, of course, my handball partner, Fritz.

As I had promised, it did turn out to be a good deal for Miller's over the long run. In later years, they concentrated most of their advertising budget on sports and prospered mightily.

In the short run, however, it turned out to be an even better deal for us. I went off to the Marines, and when I came back I found that due to the rationing of malt during the war, the output of all the breweries had been severely restricted.

Well, our contract with Miller's called for them to deliver all the beer we could sell, and the shorter the supply became, the greater the demand became at the park. Tavern owners were paying their way into the park just to load up with beer. Customers were coming in with paper sacks and carting the stuff home. We had become, to all purposes, a leading distributor of Miller's Hi-Life Beer, on a retail basis.

I was shipped back to the Corona hospital outside Los Angeles. Waiting for me was a letter from Rudie Schaffer. Rudie explained that Fritz felt it looked very bad—to both his distributors and the customers—that beer was readily available only at the park. His offer was to pay the maximum figure in the contract, plus a bonus, if we'd agree to a more equitable deal. Well, Fritz was a friend, and he was a good guy. He had helped us when we were hurting and it was incumbent upon me to return the favor.

I didn't want any bonus, I wrote back, but I did want the maximum figure, since we had already reached it.

"But having enough beer in the park is very important to our own operation," I made clear. "Especially now that our customers have come to expect it."

My proposition was that while he was to continue to keep me stocked with beer, it didn't necessarily have to be Miller's.

Boy, I'll tell you. We had beer coming into that park that nobody had ever heard of before. Miller must have sent scouts all over the state of Wisconsin, because his trucks would pull in with 10 cases of Old John's and 5 cases of East End Lager; 8 cases of this and a couple of bottles of that. We had beer from breweries that I'm sure went back to making shampoo after the war.

We were still able to serve our customers, and if we lost the outpatient trade, that was all right. I'm all for taking unfair advantage, but there is a line where sparkling opportunism becomes sheer greed.

A buck is a buck, all right. But friends are friends, too.

In the minor leagues, you used to rise or fall on your ability to develop players for the majors and sell them at the top price.

In a well-run operation, player sales, ticket receipts and radio rights contributed just about equally to your income. The best salesman I have ever seen—and this may surprise you—was Casey Stengel.

I know you don't think of Casey as either a minor-leaguer or a salesman, because you tend to forget that Casey spent 12 years as a minor-league manager. You don't think of him as a company man either, but that is precisely what Casey has always been. Casey is always very alert to the needs of what he always calls "my owners." With the Mets, he knows he is primarily a public-relations man, and he has been doing the greatest public-relations job in the history of baseball. In the minors, where he knew his owners were looking to sell players, Casey, as I quickly learned, was in a class by himself.

Rudie Schaffer hired Casey to manage Milwaukee while I was in Guadalcanal with the Marines. Being a shrewd, astute baseball man, I immediately sent out an angry letter instructing Rudie to fire him as soon as possible. At almost the same time, Casey was writing me a chatty letter to tell me about my ball club. In that letter, he told me that before the season was over he was going to sell a mediocre catcher, Jim Pruitt, to a particular team, the Philadelphia Athletics and, more outrageous still, that he was going to sell him to a particular scout, Jim Peterson.

Now Pruitt, whom we had purchased from the Sally League that season, was a pretty good hitter—but that's all he was, a *pretty* good hitter. He was also a fair enough receiver—but that's all he was, a *fair* receiver. A major-league prospect he wasn't, no matter how low the wartime standards had sunk.

"What kind of a fool does Stengel think I am, trying to con me by throwing in the scout's name like that?" I thought. "Doesn't that old fraud know you can't con a con man?"

But Stengel knew what he was talking about. Casey, whose talents are really astonishing, is essentially a teacher. As a minor-league manager, he always told his players: "Work with me, kid, and I'll get you in the big leagues." In Pruitt he had found a kid who was willing to come out every morning for special instruction.

Pruitt did have one asset. He did have a better than average throwing arm. And so Casey was out there with him every morning teaching him to snap his throws down to first and third. He kept him under wraps through most of the season, though, never letting him even try to pick a man off until Peterson came wandering through to watch us through an entire series. And then he turned him loose. Pruitt picked six guys off first and third, and before Peterson left town he had bought Pruitt for something like $40,000, plus a couple of players.

Somewhere in his travels, Casey had heard Peterson, a one-time minor-league pitcher, tell a story about how a catcher had saved a game for him by picking off three straight runners. Spotting a potential weak spot in his scouting objectivity Casey had made a mental note to fatten up a catcher for him some day.

In setting up a prospective buyer, Casey's interest lies principally in matching a player's particular ability with a buyer's particular weakness. My own interest always lay more in the more universal area of human nature. The best trade I ever made came about because I knew that Clark Griffith thought I was a disgrace to the game of baseball. Even though he abominated me, Uncle Clark had been forced to humble himself and ask me to pitch Satchel Paige in Washington at night, because one thing you've got to say for Uncle Clark, he was never a man to let his principles interfere with his profit.

But that didn't mean he didn't dislike me even more for having to come to me for favors.

I had tried to buy Early Wynn from Griffith without success until I read that his son-in-law, Joe Haynes, a sore-armed pitcher with Chicago, was going to have to undergo an operation. I called up Frank Lane and bought Haynes cheap, because I was sure that Griffith could not live with the thought of his son-in-law working for me and maybe even taking part in some of my stunts. I called Uncle Clark and, trying my best to sound like a kidnapper, I told him I had Haynes and he had Wynn and what did he suggest we do about it? What he chose to do was to trade me his best pitcher for a mediocre pitcher with an arm that had to be operated on.

Hate is a terrible thing.

8

⊖ ⊖ ⊖

New York, New York, It's a Wonderful Town The Mets Are Up and the Yanks Are Down

THIS course carries a hand-embroidered guarantee that everything you read herein is at least 83 percent true. If you follow the directions carefully and shake well before using, you will be fully equipped to seize opportunity by the forelock and stay out of jail.

There is—uh—one little codicil down here in the fine print which the attorneys insisted upon putting in just to show that they're on the job. I believe they have been referring to it by some dry legal phrase such as "escape clause." Pay no attention to it:

> There are times when the moon goes out of whack, when lionesses whelp in the streets and graves do yawn and yield up their dead.
>
> Horses neigh and dying men do groan and ghosts do shriek and squeal about the streets.
>
> At such a time the party of the first part (hereinafter known as the professor) is not responsible to the party of the second part (known hereinafter as the student).

This is the "Death of Princes" disclaimer, which dates back to a colleague of Blackstone's who practiced under the name of W. Shakespeare. It means that there are times when a phenomenon arises that goes so completely against all known laws of man and nature that a wise man stays home in bed, coughing pitifully and snarling at his wife.

I am not recommending that the hustler do this—although I do recommend that he take the elementary precaution of staying off the Senate steps.

Once or twice in the course of even the tidiest lifetime you are going to run across a phenomenon like the New York Mets which defies not only the rules of baseball but the laws of gravity. The Mets begin every season by sinking like a rock into the cellar, and their attendance goes up, up, up into the sky, bounding over the New York Yankees in a single bound.

Explain the Mets, students? The Mets are not there to be explained or understood; they are there to be loved.

But what the heck, I'll try.

Whenever anybody stops me in the street to ask whether it's more important whether you win or lose than how you play the game, I look into the deepest recesses of my heart and answer, "As my dear friend, Al Smith, once said, 'Let's look at the box office.'" (My Al Smith was a guy from the South Side of Chicago. Poor fellow just loved to stand there and look at box offices.)

It should be perfectly obvious by now to all us deep thinkers (I said *thinkers*, Mr. Frick) that the Mets cannot do anything wrong just so long as they continue to do EVERYTHING wrong. It doesn't matter whether they win or lose but how badly they play the game.

If any doubt ever existed on that score, the opening of Shea Stadium last year should have eliminated it for all eternity.

The season started in New York with less than 13,000 loyalists showing up to watch the Yankees who, as everyone knows, have the best winning record since Attila the Hun hung up his spikes. (He couldn't get along with Bobby Bragan, they tell me.)

A couple of days later, 50,000 New Yorkers showed up at Shea Stadium for the Mets' opening fiasco causing, in purest Met tradition, a historic traffic jam. This delighted the city so much that 30,000 more fans rushed out the following day to see whether they could have the pleasure of being caught in a traffic jam too. My friend Al Smith came all the way from Chicago. He has a thing about automobiles too.

The Mets, needless to say, rose to the occasion nicely by blowing the ball game. The only untoward incident came when Bill Shea, who modeled for the Stadium, threw out the first ball, and Jesse Gonder, obviously a man of limited imagination, caught it! I swear to you by the hair of George Weiss' chinny-chin-chin he caught it! I understand that Casey took him right under the stands and had a long talk with him.

The success of the Mets is a case study that should be required reading for all public-relations majors, graduate students in civic government and would-be psychiatrists. The first thing to understand is that it couldn't have happened anywhere except in New York City. No other city is so confident of its own preeminence that it could afford to take such an open delight in its own bad taste.

In order to be able to codify the rules of hustling, you have to start with the basic premise that people are basically the same (which is true), which means, necessarily, that they are the same wherever they may happen to be (which is true), which means that all cities, being composed of people, are also essentially the same—which is not true. People will laugh at the same things and cry at the same things but their personal histories can leave them aggressive or defensive in entirely different areas. What is true of people is even more true of cities.

The best way to approach the New Yorker's attitude toward the Mets is to examine the reactions of other cities to a new big-league franchise.

Baseball has operated from the first upon the theory that all that is necessary for initial success is to dub the town with the magic label "Big League" and assure the citizenry that they have just been endowed with the rare honor of playing with baseballs signed by Joe Cronin or Warren Giles. It was made clear enough, certainly, that the thought of providing an occasional big-league player to go with the franchise never entered anybody's mind.

The logic is, I will admit, unassailable. We are a label-conscious nation, possibly because our better advertisers have spent 8 zillion dollars to make us label-conscious. The *Today* program proved this conclusively by taking an atrocious straw hat off one of those tired old horses that draw young lovers and aging romantics through Central Park, sewing a Bonwit-Teller label on the inside and advertising that it had been marked down from $39.50 to $10. Needless to say, they had no trouble at all in finding a customer. It was as easy as taking a straw hat away from a tired old horse.

Some cities, like some people, are more label-conscious than others. Milwaukee, only 90 miles from Chicago, has always suffered from a "country cousin" complex, and when baseball came in to tell them they were as good as anybody else they went dancing joyfully through the streets to the box office. It took eight full years before the music stopped playing.

By one of those coincidences that make life so easy for us recorders of our times and manners, Milwaukee's debut as a certified big-league city came the day after Russia had sent the first Sputnik into outer space, one of the landmark (a wildly inappropriate word here) dates in the history of mankind. You know darn well which story the Milwaukee papers headlined. The scare headline on the Milwaukee *Sentinel* read: TODAY WE MAKE HISTORY!

If you wanted to read all that stuff about the satellite, you had to turn the page.

Houston is something else again. Houston is a small island completely surrounded by an ocean of oil. In Houston, a bunch of oil millionaires got together (there really should be a more worthy way of describing an assemblage of oil millionaires: slick of oil millionaires? goldwater of oil millionaires? deprecia- tion allowance of oil millionaires?) . . . Anyway, all these Texas millionaires, having grown weary of alternating their leisure time between counting their money and counting the traitors in Washington, got together and decided it would be nice to have a big-league team in the neighborhood. They were sure the team would be well supported because all their friends— who also happened to be Texas oil millionaires or Texas bank- ers—agreed that it would be comforting to be able to see a big- league game without having to go through all the bother of revving up the motors of their private planes.

The basic mistake they made was that they did not stop to consider that the wealthiest man in the world can only put his fanny in one seat, one phase of democracy that not even the Chairman of the House Committee on Rules is empowered to alter.

Baseball is not the sport of the wealthy, it is the sport of the wage earner. There has never been any indication that the Texas workingman has any overwhelming interest in the grand old game. Texans, as has oft been observed, have never suf- fered unduly from the ravages of the inferiority-complex syn- drome. Texans therefore didn't need Organized Baseball to tell them they were big-league fellows. They know they're the biggest of the big, and they have the mouths to prove it.

Even with a good team, Houston probably would have had its troubles. Given the very poor—and worse—exceedingly dull team which the National League fobbed off on them, Texas, with its penchant for doing things big, responded with a great big yawn. It took a $30 million astrodome to wake them up and head them toward the park.

Los Angeles is exactly the opposite. L.A. has always suffered from such a terrible case of third-degree inferiority that its newspapers find it necessary to apply poultices by proving, daily, that its horses are faster, its football players stronger, and its weather balmier. The typical L.A. headline tells the reader how bad the weather is back East.

Although it is now the second most populous city in the country, Los Angeles—which is really seven towns in search of a city—still has a small-town complex. (For a promoter, Los Angeles is as close as you can get to heaven because you have both the small-town psychology and the huge population to work with.) Los Angeles has grown so much, so fast, that it still finds it necessary to prove to itself that it is really entitled to play with the big boys, a thought which would never occur to New York or Chicago. The only way it can prove it is by winning.

And so, as important as the Big League label was to Los Angeles, it was absolutely essential that O'Malley show up with an established and colorful team like the Dodgers.

The fans ignored the Angels when they came limping into town with a bad team, leaped on the bandwagon with enthusiasm when the Angels jumped into contention for one year, and then dropped them with a thud when they reverted to type. Los Angeles is still not secure enough to support a loser.

New York had nothing to prove to anybody. New York had the Broadway theatre, the Metropolitan Opera, the best art museums, the tallest buildings. New York had everything any cosmopolite could wish for, it seemed, except a lousy ball club.

Presented with as lousy a team as the most optimistic rooter could hope for, the city responded with touching gratitude and frightening passion. The more inept the club showed itself to be (and it reached pinnacles of ineptitude previously undreamed of) the closer the city hugged it to its ample bosom.

For New York also had something else. It had the self-assurance of a town used to winners. It had the Yankees, the perennial American League pennant-winner. Before the Giants and Dodgers departed, New Yorkers had grown accustomed to an almost annual intraborough World Series. If big-league baseball was not that strong a wine, then victory was not that mad a music.

The delightful irony of the situation is that the Yankees are in the uncomfortable position of watching the Mets profit from their reputation in two almost opposite ways—which is two more ways than the Yankees are profiting themselves these days. Without the Yankees' long history of success through victory, the Mets could never have achieved their own spirited dash to success through defeat. New Yorkers can *condescend* to root for the Mets—and when you think about it there is a large element of condescension in the affection for the team— only because the Yankees are still there in the background with that history of unbroken success. The Met fan doesn't live and die with the team as he once lived and died with the old Dodgers. The city isn't deeply involved with them, it is amused by them. The Met fan puts forth his addiction as a charming idiosyncrasy.

At the same time, the Yankees were aiding the cause even further by providing the image of grim efficiency which the Mets have been able to play themselves off against. The Yankees should sue the guy who first said that "rooting for the Yankees is like rooting for U.S. Steel," because he articulated for so many people what they had already come to feel.

The Yankees always took the attitude that they were doing you a favor by permitting you to watch them perform. They would no more deign to court their customers than the Queen would deign to court her subjects when she grants her annual audiences. (But you think maybe the Queen doesn't count the house too?)

It has only been with the rise of the Mets and the fall of the House of Houk that they have found it polite to provide entertainment. This is the first year, I suspect, that they have seen a fan close up.

At this writing it hasn't worked. The Mets are a trip to the Fun House. The Yankees are still a Board of Directors meeting. I don't know about your neighborhood but it has been years since anyone rioted on my block to attend a Board of Directors meeting.

How do the Yankees fight back when their very success is working against them? They seem to be making a game attempt to match the Mets in sheer inefficiency, an ambition which—in sheer scope and grandeur—leaves one shaken to one's very foundations. But mostly they are fighting back by attempting to change their own austere, machinelike image. Maybe they will succeed. But more and more one is put in mind of that ancient form of execution in which the condemned man was tied up in such a way that the more he struggled the more he choked himself until he became, in the end, his own executioner. It couldn't happen to a nicer corporate entity.

What you had in New York—I can see now, looking back over my shoulder—was a peculiar set of circumstances which made the success of the Mets inevitable. (I do my most brilliant thinking, I find, when I'm looking back over my shoulder.)

The Mets had two great personalities going for them: a wandering holy man named Casey Stengel, and an absconding gold prospector named Walter O'Malley.

The hiring of Stengel was a masterstroke, of course, because Casey could have given PR lessons to FDR. Having been fired by the Yankees for becoming the oldest living manager ever to win 10 pennants in 12 years, he was returning to New York as a beloved and somewhat ill-used figure, full of years, honors and sympathy. (Managers, like politicians, Casey has found, are far more beloved once they are out of office.) He created a feeling, I suppose, that if he could come out of retirement in his old age and suffer through a Met ball game every day, the least the rest of the subway commuters could do was to come on out and suffer along with him.

Most of all, though, Casey gave the team its tone and its attitude. Casey has had his share of bad ball clubs during his long and checkered career, and he has always had fun with them. Casey is sort of an elf, sort of a gnome, sort of a hobgoblin.

Working in a vacuum—without a team, without a star, without any visible future—he took the sports pages away from the

Yankees, got the turnstiles to spinning and almost single-
handedly started the Mets on their way.

What more can you expect of an elf, buddy? You want him
to *win* too?

Next to Casey, the Mets' greatest asset was the old ties with
the Dodgers and the Giants. When O'Malley carried the Dodgers off to the Golden West, he left behind a large reservoir of
National League fans with nowhere to go. Their anti-Yankee
position had already become so much a part of their personality
—as a proof of their individuality, a statement of principle—that
even though the Yankees were the only team in town they were
conditioned to root against them.

The rooting interest is in the bloodstream. The old Dodger
fans could rail against O'Malley but you can be sure they had
been following the development of Sandy Koufax with almost
as much interest and pleasure as if Sandy had been setting his
strikeout records from the hallowed mound at Ebbets Field.

And once a Willie Mays fan, need I say, always a Willie Mays
fan.

With the Dodgers and Giants coming back to town for 9
games each, the Mets were assured of 18 very successful dates.
As long as Mays remains with the Giants and Koufax with the
Dodgers, there will be no need for Mrs. Payson to worry about
the electric bills.

If success was assured, however, it was a modest kind of
success. Who could have dreamed that the Mets would tempt
advertising men away from their martinis, and teen-agers away
from their phonographs? The Mets came up with their own
brand of social significance, and if you don't have social significance these days what good are you?

It was predictable that they would get the underdog crowd,
sure, but who would have thought there were any underdogs
running loose around the kennels of Madison Avenue? And yet,
along Madison Avenue, where they always march in lockstep,
it became an "in" thing to be a Met fan, to not only talk about
the latest Met desecration, but to pretend to take the Mets'

prospects seriously; to delight at the latest little foible, yes, but to become really excited about a Met victory. It was as if the young admen were displaying their magic Met decoding rings to each other as a way of putting forth proof positive that they hadn't really sold out all the way.

Nor should we forget, in this regard, that the Mets established a certain stature from the first. They were, after all, the team that was on its way to losing more games than any other team in the long and meticulously recorded history of baseball. You weren't just shuffling around rooting for a lousy team—which anyone could do—you were rooting for the most goshawful team ever.

When all is said and done, though, the impetus on which the Mets rode to glory was provided by the kids. In any other age, that might not have meant much, but today's kids, as Mort Sahl says, have the money to subsidize their bad taste. They go for bad music, bad manners and, it has become apparent, bad ball clubs.

The kids came in, took over and made their own fun. Watching them at a Met game is not too much different, I would suppose, from watching them at a rock 'n' roll show at the Paramount. They scream and they parade through the aisles waving banners proclaiming their undying devotion to Ron Hunt or Ron Swoboda, just as they scream and pledge eternal loyalty to whoever has the #1 hit record of the moment.

The kids brought their own vitality and humor and excitement into the park with them and it spilled over to the adults.

The weirdest part of it all is that the entertainment has been self-starting and self-perpetuating. The kids don't go to the park to see the game any more than they go to the theatre to listen to the Beatles. They are there to be seen and to be heard.

A situation has developed, of itself, where it doesn't matter what the Mets do. They're fun if they're in the midst of committing another offense against the noble game of baseball, because that's what's expected of the poor dears. If they rally, the kids get behind them with their "Go, Mets, Go" and try to push them home, and if they somehow do come home a winner, why that's an unexpected bonus to a pleasant afternoon.

The old baseball commandment that the won-loss record is everything has gone out the window. The team that has through herculean labors lost a total of 340 games in three years is one of the great attractions of all times.

The Mets *are* a winner. The underdog *has* won. New Yorkers can condescend to the loser and still identify with a winner because they had made the game on the field irrelevant. They had made the Mets a box-office success, a show-biz success, a psychological success. Why, they have made them the greatest success story since Margaret Truman, a poor little mezzo-soprano, overcame the incredible handicap of having her father in the White House.

The Mets are not only a sports-page success and a box-office success, they have been picked up by the New York-based comedians and converted into a surefire laugh word. And that's the real sign of national prestige.

The beautiful part of it is that once this kind of thing picks up momentum, every failure becomes an asset. Once you've got everybody in the frame of mind where they're expecting something ridiculous to happen, then ridiculous things have a way of happening. It *is* ridiculous, isn't it, that Mrs. Payson, who came into this thing prepared to throw away a few million dollars of the Whitney fortune, is in the position of making more money than anybody else in baseball?

If somebody was going to lose 18 straight games in our era, was there really any doubt that it would have to be Roger Craig, the Mets' #1 pitcher?

For the most part, the Mets were pretty alert about hopping aboard whatever promotional opportunities were presented to them. If the kids wanted their banners, the Mets were willing to put banner writing on a formal basis and hold an annual prize day. (If nobody came up with: PLAY CAREFULLY, METS, THE GAME YOU LOSE MAY BE YOUR OWN, then I've lost all faith in a free and untrammeled public-school system.)

Still, I do have to report that they missed the boat with Roger Craig. What they should have done after his string of losses had run to, say, 15, was to hold a "Roger Craig Boosters Day" or a "Roger Craig Pep Rally" or even a "Roger Craig Memorial Day," in which he would be feted (the opposite of *de*feated) and encouraged and lionized.

The real point of the promotion would be that the rain checks of the day's game would be good for any game Craig pitched until he won, thereby giving the fans a stake in his performance. The club, for its troubles, would be getting more than a modicum of goodwill and press coverage and, if the wind was right, everybody would have a few laughs. It pains me to see these rare opportunities thrown away. Do you have any idea how difficult it is for a big-league pitcher to run up a streak of 15 straight losses?

During my own days in St. Louis, when I had no Mrs. Payson behind me to pay the bills, we were so deeply in debt in so many directions that I flirted with the idea of holding a Creditor's Day, in which everybody we owed money to—from $1 on up—would be allowed into the park free and then permitted to cut up the day's receipts in whatever way seemed best to them. Personally, I favored throwing all the money onto the pitcher's mound during the 7th-inning stretch and letting them fight for it. (For *that,* I could have charged admission.)

The first flaw in my scheme was that the park held only 30,000 people, and I didn't know what to do with the overflow.

The basic disabling flaw—which I detected immediately—was that as soon as each creditor saw how many other creditors we had, they would get together in tight little groups after an inning or two (the game figured to be lost by then) and decide to throw me into bankruptcy. These creditors can get to be soreheads and spoilsports and all-around bad actors.

The Mets keep getting the ink because the writers find them fun to write about. Even Shea Stadium itself provided a few laughs. One thing you have to say for the city fathers of New York, they did build themselves a modern stadium. It opened a year late, of course, at a cost of about $5,000,000 to $6,000,000 above the estimate but that was to be expected. It is a gorgeous, three-decker stadium, dominated by a scoreboard in right field that is a riot of color, music and Rheingold ads, topped off by a television screen to enable the management to flash a picture of the batter over a closed circuit. Mostly the television circuit didn't work, but that was to be expected too.

That wasn't the most fascinating part of this miracle of modern construction. The politicos were so busy doling out all that money to the contractors, it developed, that they had built their magnificent new park in the middle of a swamp.

For a while, there was some concern—particularly among the wives and families of the ballplayers—that the magnificent new park might disappear, of a sudden, into the mud flats.

Thirty-million-dollar ball yards that convert themselves overnight into a steaming bog can be a political embarrassment in more uncharitable cities, but New York was fortunate in having a mayor who had been demonstrating for 12 years, I understand, that he was impossible to embarrass.

In any event, the Mets would not have been caught unprepared. They had protected themselves by building a scoreboard that could flash TILT in living color as soon as the third deck began to go.

What a scene for a reporter to cover. As the park sinks slowly in the west, George Weiss would be standing on top of the home dugout with a brave little smile on his face, a solitary tear in his eye and a small American flag (borrowed from the concessions) clutched defiantly in his hand. That's George Weiss for you. All heart.

Casey Stengel would, of course, be dancing a jig and delivering a farewell soliloquy on the parks he has gone down with in his long and meritorious career.

But that isn't what intrigues me most. The most intriguing part of all, something only the Mets could be a part of, is that they are playing in the only ball park in the nation that can sink while its own scoreboard plays "Nearer My God to Thee."

The luck of the Mets was never better shown than in their home parks. They were tremendously fortunate in the beginning that the razing of the Polo Grounds was delayed until Shea Stadium was ready. The Polo Grounds had a congenial National League air about it, to say nothing about the disheveled, run-down motif and the sense of imminent mortality that blended in so nicely with Stengel's shaggy, dog-eared appearance and the Mets' shaggy unkempt play.

Most important of all, the existence of the Polo Grounds made it unnecessary for the Mets to come into New York as tenants at Yankee Stadium. For the Mets to have played in that cold and massive mausoleum would have been disaster. The sheer size of the park would have swallowed them, and the shadow of the Yankee reputation would have overwhelmed them.

Setting can be everything. A baggy-pants comedian can be great in burlesque and passable on television but he had better stay away from the Plaza.

As things stand now, I think the Yankees will ultimately have to move into Shea Stadium. By the time they do, it will be so completely soaked with the personality and mystique (I've always wanted to use that word) of the Mets that the Yankees will seem to be the intruders. They will be paying their rent to the city, but in everyone's minds they will be playing in the Mets' ball yard.

It was the move to Shea Stadium in 1964, which, of course, was responsible for the leap in attendance which ended with the worst team in baseball outdrawing everyone except the Los Angeles Dodgers.

The timing was perfect, the location exemplary, the parking facilities more than adequate. A modern new park is always an attraction. Situated as it is along the Long Island parkways, the Stadium is convenient for all the old Brooklyn Dodger fans who have moved out to Long Island. The park is small enough to lend itself beautifully to the carnival atmosphere. The World's Fair, sitting almost alongside, has done no harm either.

Helicopters are always whirling over, carrying visitors to the Fair (or to the city), and the pilot always seems to linger over the park for a moment, creating the impression that some visiting dignitary (the Shah of Persia or the head of General Electric) is craning his neck over the side in the hope of stealing a brief glimpse at this thrilling contest that is taking place before your very eyes.

Shea Stadium is also bracketed by both airports, LaGuardia and Kennedy, which means that jets are always whooshing past on their takeoff paths, providing a continuous air show to occupy the spectator's time while the pitcher is running the count to 3–2. Taken all together, and added to the prevailing spirit of ease and good nature, there is the festive atmosphere of a 3-ring circus.

The most important part of last year's box-office triumph was that it converted what had been a community joke into a community enterprise.

I was sure all along that as soon as the Mets improved to the point where they were just another mediocre club, the joke would be over and everybody would turn to another channel. But they're not a joke anymore. You can't laugh off an attendance of 1,700,000. I think now that the fans, and especially the kids, have just about reached the point of involvement where they will thrill to every improvement. And make no mistake about it, as soon as Bing Devine takes over they will improve. He'll pick up a player here and a player there, and little by little they'll improve. A jump from tenth to eighth place will increase their attendance. And if the Mets should happen to get good fast they'll do the kind of business that will bring tears of joy (I think they'll be of joy anyway) to the eyes of Walter O'Malley.

My personal thrill in this inspiring tale of one team's triumph over incompetency comes from the incongruous role being played by one George Weiss. Talk about a man being out of character! It was Weiss who put the Yankees into the straightjacket of dignity and conformity they are trying so frantically to wiggle out of, and it is Weiss who has become the greatest beneficiary of their inability to do it.

I don't really want to downgrade Weiss at this stage of his life. I'd be just as happy to be able to say the old boy has done an acceptable job. Really. But he hasn't. He was hired by Mrs. Payson to build a winning team, as I understand it, not to produce the worst team in the history of professional sports.

Weiss is a fish out of water. A cold fish. Where public relations and promotion have been concerned, he has necessarily been bypassed. The Mets have an active promotional department which functions quite independently of him.

Nevertheless, it is Weiss' team. They are his Mets, this somber and humorless man, this man who spent his entire life standing four-score on the principle that baseball is a game of dignity and protocol, of pomp and circumstance. Weiss sits there in Shea Stadium and all around him there are people having fun. Shamelessly having fun, right there in the open, while a ball game is going on. The only thing Met fans haven't seen by now is George Weiss doing the Twist at home plate, a thought to make the blood run cold.

What are you trying to do, George, make a travesty of the game?

9

⊖ ⊖ ⊖

Mine Eyes Doth Tell Me So

WE are such hypocrites. When Alvin Dark was quoted as saying that Negro and Latin-American ballplayers are not as bright as whites, and are also lazy and somewhat lacking in team pride, cries of righteous indignation filled the air.

And yet, anybody who has spent any time around ball parks knows that if Dark did say what he was quoted as saying he was only echoing what was being muttered on every bench and in every clubhouse.

It was unfortunate that either Alvin did not get down to specifics or that the columnist, in quoting him, preferred to approach the issue in generalities as a way of opening up the subject to the widest possible discussion and debate.

It was unfortunate too that because Dark himself happens to come from the South, anything he might say is evaluated by a completely different set of standards than if Hubert Humphrey had said it.

Now, no one can tell me that Alvin didn't know his own ballplayers better than anyone else, or that Alvin didn't see what he saw. If he had said that Orlando Cepeda, who happens to come from Puerto Rico, or that Willie McCovey, who happens to be an American Negro, weren't the leading candidates for the Team Player of the Year Award, he'd have found any number of baseball people ready to agree with him.

Dark isn't the first manager to feel that Cepeda wasn't putting out to the limits of his capabilities. Nor would he have been the first to say that McCovey tended to lose interest in that rather large portion of the ball game when he wasn't at the plate swinging a bat.

Of course, baseball people have always said that Jackie Brandt doesn't play up to his capabilities either, and no one has ever felt it necessary to observe that they sure do grow them lazy in Nebraska. They just nicknamed him "Flakey" and let it go at that.

What you always have to bear in mind is that Cepeda may very well feel in his heart that he is playing to the peak of his ability. At first, anyway. But human nature is human nature. If you keep telling a player he is lazy he just may say to himself, "All right, I'll *show* them how lazy I can be."

It takes a little imagination to perceive that anybody who is called The Baby Bull needs coddling, and yet I have a strong hunch that if every time a Giant manager had felt like blasting Cepeda he had called in the newspapermen and told them what a joy it was to have The Baby Bull on his team, things would be a lot calmer along the banks of San Francisco Bay these days.

As for McCovey . . . well, they kept telling me for twenty years that Ted Williams took a very casual attitude toward fly balls too, but nobody even felt moved to draw any generalities about tall, left-handed hitters from San Diego.

But whatever limitations McCovey may have when he is not swinging at a fast ball are certainly not the limitations of a teammate named Willie Mays, as Dark would be the first to attest. Mays is a flaming genius in the outfield. He catches everything, he cuts off balls between outfielders, he makes the right throw to the right base. He is in the starting lineup, day after day, until he quite literally drops from exhaustion. We all know how that story reads by now. Mays collapses into a dead faint, and the Giants lose two or three games before he gets back into the lineup.

One might even say that Willie is the symbol of the team

man in baseball, just as Jackie Robinson was the symbol of the competitor.

You can tell me Latin-American players are lazy and I will listen to you politely, but please do not tell me that Minnie Minoso, whom I first signed out of Cuba in 1948, was lazy. Minnie would be in there hustling for 154 games a year. He might be carrying ten pounds of tape around his body but he'd still be giving you his standard 110 percent, because Minnie was one of the greatest competitors I have ever seen.

If we want to talk about team spirit, we can talk about Maurie Wills leading the Dodgers to the pennant, although he was sliding on legs that were raw and bloody. If we want to compare I.Q.'s we can talk about Bill White of the Cardinals, who made himself into a topflight player through intelligence and application.

I can remember a game when my dear friend Larry Doby tried to steal home against the Yankees, in a ridiculous situation, and I stated publicly that it was a stupid play. Because it was. But that didn't make him stupid, because he's not. I just wanted to know what had got into him. You can understand why stupid people do stupid things; it is always difficult to understand why a bright man does a stupid thing.

In other words, if we started to list the exceptions to the overall indictment we just might end up with a list containing more names than the non-exceptions—which would put the exceptions in the majority and make the non-exceptions the exceptions and . . . aw, let's forget about it.

The point I'm trying to make here, quite obviously, is that *individuals* are bright and dumb, selfish and self-sacrificing, good and bad. Races are just a collection of individuals.

I suppose that the Negro will know he has come to full equality when he is granted the glorious right to take all the credit for his triumphs and all responsibility for his failings. I do not expect it to happen tomorrow morning.

A home run is without color, nationality or previous condition of servitude, and so is a bonehead play. It may not be completely irrelevant that the terms "bonehead play" and "rock-head" were a part of the language of baseball while the color line still stood, pure and inviolable. If we check the record books, we may even discover that they were applied to players who were light of hue and backed to the hilt by generations of good Anglo-Saxon forebears.

The difference, of course, is that nobody has ever said, "There goes that dumb white so-and-so again. . . ."

This does not mean that I'm copping out on the subject by delivering the usual profound and resounding liberal manifestos, which are really meant to prove that I am pure of heart. I think the indictment, whether Dark made it or not, has enough merit in enough cases to be worthy of much closer examination.

We need, more than anything else, to be less self-conscious about race. It has become so difficult to discuss this subject, on its merits, because you are a loser no matter which way you go. It is an accepted part of one branch of American folklore that the Negro is almost a different species—and not a higher one. These people are willing to concede that the Negro is superior physically because he is inferior mentally, a somewhat dubious compliment.

To the other side, it is Holy Writ (couched though it may be in vague scientific terms) that there is absolutely no difference between any people anywhere, and that anyone who thinks there is, or might be, is a dirty bigot who should be stoned out of the community—presumably toward the end of keeping that spirit of scientific inquiry alive.

At the risk of being stoned, I want to stand up boldly and say that there is a difference between Black and White. Black is darker; White is lighter. If we can't agree on that we're in real trouble.

There are physical differences between races too. When I was in Japan last year to telecast the Japanese All-Star game, the one thing that impressed me above everything else was the weakness of Japanese throwing arms. Even though their ball parks are somewhat smaller than ours, no outfielder is expected to make a throw directly to a base. A cutoff man goes out automatically to relay all throws.

The way it was explained to me, the Japanese shoulder is so constructed—on a downward slope—that it is almost impossible for them to throw a ball that will rise. As soon as a boy gives any indication of having a strong arm he is pressed into service as a pitcher. And here, as it was explained to me, is the most interesting part of all. Almost all pitchers, I was told, are the fruit of a mixed marriage with an inhabitant of one of the off-shore islands. It is an infusion of blood, in other words, that changes the construction of the shoulder.

But that isn't too surprising either. Who among us hasn't observed that the mixture of Oriental and white blood produces women whose beauty takes the breath away? (I believe it is known among the more learned academicians in Mississippi as mongrelization.)

The American Negro has a physical difference too. He can run faster and jump higher.

Question (asked with an appropriate sneer): What authority do you cite, Mr. Veeck, for this flat, unequivocal and unscientific statement?

Answer: The greatest authority I know. The authority of my own observations, which means far more to me than anything out of an anthropologist's tract.

I know that Negroes can run faster because I have observed them running faster on baseball and football fields. I have observed that when the six finalists in any dash event of any national track meet (to say nothing of conference championships) crouch over the starting line, a minimum of five of them will be Negroes. Usually, it is all six.

My eyes also tell me that Negroes jump higher, because I can see that almost all the best high jumpers are Negroes, and so are almost all the best rebounders in the National Basketball Association (to say nothing of any college campus).

I am able to cite one other authority to support me. You! Almost all sports fans, and certainly all athletes, accept the fact that Negroes run faster and jump higher. Give me all the theories you can find about sociological and economic forces—and I will give you a few back—but let's not permit anybody to bull us into saying that we don't know what we are seeing.

There are sociological, economic and psychological factors that push the Negro into sports, sure. That can hardly be the entire story, though, because I am sure there are still plenty of tow-haired farm boys from Nebraska who want to win the 100-meter Olympic dash just as badly and practice just as hard as any Negro boy. They just get shut out in the quarter-finals, that's all.

After all, records are falling in all track events these days, and white runners are setting their share of the new ones. The same sociologic and economic pressures would surely apply to all events. It is only in the dashes and the high jump that the Negro has his monopoly.

In point of fact, there *is* a physical basis to account for their superiority as dash-men and jumpers. The Negro has a somewhat different bone formation in his ankle which gives him an extra cushion off which to spring.

Basketball is a game which seems to have been practically invented for the Negro. It is a game of particularly sharp reflex, of sudden spurts and quick stops, of jumping and of timing. It is therefore, logically enough, a game which is becoming increasingly dominated by Negroes. The NBA has already reached the stage where the operators, for reasons having to do with nothing more than customer identification, are willing to take a #9 and #10 man who are white over Negroes who have slightly more ability.

You will notice that I slipped in the words "sharp reflex." And I can already hear the snickering out there that goes, "Yeah, and they all have rhythm too, huh?" the implication being that anyone who dares to say that Negroes have a more basic sense of rhythm is, giving him the benefit of the doubt, stupid.

Giving myself the benefit of the doubt, I don't think I'm so stupid. The National League is superior to the American League these days because—and no one even bothers to argue this anymore except a few chronic searchers after lost causes—because the National League stocked up on Negro players while the American League was sitting back and admiring how nicely the Yankees were getting along without them.

In 1964, the National League had fifteen .300 hitters. Twelve of them were colored. The year before, the National League had eleven .300 hitters. Ten of them were colored.

It would seem fairly clear, then, that Negroes are better hitters than whites. No, not more deprived, not better motivated. We're not talking about that. *Better hitters!* Hitting is reflex and timing. In short, rhythm.

It is always possible that there are physical—meaning biological—factors involved that go far beyond our knowledge. In the first place, what *is* a Negro? We have a way in this country of arbitrarily characterizing anybody with any Negro blood in him as Negro. It would seem to me that anybody with one Negro grandparent is three quarters white and that my side is entitled to take credit for 75 percent of him. Remembering what the infusion of island blood does for the Japanese throwing arm and sighing over those beautiful Eurasian women, I have to wonder whether anybody has really conducted meaningful and objective experiments on the relationship of the *percentage* of Negro blood to athletic ability. Wouldn't it be funny if they really owed it all to us?

The real question is why there should be any question of the Negro's superiority in these directions at all. The answer, I suppose, is that both races seem to be more comfortable ignoring it. The white man doesn't like to think that the Negro is superior in a basic test of strength and skill. The Negro knows that to be superior is to be different, and he has learned that differences have a way of being used against him. Still, I have a sneaking suspicion that when Negroes gather together in the privacy of their own parlors, they are quite willing to boast about their physical superiority over their little white brothers.

As for the economic and sociological factors, they are so apparent that they are almost not worth going into. The American Negro is not as far removed from the purely physical life as the white man. He is, after all, only 100 years removed from the harsh life of slavery. He still finds himself, on the whole, limited to harsh physical work. Next time you see a crew of movers, you will notice that the white men have assigned themselves the arduous task of telling the Negro how to carry a piano on his back. This is known as integration.

Having been denied the fruits of our soft society, the Negro has been denied the luxury of growing soft in the bone and muscle. Negro athletes even last much longer than white athletes, which can only mean that the point of physical deterioration comes much earlier even in the best trained white athlete.

The economic problem is simple. The performing arts—sports and entertainment—have attracted a disproportionate share of the Negro population because they have provided the only fields to which the Negro has had free entree. It could almost be said that if a Negro has it in him to be an athlete, he has to give it a try. And because he knows there is a stone wall waiting for him to butt his head against in the event he doesn't make it, he will throw all his energy into developing his talents.

Now, that seems to fly in the face of our original theme, doesn't it? If the Negro can run faster, react quicker and is, in addition, more highly motivated, how can it also be said that he is lacking in team pride and spirit?

An entirely different set of circumstances comes into play here. We are speaking of these players *after* they have made it (and, remember, we are still talking about a *minority* of a minority). We are moving into the area of human relations now, because we are involved with the relationship between black and white in the United States. More particularly, we are dealing with the hidden emotional dialogue that passes back and forth between them below the surface, behind the spoken word.

At the root of the difficulty is the white man's belief—why is this so difficult to shake?—that the Negro should be grateful for being allowed to play in the big leagues. The same quality that the fans most admired in Eddie Stanky, his combativeness, was the very quality that they criticized in Jackie Robinson. It was as if they were saying, "What's the matter, doesn't he appreciate the chance we're giving him?"—which could only mean that they did not really believe he was as entitled to that chance as the kid next door.

By the same token, I suspect that managers and players will criticize a colored player who seems to be lackadaisical far more that they would criticize a white teammate. When a colored player loafs he is showing, they feel, that he does not appreciate what has been done for him, which—again—can only mean that they still consider him, at this hidden emotional level, to be something less than equal.

The Negro, having developed antennae which are perfectly attuned to that wave length, picks it up, understands and is not gladdened. Robinson always reacted to criticism by playing harder. But people are different. Other Negroes, finding this sort of peripheral prejudice existing at the point where they had thought they had escaped from it, react by drawing back into themselves.

It is more than possible, you know, that the Negro in the ghetto never feels rejection with quite the intensity of the Negro who becomes a celebrity in the great un-ghettoized world—as a big-league ballplayer, let us say—and then finds that all the success in the world does not make him immune from the same old slights and humiliations.

Even here, of course, human beings react in a multiplicity of ways. To find that nothing you can do can change your situation can be a great comfort to some, since it means that no further fighting is necessary. To others, it is the ultimate rejection. It was Paul Robeson, the Negro who achieved the greatest popular acclaim of his time, who became the most disaffected of all Negroes.

The white players are aware, if only subconsciously, that

what is really bugging the Negro are the conditions that have been imposed upon him as a Negro. Human nature being what it is, their reaction is to turn the situation completely around. Since his moodiness arises out of the *fact* of his being a Negro, then it becomes a simple matter for the white player to tell himself that is the *natural result* of his being a Negro. Sure, he thinks to himself, *all* of *them* are like that.

It is far more comforting, we can all agree, to blame *him* and his race than to blame *us* and our race.

So here we go again. It is now the Negro's turn to react a second time to the white teammates' reaction to him. If a man is made to feel that he is not accepted as a member of the country, the community or the team, he will come to feel that he is a member of nothing except the Negro race and that he owes allegiance to the Negro race only.

This is not an attitude that is going to leave a man brimming over with team pride.

The problems of the Latin American are somewhat different and probably even more complicated.

To give you an idea of the problem confronting him, do this for me: Take one of his white teammates away from his home and family, put him down in a Caribbean village where nobody speaks his language, have him eat strange foods which emphasize his foreignness and also upset his stomach. Have him faced, socially, in this imaginary village with completely new—and bewildering—customs which discriminate against him. Make it perfectly clear to him that he is not considered quite the equal of the natives and that while no offense is intended it would be greatly appreciated if he would be a good fellow and keep his distance.

He just might feel that he is an outsider. He just might not have any flaming loyalty to his team. He might even have trouble remembering what his team's name is.

When he does manage to find the ball park, the manager has to pass on all instructions to him in this strange language, necessitating a certain amount of sign language and a certain tone of voice that reminds him uncomfortably of the tone that is used toward a particularly backward child.

It is just possible that he might be uncertain and hesitant and, being uncertain and hesitant, he might not go about his work with his accustomed snap and vigor.

He might not even want to. If you treat a man like a migratory worker, he will act like a migratory worker.

This is the situation, admittedly carried to its extreme, that the Latin-American players have been confronted with. As they begin to come to the big leagues in greater number, they naturally tend to group together in the clubhouse, as well as off the field, much in the way American players would group together in Puerto Rico. Much, in fact, as Americans have traditionally grouped together within their own cities.

Clubhouse cliques have always been a part of the baseball scene. But this is something new; this clique speaks in a foreign tongue. This is a foreign colony setting itself up in the last American stronghold, the baseball clubhouse. You see them there, chattering away in Spanish, and every once in a while you are left with the uneasy feeling that these foreigners are talking about you and laughing at you. If they want to play here and take home our money, you think to yourself, why don't they speak English like everybody else?

If you are half intelligent you don't carry that kind of thinking too far, and yet some of the resentment remains. Enough of it remains, at any rate, so that when you can find an outlet by criticizing them for something that is obviously true, an easier attitude toward their work, you are not slow to seize upon it.

They don't hustle, They don't care. They're taking the bread out of my children's mouths. Never mind that they are also leading the team in hitting, that only makes it worse. That only shows how good they could be if they cared.

There is some truth here too. The Latin temperament *is* quite different than the American temperament. People who grow up in Latin-American countries—be they white or colored—have never been noted for their energy. There is, first of all, that enervating tropical climate which slows down the entire pace of life.

We don't see ourselves as others see us. We don't even begin to appreciate that our whole attitude toward life has been formed by that remarkable institution, the American Dream, which tells us that there is nothing we cannot do, nothing we cannot be, if we will educate ourselves, work hard and think clean thoughts. We are a nation of optimists. The American player whom we call a hustler is just the standard American go-getter transported to the baseball field. We are also a people who think in terms of the long-run because we have been granted the luxury of a stable government. We are so sure that the framework that exists today will be there always that it does not even enter our calculations.

The Latin American has no such history of political stability. His thinking, formed just as unconsciously by his own background, is for the short-run. The Latin-American player wants to be successful, sure. But he does not really think in terms of being a *big* success. The drive to keep pushing himself to rise higher and higher just hasn't been built into the marrow of his bones. He is more apt to wonder why these crazy Americans don't relax and take a siesta now and then instead of rushing around all the time, going nowhere.

The criticism of the Latin-American player really adds up to that age-old cry, "They're not like us!" And they are not. The difference in temperament could hardly be wider.

In all of these differences and all of these conflicts, as they apply to both the Negro and the Latin American, there is one constant. They have not a thing to do with basic intelligence.

There are some people who fear that the Negro will soon dominate the major leagues. I take this as a compliment to baseball, because it shows that everyone understands that ball clubs will play the best men available in every position regardless of color—and regardless of any talk about conflicts of temperament.

I, for one, don't think it's going to happen. I think that as other fields open up for the Negro, a draining-off process will set in.

Besides, as the Negro becomes more sophisticated, more successful, more middle-class, he will become less physical. He will sit at an office desk, drive to the corner for his newspaper and be privileged to enjoy the rich food we could all do so nicely without. The debilitating process will have begun. Welcome to the affluent society.

The Negro influx, I think, has just about reached the high-water mark. The present balance will hold for about five years and then begin to fall the other way.

The next influx is going to be the Japanese. The Negro ball-players reshuffled the power in the past decade, the Spanish-speaking players are reshuffling it again in this decade, and the Japanese will be coming on in waves in the next decade. *If* we can afford them.

I covered the 1964 All-Star game in Tokyo for ABC's *Wide World of Sports* and the improvement over what I had seen immediately after the war was just remarkable. Their All-Star teams are roughly comparable to the Mets or some other good AAA club. If that means they are not up to major-league caliber yet, it also means they would not be humiliated. Far from it. Their main strength is in pitching and defense, and nobody has yet refuted Connie Mack's dictum that pitching is 70 percent of the game. Any team that gets good pitching and good defense has got to look pretty good.

There were ten players I wouldn't have hesitated to sign, and six of them were pitchers. Some of the pitchers can throw very hard. All of them seem to have great control.

The best American hitter in Japan the past few years—the only .300 hitter, I believe—has been Jack Bloomfield, a second baseman who never went higher than Portland in the Pacific Coast League. What the other American players, like Darryl Spencer, Jim Marshall and Johnny Logan, provide is the long ball.

I was sitting around the lobby of the Okura Hotel with them on the morning of the All-Star game, waiting for the rain to stop. Jim Marshall told me that the only real adjustment an American player has to make upon coming to Japan is in his thinking. American hitters are all guess hitters (and I would suppose Japanese hitters are too). The Oriental mind may not be inscrutable to other Orientals but the Japanese pitcher's patterns are entirely different than those our hitters are used to.

"They get you three-and-nothing," Jim Marshall told me, "and you automatically look for a fast ball. Not in this league, though. You're just as liable to get three curve balls in a row. They'll throw you the good breaking stuff and even change speed on you, and they'll get them all over, too."

The great player in Japan is Mr. Kanada, who has won over 20 games for 14 straight years. He reminded me of a Herb Score with control, which isn't bad at all. He's smart. He knows what he's doing out there every second. When he walks a man, it's because he *wants* to walk him. He reminded me a lot of Satchel Paige in this respect, something I told him, to his delight, when I was interviewing him—through an interpreter—before the game.

Mr. Kanada receives the equivalent of $100,000 in American money, and I do not have to tell you that $100,000 over there is comparable to half a million over here.

Speaking generally, all Japanese players are higher paid than players of comparable talent in the United States. Particularly the 26 American players allowed in by the rules. The Americans are all cut from pretty much the same pattern. They are either mediocre players just over the hill or Triple-A players who never quite made it. The Japanese make life a bit more pleasant for them by paying them $25,000 to $30,000, deposited in a United States bank.

For the home-grown Japanese, the prestige is even greater than the money. We do not exactly stone *our* big-league players as they walk down the street, but Japanese players are idolized beyond anything we can conceive. Great players like Mr.

Kanada and a young first baseman with the wonderful name of Mr. Oh are followed down the street like Babe Ruth, and good players are treated like Mickey Mantle.

This, of course, is what Japanese baseball has going for it. Baseball is not just entertainment, it is a vital part of the national life. I jumped into a cab on a rainy Sunday morning in Tokyo and asked the driver just to drive me around the city. It was one of those days where the sun peeked in and out, and yet on every street corner there seemed to be uniformed kids heading for some park or lot. On every empty lot there was a game going on, and a couple of other teams waiting to take over. On every available square foot of ground there were kids playing catch or pepper. The streets themselves were filled with kids playing catch or throwing a ball against a wall.

The next Sunday, I flew back to Chicago and, as we circled over O'Hare Field, I counted nineteen diamonds. Eighteen were vacant.

We are so presumptuous that it never enters our mind that a little country thousands of miles away from Cooperstown could ever beat us in what we like to think of as our own private game. The Japanese are only an imitative people, aren't they, not quite equipped with the competitive spark, the good old American initiative, or the mental or physical agility that makes us such a superior people? Baloney. I would only remind you that Sony started by copying our television sets, and they now make the best television sets in the world. That's something for the boys to talk about at Cooperstown when the weather turns cold.

There has been, in recent times, a lively debate as to whether baseball is still our national pastime. There is no doubt at all that it is the Japanese national pastime. The *Sporting News*, a weekly, is our only publication of any size devoted entirely to sports. It has a circulation of about 240,000. In Tokyo alone, there are two sports *dailies*, the *Orion Press*, with a circulation of over 600,000, and the *Minitchi Press*, with a circulation of 540,000. Both newspapers, like the *Sporting News*, devote most of their space to baseball.

There are a few minor but interesting differences between our game and theirs. Their bats are concave at the end instead of convex, and are made of a kind of wood which is not quite as resilient as ours. The ball, on the other hand, is even more lively—if you can imagine it—than ours. The infields are skin, rather than grass, which means that there is nothing to slow down a ground ball. The infielders have to be very quick, and since people tend to develop the talents they need, they are very quick. Japanese infielders, like Japanese pitchers, are first-rate.

The hitting is not. For one thing, the Japanese are still a small race, although the great advances being made in nutrition, plus an almost fanatic interest in exercising, has made them the fastest growing race in the world. Japanese authorities maintain that in ten years they will have improved enough both technically and physically to take on the Americans.

There's one other handicap, though, which neither vitamins nor push-ups will overcome. The coaching is terrible. Through nothing more than historical accident, Japanese baseball is run by an entrenched group of managers who arrived early and have managed to convince everybody that they have special knowledge of something called Inside Baseball. Human nature being no different in Japan than anywhere else, they are not about to surrender their billing as wizards by surrendering any of their authority. The first thing any American player learns if he tries to pass on some advice about hitting technique is that his help is not wanted. As a result, Japanese ball is comparable to what Negro ball was when the color barrier was still up. A young player has to learn everything by trial-and-error, which is a way of saying that it will take him anywhere from five to ten years to learn what a couple of good coaches could teach him in a year or two.

Japanese baseball is still characterized by a great respect for umpires, with much bowing and self-abnegation. The umpires wear white gloves with their black suits, which makes them look like maître d's, and as we all know there is something about a maître d' which overwhelms all but the most reckless. A player might glance disapprovingly toward an umpire, but that's the Nippon equivalent of a rhubarb.

They still talk about that incredible day when an American diplomat, known only as Leo Durocher, attacked an umpire head on.

The umpire had blown a play at third base, calling a Japanese runner safe although, it is generally agreed in the telling, the man was lying on the ground about three feet from the base even after the call was made.

In Japan, the players and the manager accept such decisions as no more than regrettable examples of man's imperfections and fallibilities.

Durocher had been carefully instructed on the strange native habits by Frick, Stoneham, Giles and probably the State Department, but, acting on pure animal instinct, he came racing out of the dugout to deliver a dissertation in a strange and colorful patois, known to students of the Romance Languages as gutter English. While many of the shorter words could not be found in any accredited Japanese-English dictionary, an odd phrase which sounded like "you slant-eyed———" seemed to be a recurring theme.

Since Japanese umpires are unschooled in the proper stance with which to confront an enraged manager—i.e., chest-to-chest and chin-to-chin—Leo's student kept giving ground. Durocher had just about driven him back to the pitcher's mound before a certain glazed look in the umpire's eyes told him that the guy didn't understand a word he was saying.

Never a man to waste his best efforts on an unappreciative audience, Leo snarled one final snarl, and started back to the dugout.

From the very beginning, the crowd had gone into a state of shock. As Leo walked back through that incredulous silence, he suddenly remembered all those vows he had taken about not addressing an umpire, save to express his own unworthiness.

One thing you have to say for Leo; he is nothing if not resourceful. In previous innings he hadn't bothered to go out to the coaching lines but, aware that he had to do something to preserve the peace and bring the crowd out of its shock, he hustled out to the third-base coaching line at the end of the inning.

His opportunity developed immediately. Because the Japanese play on a skin infield, the dust tends to spread, and because the Japanese are very neat the umpires brush the bases off between every inning. The third-base coach has an additional duty: He is charged with brushing off the pitching rubber. As Leo was walking from the dugout to the coaching box, the umpire was moving, whiskbroom at the ready, toward the pitcher's mound.

"Hey, buddy!" Leo shouted at him.

The umpire turned back, startled, and paled again, obviously expecting Leo to make another run at him. The crowd, already in shock, gasped.

But Leo wasn't there to start anything. He took off his cap, put his feet together, and with a wide flourish of the arm he bowed deeply from the waist, an obvious and abject apology which could be seen by everybody in the park—as well as by passengers in low-flying aircraft.

The umpire, beaming broadly, bowed back. The crowd heaved a sigh of relief and, the tension broken, broke out into wild cheers.

Player development in Japan is considerably different too, in that there are no minor leagues as we think of them. The players are signed out of college or, to a much lesser degree, high school.

The colleges extend their baseball season four or five months past the school year, allowing their players to play a full season.

There *is* a minor league of sorts. Each club has its own B

team, a sort of junior varsity, and players can be moved up and down at will. If Tokyo is playing Nankai at night, their junior varsities will meet in the afternoon.

Player personnel comes high and is coming higher. Mr. Oh received a 40-million-yen bonus (more than $100,000) for signing, proving that anything Americans can do they can do too.

There is no reserve clause either. The player is signed to a 5-year contract, which calls for annual increases (much like the old 7-year Hollywood contract). When the contract expires they become free agents and are given a bonus if they re-sign with their old team. Generally, they do. There is very little shifting around, because there is no tradition of trading between clubs. I suspect that a player would lose face if he left his original team to sign with a former opponent, and I'm sure it would be considered a dreadful loss of face to be traded or sold like an animal.

With both the pay and the prestige so high in Japan, you may be wondering why any Japanese player would want to come to the United States. And well you may. It takes us right back to the underlying reason for baseball's immense popularity in Japan.

Japan is American-oriented to a degree that is almost embarrassing. Anything American is automatically desirable. They not only copy us, they want to compete with us. They cannot compete in basketball because they are not 7 feet tall and they cannot compete in football because they are not 7 feet wide. There is also soccer, of course. Soccer does draw well, and the Japanese are quite good. But soccer, which is the national sport of most of the countries of the world, has never been more than a minor sandlot diversion in the United States. Given the choice between the United States and the rest of the world, the Japanese prefer to go along with us.

Still, baseball is big business in Japan, and they are not about to sell us any of their stars. They were willing to let Murakami pitch for the Giants for a year because, quite frankly, Murakami wasn't looked upon as anything more than a run-of-the-mill prospect.

If I had my choice of any Japanese player, I wouldn't hesitate for a moment. The Tokyo Giants have this young first baseman called Mr. Oh, who cocks his front foot like Mel Ott and has that good home-run swing. When I asked Mr. Oh for the television camera whether he would like to play in the United States, his eyes lit up and he answered, "Oh yes, if I can make it."

To get the Tokyo Giants to go along, however, the approach would have to be exactly right. I would tell them that we have reached the stage where it has become important to start thinking in terms of a truly international World Series. I would tell them that the first necessary step is to convince the American public that Japanese baseball has developed to the point where it has hitters as well as pitchers.

I would try to set up some kind of lend-lease arrangement for Mr. Oh, in short, as a precursor to a World Series.

An international World Series would be very profitable and very exciting. We, of course, would be taking a calculated risk. We would be betting that we will be able to knock the Japanese over fairly consistently in the immediate years ahead. For if Japan should walk in and knock *us* over for, say, three straight years, the American fan just might drop the game like a hot potato and go over to football and basketball where he *knows* we are still supreme.

10

⊗ ⊗ ⊗

People Need People (Who Else Is There to Take Advantage Of?)

SINCE the hustler is a dedicated man, engaged in a never-ending pursuit after unfair advantage, he is, in effect, a practicing psychologist—always probing for the weak spot, the Achilles heel, the soft underbelly. But then, the athlete is a practicing psychologist too. (And he'll keep on practicing, if I have anything to say about it, until he gets it right.) Any competitive sport—or, for that matter, any competition from Karate to child-rearing—has a large quotient of psychology in it, whether it be directed outwardly against one's opponent in some loose form of gamesmanship, or inwardly toward one's own ego in an effort to bolster one's own shaky confidence. To an alarming extent, the man who thinks he is going to win usually does. The man who *knows* he is going to lose *always* does.

I have always had the feeling, amounting to a certainty, that we have not even begun to scratch the field of psychology. This blind faith in the scientific method did not come about through my occasional jousts with the practitioners in the field, I must admit; it goes back to my early impressionable days in Chicago when I was intimately involved in a pace-setting program set up by Mr. Wrigley, owner of the Cubs, and Dr. Griffith, head of the psychology department at the University of Illinois. (The program set such a killing pace that nobody seems to have ever followed us.)

What we hoped to do was to combine psychological tests, physiological tests (reflex, sight anticipation, etc.) and the usual baseball aptitude tests (running, hitting, fielding) and come out with a complete profile of each of our prospects.

Our basic premise was that this complex of tests would enable us to eliminate the 95 percent who had no chance of going all the way to the majors and concentrate our full efforts upon those remaining 5 percent whose future was obviously bright.

My first job was to get the local high school coaches to send us their best 3 or 4 kids and to supervise the building of the clubhouse in which we were going to install both our kids and our testing equipment. (The clubhouse, incidentally, is the one the Cubs are now using themselves.) Today, need I say, the best-looking high school prospects wouldn't submit themselves to such indignities for less than $50,000 plus fringe benefits. In those days, we just gave them carfare to come to the park every morning throughout the long summer, and they were not only delighted to have the opportunity, they were downright flattered at our interest.

Just before the season ended, the psychologists picked their starting lineup, based upon their tests, and the scouts picked their team based upon their eyesight. (I once asked Jack Doyle, whom I consider the greatest scout who ever lived, why he had signed Gabby Hartnett. "Because he had a good Irish puss," Jack said. Even today, when most clubs have their scouting reports laid out so they can be fed into IBM machines, you will sometimes see the remark, in amongst the assessment of a prospect's physical abilities, "has good face." It is, of course, more complicated than that. What Doyle really meant—whether he knew it or not—was that out of his years of experience he could see that Hartnett, in his actions, his bearing and his performance, *looked* like a ballplayer.)

The anticlimax to this excursion into the Brave New World

was that the scouts' team clobbered the psychologists' team. About 10 of the players picked by the scouts eventually progressed up to the high minors. Of the players picked by the psychologists, the scoreboard read zero.

And yet, I have always felt that it was a most fascinating and farsighted—if not necessarily far-reaching—experiment. Psychological testing was in the fire-and-wheel stage in those days; it had barely crawled out of the cave. In my last year with the White Sox I got together with a team of psychologists from Illinois Tech to fool around with the same type of problem, because I wanted to find out just how much the testing methods had improved. Unfortunately, I became ill and the program had to be cut short.

The limitations would seem to be self-apparent, which means that the challenge is immense. Is there any way you can really devise a complex of tests, however ingenious, that will measure a young boy's guts and desire? Is it possible to measure the will of a young Eddie Stanky and, having measured it, to correlate it with his rather unimpressive skills?

Because on the basis of raw natural ability, Eddie Stanky had no right to make the big leagues at all. When I bought Eddie Stanky for the Milwaukee Brewers in 1942, he had been in the minor leagues for 7 years without ever having risen above Class B (which in those days was the third lowest of the eight minor-league classifications). By all the normal rules of baseball, he had no right to rise very much higher. But Eddie hit .342 for us that year, and the following year he was in the big leagues. He remained in the big leagues for 11 years.

Not only had Eddie worked to develop every scrap of skill he possessed, he had developed the best psychological gambits to enhance those skills. His greatest asset was his ability to work the pitcher for a base on balls and he worked harder to get that base on balls than Babe Ruth ever worked to hit a home run. Stanky was one of the few batters I ever saw who tried to goad the pitchers into throwing at him. The only thing that pleased him more than to be knocked down was to be knocked down twice, because that meant he was starting off with a 2-0 count. When the count ran to, say, three balls and one strike, he would spin the bat up under his arm like a captain of the cavalry as he glared out at the pitcher—the most insulting and contemptuous gesture I have ever seen on a ball field. Eddie was out to get the pitcher so mad that he couldn't see straight, let alone throw straight.

When he did get himself one of those bases on balls (and he got himself 148 of them one year at Brooklyn) he would grasp his bat tenderly between his fingers and let it drop $\frac{1}{16}$ of an inch from the catcher's toes (and sometimes $\frac{1}{8}$ of an inch closer). Only the instep of the catcher's shoe isn't protected, you must understand, and Eddie was careful to drop it right where it hurt—just to encourage the catcher to make a mental note to sit that wise punk down the next time he came to bat.

Stanky would get the opposing pitcher in a mood where his only concern was not letting Eddie work him for a walk, which meant that Eddie would not only be drawing a record number of walks, he'd be getting a lot of excellent pitches to hit.

Eddie worked so hard to encourage people to hate him that he could not seem to reverse his field when he became a manager. Like so many other thinking ballplayers, Eddie had come under the influence of Leo Durocher, and Leo had always used the goad, the whip and the tongue (particularly the tongue) wherever he thought it would do him any good. The difference was that Eddie Stanky wasn't Leo Durocher, he was Eddie Stanky. Durocher picked the time, the man and the spot with exquisite care, while Stanky's style, as you can see, was always direct and blunt. All I can say is that if Eddie set out to make his players hate him, he succeeded beyond his wildest dreams.

Leo was a constant goad as a player too, but he could pull his capers off with such style—with such impudence really—that as much as it might enrage his victim, it made a good story afterwards. And you could be very sure that if nobody else spread the story, Leo would.

One of his favorite targets was Fatty Fothergill, the Detroit outfielder. Fothergill, as his nickname would imply, was a short, fat man. He was also a tremendous hitter. Fothergill is one of those forgotten players—that name makes him sound like an English cousin written into the *Our Gang Comedies*—but over one 5-year period his batting average came to .350.

At the end of one season, with the Yankees battling for the pennant, Fothergill came to the plate in the ninth inning, with two men out and the winning runs on base. All of a sudden, Leo bellowed, "Time!" and went racing in toward the plate, his face red with indignation and fury. When he got up to the plate, he screamed at the umpire: "There's a man batting out of turn here!"

The umpire pulled out his lineup card, studied it carefully and said, "Have you lost *all* your marbles, Durocher? Fothergill is the right batter."

"Fothergill?" Leo said, clearly astonished. "Is that Fothergill? Oh, I'm sorry. From where I was standing, it looked like there were *two* men up there."

Well, Fothergill was so mad that he had to be restrained. After Leo trotted back to his position, Fatty continued to glare out at him while three straight strikes whizzed right on past him. Then he dropped his bat and went racing up the base line to try to get his hands on Leo before Leo could make it back to the dugout.

Stanky didn't have that kind of dramatic flair. With Stanky, it was all analytical. In all fairness to Eddie, I know that he has very carefully analyzed his failure and that he understands where he went wrong. I'd like to see him get another shot at managing because I'm quite sure he'd be one of the good ones.

As for Leo, well . . . can you think of any other business where the man who is recognized as the best in his field hasn't been able to find anybody to hire him for a full decade?

At any rate, to get back to our experiments in Chicago, Dr. Griffith was a strange and wonderful fellow, almost a novelist's version of a psychologist. The inconsistencies of ballplayers, particularly of pitchers, was a challenge not only to his scientific background but to all of his instincts. He could see readily enough where the regular players might go stale from time to time out of sheer physical weariness, but since pitchers could always be presumed to be well rested and physically strong whenever they were called upon, he believed it was only a matter of propping them up psychologically so that they would be mentally primed for the great effort. Mr. Wrigley, who was just as intrigued by his theories as I was, had given him a free hand, which meant that Charlie Grimm was the only manager who had to clear his rotation with a psychologist.

(Wes Ferrell, the old Cleveland and Red Sox pitcher, adhered to a somewhat more exotic school of science. Wes was a student of astrology and he preferred to have his starting assignments guided by the stars. This may be difficult to believe but there were managers, like Joe Cronin, who were so unsympathetic as to insist that he take his regular turn even when the stars forecast disaster. And yet, can you really laugh it off? If a man truly believes that his prospects for success are favorable due to forces beyond any man's control, isn't he going to go out there and pitch with ease and confidence? And isn't he, therefore, bound to be that much more successful? Ferrell, after all, had six seasons where he won 20 games or more, and in two of those seasons he won 25. Give a man a zodiac and a good curve ball and who knows to what heights he can aspire.)

Larry French, a somewhat inconsistent left-hander, was a particular project of Dr. Griffith's. Once, when we came into New York for a crucial series, Dr. Griffith informed Grimm that French was all wound up and ready to give forth with his very best effort. Charles pointed out patiently that while he was overjoyed to hear that French was such a cooperative subject, he had not planned upon using him in New York since it had been established rather conclusively through the years that the Giants had developed this unfortunate habit of clobbering him.

But that, of course, was the old unreconstructed French. Larry was now ready to face the enemy with a smile on his lips and confidence in his heart, Griffith insisted, and so, much against his better judgment, Grimm had to start him.

The Giants, buoyed perhaps by the wholly unexpected appearance of their old buddy, scored 7 runs in the first inning.

Unfortunately, Dr. Griffith couldn't make it to the park until halfway through the game, and his confidence in his testing was so great that he made no connection between the absence of French and those 7 big runs on the scoreboard.

At the Commodore Hotel that evening, Griffith came bursting into Charles' room and demanded to know why he had not started French after the good doctor had nurtured him to his peak efficiency all through the week.

Now, Grimm is a man of tremendous strength, particularly in his arms and hands. He also happens to be blessed with the best disposition of any man I have ever known—which proved to be a blessing for *me* on a few hundred occasions that come quickly to mind. The only time I ever saw Charles lose his temper was in the hotel room that night. "You jerk," he shouted, making a lunge for Dr. Griffith, "who do you think gave them those seven runs?"

If somebody hadn't thrown himself in front of Charles, he'd have picked up the good doctor and pitched him bodily out of the room.

Still, I have always felt that this was a field well worth further study. In the spring of 1960, I had a memory expert come down to Sarasota to work with our catchers so that they would be better able to remember what our pitchers threw in the course of a game and what the opposition batters hit.

I also made a stab at sleep-teaching. It seemed to me that slumps had to be caused, to some degree, by nothing more than the physical and mental weariness that overtakes a player during the long season. The records weren't designed to hypnotize our players into thinking they were the greatest hitters since Babe Ruth. All I wanted to do was have them wake up every morning thinking that today was the day they felt better than they had ever felt before. There has to be something to it. If it does nothing more than keep each player from having one off-day during the entire season, it is obviously well worth the time and effort. What time? What effort?

Most of the psychological gambits, however, involve the relationship between competing players rather than what might be called a doctor-patient relationship. Since baseball is essentially a walk-down on Main Street between the pitcher and the batter, there can develop fascinating running battles having very little to do with basic talent. The classic example was the ability of one Hub Pruett, a lousy pitcher, to strike out one Babe Ruth, a pretty good hitter, almost as if it were by vote of Congress.

To some extent, sheer craftsmanship is involved. Certain batters hit a certain type of pitcher and cannot hit another type of pitcher. Generally, however, these phenomena are inexplicable save on the grounds that one man achieves a kind of moral supremacy over the other.

Joe DiMaggio had trouble hitting Satchel Paige, partly—I suppose—because Satch made him wait. Satch once committed the ultimate insult of walking a man deliberately to get at Joe, and then getting Joe to pop out. It was DiMaggio's temperament to be a solid professional, to show no emotion, but you knew that Joe burned inwardly at that gratuitous slap and was hurting to get back at Satch. And so Satch would fiddle around on the mound until he saw he had Joe anxious, then he'd give him the three loop-de-loop windups and have Joe ready to catch the ball in his teeth and spit it out by the time it got to the plate.

On the other hand, Mickey Vernon owned Satch, lock, stock and mustache. It started when Satch and Feller were barnstorming with their All-Star teams, and Vernon hit everything Satch threw at him. It continued when Satch signed with us in Cleveland, and Vernon continued to hit him like he owned him. Satch fears no hitter who ever lived—except Mickey Vernon. I have seen Satch come into a game with the bases loaded and his team two runs ahead and deliberately walk Vernon, forcing in a run. That seemed to me to be a rather foolhardy way to handle the situation, but Paige just said, "That's a fellow I can't get out. I tried him every which way. He always seems to think with me, and you know that anybody who thinks with old Satch has to be a pretty good hitter."

Usually, the batter is bursting with confidence when he's up there hitting against his own little lamb—that's one of the reasons he maintains the franchise. But Mickey was different. I once asked Mickey about his peculiar ability to bomb Paige and he told me that he never could quite understand it himself. Every time he faced Satch, he said, he thought the time must be on hand for Satch to begin to even up. So here is a unique case where both the hitter and pitcher seemed to be thinking negatively, with Satch's negative thoughts overpowering Vernon's.

What usually happens is that the guy who's taking the beating gets so frustrated, so worked up, that he makes things progressively worse for himself. Hank Greenberg (a Hall-of-Famer) could always hit Ted Lyons (another Hall-of-Famer), although Lyons, who was exceptionally smart, seemed to be just the kind of pitcher who should have been able to stop a power hitter like Hank. Hank would always get the hit to beat him, though, and it just killed Lyons. He'd throw everything he had at Hank, including an occasional curve ball at his feet to keep him skipping, and then late in the game Hank would hit one.

Lyons pitched for the White Sox in old Comiskey Park, and since the White Sox were very weak at bat and the park was about the size of an airport, he almost had to pitch a shutout every time out to get a tie. He once went something like 17 scoreless innings against the Tigers, and then Hank reached out for a good curve ball and hit a monumental drive into right center for a game-winning triple.

The next time the Tigers were in, Charlie Gehringer (still another Hall-of-Famer) was called safe on a close play at first in the very first inning. The White Sox were a scrappy, fighting team under Jimmy Dykes, even if they couldn't hit. They were all out screaming at the umpire, with Lyons contributing more than his share. Meanwhile, Hank is standing at home plate waiting for things to quiet down so he can go to bat. And he's thinking to himself: Lyons is going to be so mad when he gets back on that mound that he's going to just rear back and fire that first pitch as hard as he can.

So Hank sets himself for a fast ball, Lyons fires it down the middle and Hank hits it up into the upper deck in Comiskey Park, the closest thing to unexplored territory in any big-league ball park.

Lyons was so mad that he wanted to fight. The first inning, and he knew darn well the ball game was over. While Hank was running around the bases, Lyons was turning with him, screaming insults and abuse every step of the way. If there was any decent way he could have done it, Ted would have run over and tackled Hank or hit him or broken a bat over his head.

Slumps and rallies are brought on primarily by psychological factors too. Hank Greenberg and I used to discuss it often, and Hank—who should know—always felt that slumps and streaks were brought on by the way a pitcher or a batter reacted to the bad days that all ballplayers have over the course of a season.

His favorite example of how mental attitude can affect performance centers on JoJo White, his roommate with the Tigers. JoJo lost his starting job, became the team's number one pinch hitter, and got about 7 straight hits.

"JoJo," Hank told him, "I can't for the life of me see how you do it. I know I'd be a terrible pinch hitter. How can you just walk up there cold, always in the clutch, without having any chance to find out what the pitcher's throwing or how he's thinking and keep banging out those hits?"

"Nothing to it," JoJo told him. "I come off the bench and I'm strong and I'm fresh. That pitcher doesn't know what I'm thinking but I know he's thinking that he's going to get that first pitch in there while I'm still cold. And so, boy, that first good pitch I see, I just whack it."

Either the conversation jinxed him or the law of averages began to take its toll, because JoJo went hitless in about his next dozen tries. Sitting in their room one day, Hank casually mentioned that his theories didn't seem to be working anymore.

"Well, how can anybody expect a guy to go up and pinch-hit?" JoJo said. "You come off the bench, you're cold. You don't know what the pitcher's going to throw, you've had no chance to look the ball over. He's nice and loose. He's worked himself into his groove, so he can start you off with either a curve or a fast ball. Before you even loosen up you're behind in the count and now he can really go to work on you and make you hit his pitch. . . ."

There have been more nostrums prescribed for shaking a batting slump than there have been for anything except the common cold. Both, you will notice, are still with us. Most slumps do *not* begin with the batter losing his timing. Quite the contrary, they usually begin with the batter hitting the ball well. He hits two or three balls right on the nose for two or three days, but either they go right at somebody or somebody makes a fantastic play. He hits the usual amount of dunkers, too, but none of them drops. Day by day, his worries increase, and the more he worries the worse he gets. His thinking goes something like this:

After the first day, he says to himself, "Well, 0 for 4 today. I got to get a couple of hits tomorrow to get the average back up there."

By the second day, he's something like 0 for 8 and now a desperate gleam appears in his eyes. I got to get myself a hit tomorrow, he's thinking, or the average will really be dropping. After the third day, he thinks, Oh my gosh, I'm 0 for 13. They're catching everything I hit. *I got to get lucky."*

The next day, he'll hit only one good ball but it doesn't fall in, and now he's mad at the world. He doesn't care now whether he gets a hit or not tomorrow. That will show them. And when you Don't Care, buddy, you Don't Hit.

The Don't Care stage lasts only a day or two, and is followed by a period of self-analysis. Deep in a slump now, the hitter tells himself that he's got to keep bearing down out there. But by now he's either overanxious and swinging at bad pitches or he's overcautious and taking too many good pitches. Either way, he comes back to the bench second-guessing himself. He isn't really *bearing down* at bat, he decides, he's *pressing*. (The difference is quite easy to tell. When you're hot, you're bearing down; when you're cold, you're pressing.)

He is aware that he isn't swinging at the pitches he usually swings at, so he decides he must be doing something wrong mechanically. This is the point at which he inevitably turns to the Guy Behind the Batting Cage. "Watch me up there, will you," he says, "and see if you can tell me what I'm doing wrong."

Usually, he is asking this favor of his buddy, who has never been known as a scholar of hitting or anything else, or of a shrewd old utility infielder who has earned a reputation for being smart although he has never hit over .232 in his life. (If he wasn't smart, how could he have stayed in the big leagues this long with a .232 average?)

"Listen," our man says, "I don't feel comfortable up there. Are my hands right? Watch my feet, will you, I've got a feeling that maybe I'm overstriding."

The guy watches him closely throughout batting practice and tells him that he's got his elbows sticking out, or he has a hitch in his swing (he's had that hitch since high school and it didn't stop 12 clubs from offering him more than $50,000).

But whatever other pearls of wisdom the Guy Behind the Cage may drop, he will invariably include one of two things. He will tell him: 1) You're moving your head, or 2) You're taking your eye off the ball.

He's right, too. I would suppose that it's almost impossible to hit a ball without moving your head, and in the entire history of baseball there have only been a handful of hitters who could actually follow the ball right into their bat.

By now, our guy hasn't got too much time to concentrate on hitting the little white baseball. He's too busy worrying about his elbows and his feet and his head and his eyeballs. He's so completely fouled up at this stage of the slump that he can no longer remember just what he did do with his hands and his feet and his elbows when he was hitting.

I have always maintained that the best remedy for a batting slump is two wads of cotton. One for each ear.

The day finally comes, though, as it must to all men, when he gets himself a couple of hits and stops outthinking himself. If slumps usually begin with hard-hit balls being caught, they usually end when a dunker drops in front of an outfielder or a squibbler sneaks through the infield.

The difference between the .300 hitter and the .250 hitter is only partly in strength and reflex. It is also in the ability of the good hitter not to let a bad day or two get him down. The .250 hitter gets killed by a couple of bad days because he lets them develop into slumps. The .300 hitter always figures that if he didn't get his hits today, he'll get them tomorrow. Ted Williams always felt that any pitcher who held him hitless was lucky. He never doubted for one second that given any kind of an even shake he'd bury any of them.

The difference between the *good* hitter and the *great* hitter is that the great hitter is never satisfied with the 2 for 4 days. I know that big-leaguers are all competitors and all that, and yet when they start off the game with a couple of hits there is an irresistible feeling—human nature being what it is—that no matter what happens they've insured themselves a pretty good day.

You will notice that the hit column in a box score tends to even out as the game progresses. This is easily attributable to the law of averages, of course, but I am convinced that psychology plays at least as great a part in it. The guy who says to himself, "Well, I've got my two hits . . ." isn't going to be too unhappy when the pitcher salvages a couple of outs on him toward the end of the game. If he does happen to go 3 for 3, this same batter is going to think to himself, Gee, this guy is probably going to lower the bridge on me next time. I'd better be a little loose up there. (At that point, you can forget him.)

If the same guy has gone 0 for 3, he's a different batter altogether. He's not worrying about anybody knocking him down now. He isn't even worrying about getting hit on the head. He wants a hit so bad that he'll stay in there even if they're throwing hand grenades at him.

One of the reasons Ty Cobb was such a great hitter was because he never permitted himself to let down psychologically; he never gave ground. When Cobb had 3 straight hits on the day, he'd start revving himself up. "The day is going to come," he'd say to himself, "and you *know* it's going to come, when you've gone 0 for 3 and you'll be up here in this same part of the game desperate for a hit. But if you've gone hitless through the game it's probably because your timing is off, and that will be the day when you'll look back on this game today—this time at bat—and say to yourself that if you'd only got that fourth hit that day when you were hot, you wouldn't need this hit so much right now. So you just better get this hit and put it in the bank for the time when you'll need it. And if you come up to bat again you better store away another base hit too."

What Cobb was doing, with malice aforethought, was putting himself in the same frame of mind he'd have been in if he had gone hitless.

In personality, Stan Musial was the direct opposite of Cobb but they shared that same quality of turning the good days into great ones. When Musial was 3 for 3, you could just see the determination crackling out of his pores as he stepped up for the fourth and fifth time. Great hitters are greedy hitters.

I don't think that an individual batting streak, like Joe DiMaggio's record of hitting in 56 straight games, is psychological at all. It's pure ability. DiMaggio had the uncommon gift, for a power hitter, of hitting the ball right on the nose 3 times out of 4. Since he hit with such power, the ball didn't hang in the air to be caught or take the one extra bounce that permitted the infielder to go into the hole and make the play. Unless all three of those hard-hit balls went right at a fielder, DiMaggio was almost impossible to shut out.

He was stopped finally when Ken Keltner did make three great plays on him at third base. The most remarkable part of that streak to me was that after hitting in 56 straight games, he did not suffer the almost obligatory letdown. I don't know whether Joe had any system for battling human nature, or whether he was just the exemplary, unemotional craftsman he appeared to be on the surface. At any rate, he went right back out there in the second game of the doubleheader and started a new streak that carried to 37 games. To me, that was just incredible.

When a team wins a lot of games in a row, there is an even stronger psychological factor. To win 15 games in a row you have to have a pretty good ball club. No question about that.

What happens when a team goes on a long winning streak is that it wins all those games it would normally have lost by one run. Somebody steps up and whacks one out of the park in the last of the ninth. A ball drops behind second base while three fielders stare at each other blankly. A ball drops a fraction of an inch inside the foul line instead of a fraction of an inch outside. They walk your #8 batter to get at your pitcher, and your pitcher clears the bases with a 400-ft. double.

Actually, a game won on a bad bounce helps you more than a game won by a solid base hit, especially in the early stages of the streak. We are all basically superstitious, deny it though we may. Once your whole team begins to think, Boy, they're beginning to drop in for us, you're on your way. Pretty soon, you expect them to drop in for you, and now you're really rolling. And, finally, the opposition begins to wait for them to drop in for you, and once you have them in that frame of mind, you are simply unbeatable.

That is precisely what happened to us in Chicago in 1959, except that nobody stepped up and hit any balls out of the park. We had a team that had no right at all to win the pennant. We were a club that knew every time we went out on the field that we couldn't possibly win by more than 2 runs. By all logic, we were the ones who should have been playing scared. What happened was exactly the reverse. Once we got rolling, we sat back, utterly confident that the other side would eventually make the mistake that would start us on our way. By the end of the year, the other team was waiting for itself to make a mistake, which meant that it was only a matter of time before they made it. We'd win one day on a swinging bunt, the next day on a passed ball, and the day after that when somebody would lose a fly in the sun. As soon as any kind of an opening was presented to us, our fans would begin to chant "Go, Go, Go . . ." and the other team would think, Oh, oh, that's all they're going to need. . . .

Anybody who has ever been to a ball game knows that you can feel an imminent rally in the air. It runs through the park like electricity. If we know we're going to score and they know we're going to score, you can bet your sweet life we're going to score.

Everybody kept saying how lucky we were and, up to a point, we were. The point where luck ceased to be the prime factor was the point where our own confidence—which was far greater than our skill—took over.

The Phillies' collapse at the tag end of the 1964 season was the same thing in reverse. The Phils, who looked like a shoo-in, suddenly lost four straight and you could feel them thinking, Oh no, it isn't really possible that we could blow this thing, is it? The Phils would score a few runs early and then sit back, waiting to see whether the runs were going to hold up. Once you do that, you can be assured that they won't. At the end, everything happened to them that happens to a collapsing team. Every time the other side blooped a ball it fell in. Every time the Phils needed a fly ball, you could be sure they weren't going to get it. Everybody in the country knew they were going to blow it, and—while they can hardly admit it even to themselves—the Phils knew it too. Mauch had panicked and messed up his pitching staff, and he refused to back away from his command decision that Frank Thomas, a non-fielding first baseman with a bad arm, was going to win the pennant for him. The team lost confidence in the manager, in itself, in its destiny.

It has always seemed to me that rallies begin in the pitcher's box far more than in the batter's box.

You will find, for instance, that most runs are scored in the first two innings or the last three. I am not going to bother to check the statistics that are undoubtedly kept in the radio booths in the land, because the statistics just might show I was wrong and then where would we all be? On the other hand, if I were not such an honorable chap, I could simply shower you with figures, like: "An exhaustive study conducted under a Rockefeller Foundation grant shows that 23.7 percent of the runs are scored in the first inning, 13.3 percent in the second inning and 7.1 percent in the third. Surprisingly enough, 28.9 percent of the runs occur over the final 3 innings. The team of highly trained engineers who conducted this study found it amusing that 0.7 percent of the runs were scored in extra innings." (This is known as Statistmanship and is highly recommended.) I am not doing it here only because I know that this class is too bright to fall for any such obvious ploy. (This is known as Lullmanship and is even more highly recommended.)

Most pitchers are geared—either consciously or unconsciously —to pace themselves over the full 9 innings, which means they are psychologically geared to hold back a little at the beginning.

If the first two batters whack him for base hits while he's holding back, the pitcher has something to start worrying about. He thinks, If this next guy whacks it out of the park, I'm out of the game and won't that look great in the box score? So he pitches very carefully to the next batter and the next thing he knows he's walked him. Now he's got to really bear down, and, unfortunately, he hasn't had time to hit his groove. The chances that he's going to lay one right in there are very great and— boom—that's all for today.

It is possible, I know, to argue that the big first inning isn't psychological at all. That it simply proves that the pitcher isn't warmed up yet.

Quite true. But you have to remember that this purely physical problem of the pitcher has its own psychological effect on the hitter. The batters, being perfectly aware that pitchers tend to have their troubles in the first inning, are watching very carefully for any sign that the pitcher doesn't have it that day. Once a couple of batters get base hits, the rest of them are running up there like tigers, because they're all anxious to get in their licks before he's pulled out of there.

At that point, it doesn't really matter whether the pitcher has good stuff or not. Once the batters are running up to the plate in that kind of aggressive, bloodthirsty mood, their chances of hitting him have improved about 100 percent.

Let us suppose, on the other hand, that the pitcher weathers the first couple of innings or starts off strongly and sets them down easily. The pitcher will now groove down, fall easily into his natural rhythm and breeze through the middle innings.

An exhaustive study recently completed by the Rockefeller Foundation tells us that 30 percent of all baseball games are decided by a single run. This means that there invariably comes a time in the final three innings when the pitcher is confronted with a crucial situation which he will either survive and go on to win the game or which will destroy him and send him into the showers.

What happens is that he gets a little tired (which is physical) and gets a little careful (which is psychological). When pitchers get careful, they tend to aim the ball instead of throw it, and when they aim the ball they are not long for this world.

And now you have a repetition of the first couple of innings. The other team is looking for any signs of weakening, and once they think they see it, the saliva begins to flow again.

The manager will come out to ask the catcher if the pitcher still has his stuff. Maybe the catcher says he has. Maybe the pitcher says, "I feel great, Skip." But none of that matters. All that matters is that the other team is convinced that they are getting to him. The only real benefit the manager derives from talking to the pitcher is that he gets to stretch his legs and keeps the other side's hungry hitters away from the plate for a while.

So what you have is a mixture of the physical and the psychological. Sure, the pitcher is beginning to tire. The old cliché about the batters beginning to catch up to him may well be true. The hitters have been studying him, after all. They know what he's been throwing. More particularly, they know which pitch he's trying to set them up for in the clutch situations.

But the smart hitters have been setting up the pitcher too. Hank Greenberg, whose sheer intelligence as a hitter was always overlooked because of his size and power, would deliberately look bad on a certain pitch in the middle innings (especially during the latter part of his career) in order to trap the pitcher into throwing that pitch to him in the late innings when a home run could very well mean the ball game.

Nobody ever averaged more RBI's a year than Hank, and I can't think of anybody who won more ball games with late-inning home runs. Hank would be up there on his last time at bat, watching the pitcher work the countdown in order to set him up for what he fondly believed was *his* pitch—while all the time, Hank would know precisely what pitch he was being set up for.

Would you call that psychology, though, or would you call it craftsmanship? Well, it's psychology to this extent: Hank has been psychologically pitched to ease up in the middle innings and to bear down when he steps up that last time. The whole rhythm of the game, as far as he has been concerned, has built up to this one time at bat. Just think what joy and confidence it must give a batter to be aware that he knows what the key pitch is going to be.

It can work the other way too, of course. The pitchers are far from helpless. Gus Wynn always liked to throw his curve ball high, which is precisely where the book says you are not supposed to throw it. A high curve tends to hang up by the eyes where the batter can take a good look at it, and an even better swing. Wynn kept them from digging in by fostering stories about his meanness, which didn't really need that much fostering. Gus was never reluctant to concede that he was mean enough to knock down his own mother. "But only," he would add, "if she were digging in at the plate." He also did nothing at all to discourage the story—which is still believed by an astonishing number of people—that he took his teen-age son out to the park for batting practice one day, and when the boy hit one of his pitches off the wall, Gus promptly knocked him down with his next pitch. "What was I supposed to do?" Gus is supposed to have said. "The little so-and-so hit my *curve ball.*"

Nobody ever had more of an edge on the batters, though, than Ryne Duren. Ryne threw a faster ball and wore thicker glasses than anybody else in baseball, and that's a pretty fearsome combination. Ryne was in our farm system when I took over the St. Louis Browns, and the scouting report on him read: "He can throw a ball through a brick wall but he probably can't see the wall."

A man who has difficulty seeing a brick wall figures to have to squint a bit to make out the bare outlines of the batters, especially the skinny ones.

When he was at San Antonio, we decided to fit him with contact lenses. His eyes turned out to be allergic to the lubricant or something, which was particularly unfortunate in that he hadn't bothered to bring his regular glasses along. Just before the game, Bill Norman, who was managing at San Antonio, phoned to ask me whether it would be all right to pitch Ryne without glasses.

"Sure," I said. "Just make sure he throws the first pitch on top of the screen and the second one right through the on-deck hitter's circle."

Ryne went out there, *sans* glasses, threw the first pitch on top of the screen and the second right through the batter's box. With the enemy batters practically running for cover, he then proceeded to pitch a shutout, striking out 15.

Ryne, a bright, fun-loving guy, knew what he had going for him with that bad eyesight, which was not nearly as bad as it was reputed to be—mostly because nobody's eyes could be that bad.

Whenever he was having a little trouble, he'd help the legend along. He once took off his glasses during a hot, humid night, and flung them over toward the dugout. Just in case anybody missed the message, he got down on his hands and knees at the end of the inning and began to crawl around, in full sight of the players, feeling around for them. The opposing players laughed uproariously. They also stayed loose.

He liked to tell stories, with a feigned innocence, about how he had taken off his glasses while washing his face in the men's room, bumped into a mirrored door as he was reaching for a towel and, seeing his reflection about an inch in front of him, apologized.

When Ryne got his big chance with the Yankees, his control turned out to be surprisingly good. Except when he was warming up. For some reason that defies explanation, Ryne's first warm-up pitch always seemed to hit the top of the screen and his second warm-up pitch would go right through the batter's box.

11

⊖ ⊖ ⊖

Harry's Diary—1919

TO be a hustler, you have to have a profitable field of action. The greatest poolroom hustler in the world wouldn't walk out of a monastery independently wealthy unless he measured his fortune in cassocks and quills. Although, now that I think of it, I wonder what an illuminated script does go for these days.

To operate effectively in baseball you must have strong leadership, an elementary fact of life which baseball owners are not always quick to understand, possibly because they don't want to.

In these days of corporate ownership, the Commissioner has become of particular importance to the hustler. Corporate ownership brings company men, company policy and company cards with little holes in them. Corporate ownership, in short, brings committee-think, and with Comthink comes the banishment, discouragement and attrition of colorful characters. The hustler is dependent upon colorful characters, because color is what is salable.

Corporations don't want to be regulated. They don't want a Commissioner with any powers. They want Frick. They *like* Frick. The hustler needs a Commissioner who will throw his weight against the stuffiness, the routine, the deadly boredom of the executive suite. He needs a Commissioner who will help baseball, in spite of itself.

There is no reason why the Commissioner himself shouldn't be a colorful and, even, controversial figure. He should not be a figurehead, he should be a fountainhead—a fountainhead of ideas. He should tour the cities—as Landis did—bringing publicity and the impact of his personality wherever he goes.

Judge Landis was colorful in himself. He was not only a dynamic personality, he had a Shakespearian bearing and a most commendable instinct for the center of the stage. If you lined up pictures of 100 men throwing out an opening game ball, and asked a foreign visitor to pick out the man who looked most like a Lord High Commissioner, he would unhesitatingly point to Kenesaw Mountain Landis. The case for picking a man solely by name should not be lightly dismissed. Men with colorful names tend to live up to them.

I had a somewhat more complicated plan which I tried to smuggle in to the owners. Instead of sending a scouting expedition onto the beach to look for a 93-pound weakling—the most logical way of finding a Commissioner in the Frick tradition—I wanted them to hire an independent executive employment agency to seek out and interview the men who best met the job specifications given to them by the owners. The three men selected as the best prospects would then be interviewed by a committee of baseball owners who would make the final choice.

The kicker in here should be readily apparent. Once the owners were forced to write out the qualities they wanted in a Commissioner, no man would have the raw courage to say he wanted someone just like Frick. They would be forced to list the sterling qualities that a Commissioner really should have.

It is useful, in this context, to examine the noisome and gamy events through which the scepter and mace were first handed over to Kenesaw Mountain Landis, that craggy old jurist who believed that baseball owners lived far happier and more rewarding lives if they were kept in constant terror. It is particularly appropriate in this classroom, because I have recently come across some new information which I have been anxiously awaiting the opportunity to exploit.

The new information is contained in a journal kept way back when by Harry Grabiner, the one-time White Sox secretary. While it is sometimes frustrating in its brevity and shamelessly self-serving, it does shed new light upon several aspects of the hiring of Judge Landis after the Black Sox scandal. Although I have no intention of retelling the story of the 1919 Series, since Eliot Asinof covered it all quite brilliantly in *Eight Men Out*, there will be points at which the two subjects quite naturally coincide.

Harry Grabiner had been a friend of mine from the time I first began to work for Phil Wrigley, across town. Years later, he became my partner in the Cleveland Indians, and from time to time, in relation to somebody who might come up in ordinary conversation, he would say, "Yes, he's in the diary."

I never pursued the matter particularly, partly because we had enough to worry about during those hectic days in Cleveland but mostly, I suppose, because I assumed that if Harry wanted to tell me anything more about it, he would.

Much later—ten years later, when I bought the White Sox— I remembered those casual references and, out of normal curiosity, I conducted a fairly thorough search of the dead files.

I found that while the files were in perfect order up through 1919 and picked up nicely again in 1921, there was nothing but empty air in between. Somebody, it was obvious, had very carefully destroyed or removed the files of those crucial two years. I was sure it hadn't been Harry, since he had always spoken of his diary as if it were still in existence.

Accompanying me on some of those expeditions into the archives was my nephew, Fred Krehbiel, an inquisitive young fellow with a remarkable talent for liberating lost, strayed or lonesome objects. Freddy's nose for the unattached and the misplaced is so keen that he has occasionally been known to

find things before anyone knew they were missing. I predict
great things for the young gentleman.

Fred kept working for the White Sox, on and off after I departed, and less than two years ago he conducted his own
meticulous search through the dusty dead files—which are kept
in a storage room underneath the stands at Comiskey Park.
Against the far wall is an old wooden trestle table. For some
reason that must have seemed good to him, Fred pulled the
table out and there, trapped in a hole in the wall that had been
covered over by the leg of the table, he found two old notebooks, one a hard-cover ledger book and the other a long, old-
fashioned legal pad. A quick reading of the ledger told him
that, by some incredible luck, it was one volume of the journal
Harry had told me about.

A quick reading of Harry's journal also lets you know, very
quickly, why the cupboard had been stripped so bare. For the
very first paragraph shows, beyond any doubt, that the White
Sox front office had more than some inkling what was going on
from the very first game of the 1919 World Series.

The legal pad, which was really for briefs to be submitted to
the High Court of Chancery by the fine old firm of Kenge &
Carboy, Barristers, contains the Constitution and By-Laws of
the Brotherhood of Professional Baseball Players, written out
with scrupulous care and noteworthy, in part, for some fairly
imaginative spelling.

Now the Brotherhood had been formed back in 1890 when
many of the leading players, in protest against having the reserve clause shoved down their throats—to say nothing of the
unilateral setting of salary rates—broke away from the old National League and formed their own Players' League, a one-
year disaster. Charles Comiskey, as manager of the St. Louis
Browns, was not affected by the owners' action at all, and yet
he had quit his job and thrown in his lot with the players.

The fact that he had kept the By-Laws through all those
years—for all I know his may have been the hand that set

those By-Laws down—would seem to indicate that the Old Roman had been rather proud of his one foolish descent into altruism. Of course, the fact that he had dug it out and, presumably, placed it in with the Black Sox material would also seem to indicate that he had been fully prepared to use it to his own advantage to prove that he had always been sympathetic to the just aspirations of the workingman.

For it had been readily established by 1919 that Comiskey, the cheapest skate in town, was paying the best team in baseball disgracefully low salaries. Harry, in his careful way, had tucked the salary list for 1918 and 1920 into the ledger, although—maddeningly—the 1919 list is missing.

Eddie Collins was getting $15,000, in both 1918 and 1919, the only big-league salary on the list, but that was only because Comiskey had bought Collins—along with his salary—from the Athletics.

It wasn't a young team either. Ray Schalk, a great catcher, was in his eighth season with the White Sox. Ray was on a three-year, $21,250 contract ($7,083.33 per year), and you could see in that figure the haggling that must have taken place.

Joe Jackson, one of the great hitters of all time, was in his tenth year as a big-league regular. Behind him were years where he had hit .408, .395 and .372. His salary in 1918 was, believe it or not, a big $6,000. Since he was hurt almost the entire 1918 season, it could hardly have been any greater in 1919.

Eddie Cicotte was in his thirteenth year. He had won 28 games for the pennant-winning White Sox of 1917. What was his salary in 1918? It was $5,000, although Harry's sheet notes that he also got $2,000 for signing. Isn't that cute? Instead of paying Cicotte $7,000 and establishing a base off which to negotiate the following year's salary, they had held it to $5,000 and put the raise in the form of a bonus.

As for the rest of the fixers, Buck Weaver, one of the great third basemen of all time, was getting $6,000, a tribute to his powers of negotiation.

Lefty Williams, having won 17 games in 1917, was getting $3,000, and since he was out most of 1918 too, it is quite dubious whether he was getting any more in 1919 when his record was 23-11.

As for the others: Chick Gandil, the first baseman and ringleader, $4,000; Swede Risberg, the shortstop, $2,500; Frank McMullin, utility infielder, $2,750. Happy Felsch, a great center fielder, who was off two consecutive .300 years, was on a 2-year contract (1918–1919) at $3,750 a year. Pants Rowland, having managed the team to a pennant in 1917, was being paid $7,500.

So to me there is something almost eerie, as of some unseen hand, that coupled these two notebooks together, one showing Charles A. Comiskey at his best and the other at his worst.

Think how it must have been. All those books, records, reports and file folders piled on the table to be taken away and tucked from sight. You can see a pile of them, somehow jogged loose, tumbling behind the table. You can see someone pulling the table out just a little to retrieve a book or two he sees tucked behind a leg. You can see him quickly shoving the table back against the wall, trapping the two that had caught in the hole and sealing them in for 30-odd years until Fred unaccountably decided to pull the table out.

Harry's journal is in a rough diary form. But it is clear enough from his directions for spacing, for the rearranging of paragraphs and from his references to attached investigative reports that it is a rough copy from which a smoother, edited copy is to be typed.

Because it is a rough copy, it tells us something the final version would not. Despite the diary form, it is perfectly evident that Harry sat down after the World Series was over to get the first part of the story down on paper, possibly at the direction of Charles A. Comiskey (who is always referred to as CAC), and certainly for his eyes alone. Harry himself is always referred to as HG.

Harry Grabiner's journal begins:

The first intimation that there might be something wrong in the World Series and that the baseball players might be implicated therein was really brought to our particular notice when Mort Tennes (*editor:* actually, Monte Tennes) called me on the telephone in my room at the Sinton Hotel, Cincinnati, after the first game and stated that he wanted to talk to me and tell me what he knew concerning the World Series. Coming from this man who is a gambler of national reputation, rather than meet him myself I delegated Tip O'Neill (*editor:* a White Sox official) to meet him in the lobby the same morning and secure from Tennes the news of importance that he possessed. He stated that from the way the betting turned from the White Sox being 7-5 favorites night before the first game to the choice being given to Cincinnati at 7-5 immediately before the game started was evidence that something was wrong and further that a certain party made Tennes a wager of 1000 against 15,000 that Cincinnati would win four straight games did not look right to Tennes, especially in view of the fact that it was necessary for the certain party to go everywhere to secure and collect the 1000 dollars . . .

Tennes said that while everything he said was without any proof nevertheless being a gambler by profession it was apparent to him that the White Sox had been reached.

Before he closed off, Harry added virtuously for the record, "I was astounded to hear nor could realize that such conditions could exist."

Realizing that such conditions did exist, what did he and Comiskey do? Well, when the teams returned to Chicago the following day (Oct. 3) for the third game of the World Series, he called John Heydler, president of the National League "and explained fully to him what I had heard."

Heydler, as president of the National League, was one of the three members of the National Commission. Ban Johnson, the American League president, was a bitter enemy of Comiskey's, and Garry Herrmann, the chairman, was, by the luck of the draw, also the president of the Cincinnati Reds, a coin-

cidence which made Harry reluctant to consult him. "Furthermore," writes Harry, "I had no confidence in his integrity. . . ."

> Heydler could not believe that there could be anything wrong as
> he said rumors regarding World Series had always cropped up
> but I insisted that as my duty to baseball that if anything did
> exist expedient action should be taken and that it was most es-
> sential that this information be given to him, as I could not con-
> sistently divulge this to Johnson or Herrmann having no faith in
> either man. Heydler pointed out that the games looked to him as
> tho they were played honestly that nothing flaringlly [sic] stood
> out in either game one or two that might look suspicious.

Flaringlly is a great word there; halfway between flagrantly
and glaringly.

> Oct. 4. The rumors were still persistent on the night of Oct. 3
> especially after the White Sox lost so I called Mr. Heydler again
> at the Congress and stated that I would like very much to see
> him in my office.

Heydler asked Harry if he had any objections to his talking it
over with Ban Johnson, and Harry told him he was perfectly
free to use his own judgment. "I impressed on him strongly
that if anything wrong did exist regardless of whatever cost to
the White Sox, I wanted it eliminated for if there was anything
wrong in baseball that the game was big enough to stand it
being cleaned."

And then Harry adds, in an obvious insertion, "Heydler never
referred to the matter again either during the Series or after and
he stated that he would let me hear from him."

It is to be noted that there is one thing neither Harry nor anybody on the White Sox ever bothered to do. They never called
in the players to warn them they were being watched nor did
they direct the manager to warn them.

Instead, Harry is doing his best at all times to put the blame
elsewhere, particularly upon Comiskey's enemies. Despite his

wonderment that "such conditions could exist," he writes: "Blame Johnson and Herrmann for if they had acted on the Chase matter instead of whitewashing him, it would have been an object lesson and nothing of the above talked nature would have come up."

The Chase referred to is Hal Chase, who started by throwing games for gamblers and then apparently went into business for himself, recruiting others when he discovered that there were limits to how effectively a first baseman could control the game. The case had burst into the open when Chase offered a young relief pitcher, Jimmy Ring, $150 to lose a game. Ring did lose, even though he was doing his best, and when Chase slipped him the money the following day the young pitcher, "incensed," to use Harry's term, reported it to his manager, Christy Matthewson. But it was neither Herrmann nor Johnson who had direct authority over the subsequent hearing. It was Heydler who would have had to clear Chase.

When Cincinnati dropped Chase anyway, he was promptly picked up by John McGraw of the Giants.

The fascinating part here is that Harry seems to indicate later, again through indirection, that there was more to the shift than met the eye, for he writes, "Matthewson implicated in not giving all matter in the Chase case." Given Matthewson's reputation this is hard to believe.

With the Series at an end, Harry writes that the fact that the White Sox, who were the much stronger team, lost 5 games to 3 "brought out much further comment and ugly rumors."

The next item reads: "Mrs. Kelly at whose apartments the Cicottes live said that she overheard Cicotte state to his brother while in the bathroom, 'The hell with them I got mine.'"

It was almost a full year later before Mrs. Kelly, called to testify before the Grand Jury investigating corruption in baseball, became "the mysterious Mrs. Kelly." Mysterious to the press, perhaps, but certainly not to the Chicago White Sox.

And the White Sox had far more than the word of a landlady:

After the Series was over, same ended on the 9th Oct., the rumors were so persistent though nothing could be substantiated. Manager Gleason was called on the phone by Max Ascher and Sam Pass, two very enthusiastic White Sox fans who also wagered very heavily on the White Sox to win ... they advised Gleason that they had something of great importance and arranged to meet at Comiskey Park Friday after the Series was over which meeting was attended by Gleason, Grabiner, Max Ascher, Elliot.

Ascher said that Elliot was a great friend of Redmon of E. St. Louis, who (Redmon) was crossed in the betting would tell everything if he (Elliot) would so advise and that Redmon was very sore having lost $5500 and if that was not made good that he would spill the beans 100% and even go so far as sit in a room and let some of the implicated ballplayers get a flash at him. Elliot said that Redmon was in the room with the ballplayers at the time that fixing was done and while he would not implicate a single gambler he would go all the way regarding the ballplayers.

Tip O'Neill, Kid Gleason and Elliot met Redmon in E. St. Louis on Sunday night, October 12. Redmon denied being in the room with the players, but said he could put them in touch with another gambler, Carl Zork, who had been. Redmon's story, as detailed by Grabiner, was:

The players were supposed to have received $15,000 per game from the gamblers. The go-between for the players was supposed to be Gedeon (*editor:* the second baseman for the St. Louis Browns) and Bill Burns (*editor:* a one time knockabout big-league pitcher) while Abe Attell was to handle the betting. The gamblers who paid for the fix were Zork, Redmon, Franklin, a St. Louis mule buyer, and 2 Levi brothers from Des Moines. The name of Rothstein was also mentioned. The players on the White Sox mentioned as being implicated being: Williams, Jackson, Felsch, McMullin, Risberg, Gandil, Cicotte and Weaver, the last two both being crooked in the first game and then turning. The meeting at which the plans to fix the Series was supposed to have

been held was at the Sherman House the Friday before the Series
opened and was attended by all of the above players in addition
to Attell, Zork and Gedeon.

The information isn't completely correct. Cicotte didn't "turn,"
it later developed, he double-crossed the gamblers by winning
his second start after they had double-crossed the players by not
paying off as arranged. As for poor Buck Weaver, there was
never the slightest evidence at any time that he did anything
except sit with some friends and refuse to go along with the fix.

It is possible that Redmon and his syndicate did lose $5,500,
it is also possible that they didn't. What does seem quite certain
—if not directly stated—is that Redmon was selling the White
Sox information for $5,500.

It is also perfectly clear that Grabiner had all the information he needed immediately after the Series to break the scandal
open. The only trouble was that by breaking it open he'd wreck
his own team. On October 15—three days after Gleason and
O'Neill had heard Redmon's story—Charles A. Comiskey angrily
denied that there was any truth to the rumors that the Series
had been thrown and offered $20,000 in reward money to any-
body who could offer him proof to the contrary.

Two men immediately popped up to claim the reward. And
who were they? Well, the first was Joe Gedeon, who had been
in with the Redmon group, and the second was Redmon himself. According to the newspapers, Comiskey decided their evidence was inconclusive and refused to pay the reward. In view
of what Harry has written, though, there can be little doubt
that another payoff was made. Comiskey may have been able
to turn Gedeon away—if only by reminding him that if the
White Sox players went under, Gedeon would go under with
them. But Redmon's quick appearance would indicate that
Comiskey was told that he had better pay off. His angry denial
and his offer of a reward—after he had all the information—
could have left Comiskey himself at the mercy of the gamblers.

It is conceivable that Comiskey had left himself open to

blackmail from all sides. If the battle for the Commissionership had turned out differently he might very easily have lost his ball club. There is some reason to believe, putting bits and pieces of Harry's journal together, that at least one owner might have tried to take advantage of his situation.

Nobody knows better than Comiskey that he has made a bad mistake. He begins to protect himself by hiring investigators, not only to dig up all possible information about his own crooked players but to arm himself with information about everybody else's too. The Old Roman is putting himself in a position where he can tell his fellow owners that if whistles are going to be blown he has a sharp and piercing whistle hanging around his own neck.

The name of John Hunter, an investigator, begins to weave through Harry's journal as information begins to come in:

Knabe (*editor:* ex-big-league second baseman) who intended betting on the White Sox was told by catcher Killefer (of Cubs) to lay off as the White Sox had been gotten to.

Rumors are that games were thrown during 1919 season by Chase and Zimmerman, Giants; Hendrix, Killefer, Cubs.

Rawlings Boston National in addition to other players mentioned and also the Yankees, Cleveland, Boston American League clubs; St. Louis National, NYC National, Phila.

Investigated Chgo banks of Sox players nothing irregular found.

Bank acct. McMullin Los Angeles nothing irregular.

Felsch purchases automobile—$1800.

Hunter working with McGinnis, St. Louis, Tennes, Chicago (*editor:* two gamblers).

Hunter personally gone to Coast 11-18-19.

Felsch being followed.

No expense spared in investigating. Gandil would return if anything about him was said.

That last is interesting. Hunter, having gone to the Coast, has undoubtedy talked to Gandil. Gandil has either denied the charge (which, considering the evidence Hunter could throw at him, seems inconceivable) or Hunter has assured him that the White Sox are going to try to bull it through, and Gandil has agreed to go along with them for their mutual protection.

Now, Gandil had been the big money-winner in the fix. Gandil had got out with $35,000. Immediately after the Series, he had left to play winter ball on the Coast. Boots Weber, who was running the Los Angeles franchise, was operating the club. Later, as Chicago general manager, Boots became my close friend and tutor. He once told me that when he met him at the railroad station, Gandil was carrying a little black bag (obviously, he had read the Chicago papers well and knew where hot money was supposed to be kept). Boots took Gandil right to the ball park, just to show him what it looked like. On the way out, Gandil parked the rest of his bags in front of the streetcar, but he kept the black bag tucked between his legs.

Whenever he sat down in the clubhouse, he'd wrap his legs around the bag again, and finally, when Boots brought him to his room in the hotel, Gandil quickly put the bag in the closet.

"Boy," Boots finally said, "that bag must be valuable."

And Gandil told him, "You have no idea how valuable it is."

Gandil, being the smartest of the lot, was the only one who didn't send back his contract the next year. That alone would seem to indicate that Hunter had told him that they knew. As a matter of fact, what else was there for Hunter to tell him?

Harry not only had Hunter in California at this point, he had a man in St. Louis and a man in Philadelphia. The man in Philadelphia came up with some information fast:

Baker said Alexander and Killefer traded after they were crooked

Baker would be William F. Baker, owner of the Phillies. Since he had also been Police Commissioner of Philadelphia, his sources of information would be exceptionally good. Alexander, who had a string of three consecutive 30-victory seasons, and Killefer had been traded to the Cubs together in 1918.

Harry then notes that Hunter called in from California, December 15, 1919, and while he doesn't say what information he passed on, the next item reads, "Conference in Chicago Redmon and Felsch."

That is subject to two possible interpretations too. Perhaps they were still following Felsch and tracked him to a meeting with Redmon. Except that Harry doesn't say meeting. He says "conference," which gives the sense of prearrangement. It leaves the impression that the White Sox have brought Redmon and Felsch together (Felsch being a Milwaukee boy and the most readily available of the fixers) to make sure Redmon's story was true before they paid him off.

Redmon is apparently dissatisfied. Because with the year coming to an end, we get another curious juxtaposition.

> Story in papers on 30th, [by] Spunk Sheridan
> Redmon interviewed by Johnson.

If Redmon has told his story to Ban Johnson, Comiskey's great enemy knows that the Old Roman has been covering up. And sure enough, there is one final line as the year comes to an end:

> Tearney states that he was told by Hickey and Ewing that Johnson said that the Series was crooked but that he would fix things.

Nevertheless, the White Sox went ahead and signed all their players for the coming season (except Gandil). Johnson could hardly come right out and blow the whistle, after all, since the White Sox could prove that he had known about his share of fixes too.

The situation is so completely reversed, as far as Comiskey's relationship with his players now, that he is actually giving them the raises they have always deserved. He not only signs **Buck**

Weaver to a two-year contract at $7,250 a year, but there is a notation alongside his name on Harry's 1920 salary list that reads, "10 Days' clause out." This means that the White Sox have eliminated the routine clause giving the club the right to cancel the contract on 10 days' notice, something unheard of in baseball. Weaver, in short, has been guaranteed the two-year salary no matter what happens.

Joe Jackson, the world's worst negotiator, gets a three-year contract at $8,000 a year.

Eddie Cicotte is jumped to $10,000, and while he certainly is entitled to it off a 29-victory season, it is, by Comiskey standards, a huge salary.

The badly underpaid Lefty Williams finds his salary doubled too, from $3,000 to $6,000 and, according to Harry's sheet, he will also be getting a $500 bonus for winning 15 games and another $1,000 if he wins 20.

Felsch goes from $3,750 to $7,000; Risberg from $2,500 to $3,250, and even McMullin, the utility man, jumps to $3,600.

The White Sox seem about to brazen it through. If it were not for Ban Johnson they might have succeeded.

But now a series of coincidences develops that turns the feud between Johnson and Comiskey into a battle to name the new Commissioner, and it is on this front that the battle is going to be fought out.

One of Harry's brief notes during the time the material from his investigators was pouring in was a rather mysterious: "Magee stopping check for $50 in Chase case."

Leo Magee was an infielder for the Cubs who had got himself involved with Hal Chase (a teammate at Cincinnati the previous year) and—possibly because he seems to have been naïve enough to do business by check— the Cubs felt they had enough evidence against him to hand him his unconditional release. When nobody else picked him up, Magee, well aware that he was being blacklisted, sued the Cubs to collect on the second year of his contract.

He lost his suit—taking Hal Chase right out of baseball with him—but the first positive proof of gambling had hit the papers.

The Cubs were run by powerful men, not only powerful men in baseball but powerful men in the national life. The largest stockholder next to Wrigley was Albert D. Lasker, head of Lord & Taylor. Lasker and Wrigley were members of a 6-man group of movers and shakers who met at the Chicago Athletic Club every noon (the others were Charlie McCullough, Adolph Spielman of Tablet & Ticket Co., a printing house, A. D. Plamondon, a painting contractor, and W. M. Walker, owner of the largest fishery in Chicago. By coincidence, the Republican Party Presidential convention was being held in Chicago in 1920. The Wrigley-Lasker group, looking for a candidate to back, decided over the Caesar salad to try to put over Warren G. Harding, the amiable senator from Ohio. Their relationship with Harding was not completely divorced from baseball. Harding owned the Marion ball club in the Ohio State League.

Lasker was more deeply involved in trying to clean up baseball than one might expect in a minority stockholder. As an outsider, he could clearly see that much of baseball's troubles were traceable to the weak, backscratching, politicking National Commission. When whispers of widespread fixing began to spread during the 1919 season, Lasker had advanced a simple plan for hiring a chairman, of indisputable stature and integrity, from outside of baseball. In this, he had a natural ally in Barney Dreyfuss of the Pittsburgh Pirates. Dreyfuss hated Garry Herrmann with a fierce white hatred on the highly moral grounds that Herrmann, who should have been favoring his own league, was so completely dominated by Ban Johnson that he always ended up voting with the American League. This particularly incensed Dreyfuss because it had been Herrmann's vote that had cost the Pirates the services of George Sisler in a contract dispute with the St. Louis Browns.

If I were Dreyfuss I'd have hated Herrmann with a fine white hatred too.

Lasker, in the summer of 1920, was backing Warren G. Harding for President of the United States and Judge Kenesaw

Mountain Landis for Commissioner of Baseball, which seems to indicate a somewhat inverted sense of values. This stunning reversal, we are happy to report, has not influenced the subsequent quality of the occupants of either position.

The Cubs and the White Sox were natural collaborators, not only because they shared the same city and the same problems but because they shared the same firm of attorneys. Once the White Sox were in trouble, both Comiskey and attorney Alfred Austrian could see all the advantages of underwriting the Lasker Plan. By bringing in an independent force to replace Herrmann, Comiskey would be reducing Ban Johnson's authority. And by allying himself with the National League, he was giving himself a base from which he could fight back against Johnson.

The strangest part of all was that during most of the 1920 season it was the Cubs who seemed to be having the trouble, not the White Sox. The White Sox were in first place, attendance records were toppling, and although they were still throwing a ball game here and there, they were so superior a ball club that they were able to win just about whenever they pleased. If everything had continued to go along that smoothly they might have been able to win another pennant, throw another World Series and, off their unfortunate experiences in the previous one, make certain they got all the money.

Everything was going along so well that Harry finds nothing to record in his journal through the early months of 1920 except the notation about the Magee trial. And then, out of nowhere, comes: "Cubs scandal—story and investigation."

Harry had good reason to be concerned about anybody's scandal, and particularly about a scandal cross-town. Before the week was over, the Cubs' scandal had put the White Sox in the soup—which is, from all the evidence Harry later was able to dig up—precisely what it was supposed to do. For the master chef who had mixed the ingredients was Ban Johnson.

What had happened was that a late-season (August 31) game between the Cubs and Phillies had brought forth a tremendous amount of smart money on the last-place Phillies. A telegram had been sent to the Cubs office before the game warning them that a fix was in, and since the highly suspect Claude Hendrix was scheduled to pitch, he was very quickly replaced by Alexander (Alex having apparently mended his ways if they ever needed mending, which I doubt). When the Cubs lost anyway, wires and letters were sent to newspapers across the country informing them that the gamblers had cleaned up.

This time the papers broke the story big. A Grand Jury was impaneled to look into the matter, but instead of investigating the Cubs-Phillies game, the presiding jurist, Chief Justice Charles MacDonald, very quickly focussed upon the 1919 World Series.

The investigation Harry writes of in his diary had shown that the names attached to all those wires and letters had been phonies. The fine hand behind it all was, again, undoubtedly the hand of Ban Johnson.

It may seem strange that Johnson had gone almost a full year without making his move. But Johnson was hardly in the position to go around casting first stones. A direct attack from him would bring a direct counterattack, and in the general mudslinging not only Johnson and Comiskey but all of baseball would be splattered. As Harry's journal develops we can see that Johnson had waited patiently until MacDonald took the Bench. Johnson's confidence in the judge was perfectly understandable. He was merely promising to make Judge MacDonald the head of the new Commission.

With the convening of the Grand Jury, Harry takes pen in hand and resumes his journal:

Sept. 18. Conference with Austrian who has matter in hand with Hoyne (*Editor:* the states attorney) and MacDonald. First intimation that Cubs did not want Landis in 1919.

OK. An interesting beginning. The White Sox are hardly panicking; they don't really expect this investigation to hurt them that badly. Reading between the lines, it is almost impossible to avoid the impression that Austrian and MacDonald have had a practical talk about MacDonald's chances of becoming Commissioner.

Why do I say that? Well, for one thing I know what is coming later. For another, I know for a fact that the Cubs were for Landis from the beginning. I know that my daddy, who became president of the Cubs in 1919, had not only wanted Landis, a personal friend, he had plumped from the beginning for making him the sole Commissioner with total power.

For Austrian, whose sole interest is the protection of his client, there is obviously nothing to be lost by playing along with MacDonald. There is nothing to be lost for his client, Charles Comiskey, and, just as important, there is certainly nothing to be lost for Alfred Austrian. Austrian is going to have to deal with the new Chief Justice on other cases, for other clients.

There is no reason to believe that Austrian confided this strategy to Harry Grabiner. To Austrian, the practical lawyer, these baseball people must have seemed like fractious children, permitting personal piques and animosities to threaten their valuable property. Harry's greatest virtue was his loyalty, but it was the kind of intense loyalty that made him see all issues in black and white. In Harry's world, his side was always totally right and the other side was always totally wrong. To a man like Austrian, there is no right or wrong, there are only tactics, stratagems, techniques—and results.

Let's face it: to Austrian, Harry must have seemed like nothing more than a narrow, parochial baseball man.

If so, he underestimated him. As the weeks go on, we see that Harry has hired an investigator named Soule to dig into every facet of Johnson's plan. In short order, Harry simply passes the word on to CAC that Austrian is still insisting that MacDonald is their friend, and then adds somewhat dryly: "See Soule reports."

With baseball under fire, the National Commission collapsed, leaving the game to face its most critical moment without even a figurehead leader. In today's crisis, they are doing it much better. They do have a figurehead leader, albeit a lame-duck one. It is possible to argue that a lame-duck figurehead isn't *that* much of an improvement, but only if you're one of those chronic malcontents.

In Chicago, both teams leaped upon the Grand Jury hearing as a way to breathe life back into the Lasker Plan:

Sept. 22. Conference with Wrigley, Lasker and Veeck, HG at Austrian office. Cubs officials particularly Lasker willing to go to extent of closing their ballparks in order to put baseball on clean basis. They also joined with CAC in coming out for Landis for chairman. Veeck to get Dreyfuss, Ebbetts and Baker (*editor:* Pittsburgh, Brooklyn and Philadelphia) to attend meeting with Chicago, Boston, N.Y. relative to working out plans to rid baseball of its present evils and secure proper person as chairman of Nat. Com. with revisary powers.

Sept. 22. 2 P.M. CAC appeared B4 grand jury testifying as to his knowledge regarding crookedness in baseball. was on stand one hour, was cheered upon leaving. Afternoon papers carried story.

Sept. 23. Morning papers in headlines reflected and asserted World Series 1919 were fixed.

So it was finally, almost one full year later, out in the open. The eight White Sox players were finally suspended, and the White Sox pennant chances went with them.

On September 26, Hartley Replogle, the assistant states attorney who was presenting the case to the Grand Jury, came to Comiskey Park and, according to Grabiner, asked: "You're not sore at me?" He also informed them that "someone was allowed to coach and handle the investigation." The mysterious someone, we gather, is Ban Johnson.

It's rather odd, of course, for a prosecutor to drop in on the people he is investigating so that he can apologize to them and then, to show his goodwill, pass on some useful information.

It leaves the unmistakable impression that Replogle had gone much further than his boss, Hoyne (whom Austrian felt he had "in hand"), had expected.

(A full year later, on December 23, 1921, a momentary armistice was called to permit the American League to hold its annual meeting. With the players finally about to go to trial, Harry records the remarkable statement: "Austrian told Miller that he would not stand for Replogle in handling any of the players prosecution."

(Miller is Ban Johnson's lawyer, and that little exchange with Austrian makes it perfectly clear that while Johnson may still have been calling the shots, Austrian had an—ahem—fairly strong voice in court himself.)

> Sept. 27. Austrian office. met Dreyfuss, Lasker, Veeck, CAC regarding plans to secure new Commission. Papers were signed by Veeck, Dreyfuss, CAC.
>
> Nat. Com. meeting called. no one attended.

It is on September 28 that the lines begin to tighten, as all parts of the drama come together:

> Fleming called at Comiskey Park regarding Patterson, Ball and Johnson.
>
> Austrian. Conference Gleason, CAC, HG, later sent and secured Cicotte who gave oral confession. was then taken to Grand Jury.
>
> Jackson taken by Gleason to Austrian who also confessed then taken to Grand Jury.
>
> Jackson stated Williams also wanted to testify.
>
> McGraw meeting and pledge at Auditorium.

The item that looks most important is actually the least important. Comiskey (or Grabiner) had been very careful to have the players talk to nobody except the investigators so that the

White Sox officials would remain in a position to deny that the players had ever confessed anything to them—the smart way to handle the situation once the decision had been made to try to hold the team together. With the calling of Cicotte, the decision has been made that the White Sox had better feed the players to the Grand Jury themselves, rather than have it appear as if the Grand Jury was calling them in over their head.

The meeting with McGraw is far more important. With McGraw's pledge of support, they have brought the Giants into the fold for Landis and begun to extend the group beyond the original hard core. To elect Landis, they are going to need a solid National League front.

But that isn't the most important development from Harry's point of view, either. Fleming is most important of all to him, and his name is going to appear with frequency. He is the operator of a very successful coal company, and an extremely close friend of both Grabiner and Comiskey—besides being the Number 1 White Sox fan. Most big-league clubs had one of these wealthy young guys floating around the edges in those days. As a matter of fact, most big-league clubs have them floating around even today. Fleming is invaluable because, it becomes increasingly apparent, he travels with Johnson, Patterson and Ball and reports back to Harry. Fleming is the guy who gave the White Sox the little added edge they needed. Through him they always knew what Johnson was planning and, to make it absolutely perfect, Johnson never knew that they knew.

Phil Ball is the owner of the St. Louis Browns. I cannot figure out who Patterson is, except that, from everything Fleming says, he would seem to have been Ban Johnson's candidate to replace Comiskey as the owner of the Chicago White Sox.

Johnson's plan as it unfolds here was to harass and humiliate Comiskey, through MacDonald and the Grand Jury hearing, so that Comiskey would be only too happy to sell out. The plan, always referred to by Grabiner as "the Conspiracy," was hatched in June, we learn from Fleming, "at a party at the Wayside Inn at which Patterson, Ball, Johnson remarked that Comiskey has a wonderful plant and a great money-maker but after we get through wrecking it we will be able to buy it at our own price."

There does not seem to be the slightest doubt that this was indeed Johnson's plan. Two days after Fleming called in, Lasker —whose sources would be unimpeachable—checked it out and passed the word on to Harry, through Austrian, that the story was true.

The fight to name the Commissioner becomes the fight to control the White Sox franchise. If the Sox can get in their own man, Landis, they are safe. If Ban Johnson succeeds in getting MacDonald in, Comiskey is in trouble.

But, of course, Johnson was working under an impossible handicap anyway. When he pushed the investigation into Chicago he was moving into the enemy camp. Austrian may or may not have been neutralizing Judge MacDonald, but he was certainly being fed information by the states attorney:

> Oct. 10 Saw Austrian. (information) from Hoyne who said Johnson said in 1917 Sox players gave Detroit 50-dollar suit each to throw games.

True or false, this tasty little item shows us more than anything else what the climate was like in those days. At any rate, Detroit conveniently lost two consecutive doubleheaders and the White Sox went on to win the pennant rather easily.

Luckily for all of us who have faith in the essential honesty of man, Johnson was anxious to alert the citizenry to this kind of thing, even if it took him three years to get around to it. To be completely accurate, though, we are forced to report that Johnson never did alert the public. Neither, we must say, did the states attorney or the Chief Justice. It was seven more years before that story came out into the open.

> Oct. 13. Saw Fleming, reiterated regarding Patterson, Ball, Johnson. Worked out editorial matter with Walter Howey.

Walter Howey was editor of the Chicago *Examiner*. From Harry's happy tone, it is evident that Howey is going to give Comiskey a good press. Ten days later, there is the follow-up little note: ". . . splendid editorial in *Examiner*."

As the diary jumps along, in its elliptical way, from one name to another, there are a couple of widely spaced references to Phil Ball that set you to wondering. The first comes on October 25, as the Grand Jury hearing is reaching a height:

> Saw Fleming who indicated that Ball could be stopped through Kearney by withdrawing labor support from his ice plants now in construction. (This would bring Ball to you.) Told Fleming not to proceed along those lines as you would not want any part of Ball.

Now, that's odd. With this chance to neutralize Ball, one of the triumvirate involved in the Conspiracy which occupies most of Grabiner's thoughts, Harry not only calls Fleming off, he does it without even consulting Comiskey. Let's have no nonsense about conscience here, either. These boys are fighting for their lives and they are using every weapon at their disposal, not excluding making deals with the presiding judge.

Now let us jump ahead to November 12. Ban Johnson has been routed and his followers (known as "The Loyal 5") have come together with the supporters of the Lasker Plan to accept Judge Landis as Commissioner. How does Harry begin his report on this meeting that changed the face of organized baseball? Why, he starts it by writing, with obvious relish: "CAC called Ball in his true name, a crook."

Now that's pretty rough talk. What had Ball done that has left Comiskey (and Grabiner) so bitter that with all the conspiracies, name-calling and double-dealing that had taken place he finds it so soul-satisfying to single out Ball in the presence of all the other clubowners?

There's a clue, it would seem, in that quick rejection of the perfectly good gambit for bringing Ball to Comiskey by hitting him through the labor union. There would be only two reasons not to have gone along. The first would be if they already had Ball on their side. (He would be a crook, quite obviously, if he had sold out to them and had then reneged.) But that can't be, because Fleming keeps reporting on the Conspiracy to the end.

The other reason would be if Ball had something on Comiskey so serious that they wouldn't dare push him to the wall. You can't blackmail a man—which is precisely what Fleming is suggesting—if he is in possession of information he could use to blackmail *you*.

And now you remember an item that had seemed a little puzzling in the first reading of Harry's journal. Less than a week before Fleming came to him with the information that they were in a position to strike Ball's plants, Harry had written:

> Oct. 19. Conference with Austrian at 11 A.M. Bill given for $10,000. Talked regarding drawing up will at a near future date. MacDonald thought to be absolutely for us by Austrian although CAC was under impression that MacDonald was not.

Austrian, as the White Sox lawyer, is undoubtedly on a retainer. If there have been some unusual expenses why doesn't he just mail them the bill? To have handed Harry the bill like that leaves little doubt—especially since Harry feels it is important enough to jot down in his journal—that it is for a service so special that they would all just as soon keep it off the official records.

And more especially, too, since it is followed by the gratuitous remark about drawing up the will, a note which hints of danger. The only indication of what may have been involved comes in the final line where we learn that Austrian is still trying to sell them MacDonald, and Harry—who is in possession of information about MacDonald's relationship with Ban Johnson—isn't buying. He isn't buying and he hasn't enough faith in Austrian to let him in on that information.

The next day Harry is back in Austrian's office:

Oct. 20. Conference with Austrian. Paid him bill $10,000. Told him of our suspicions founded on fact from Fleming and of our report that Grand Jury was to make report and in same with aid of MacDonald, was to put Johnson on a pedestal as the savior of baseball and the reward for so doing to MacDonald presumably was to place him on Commission.

The $10,000 is being paid the very next day and, again, delivered by hand, an indication that Austrian has quite probably paid the money out of his own funds.

This time, Harry, quite obviously on instructions from Comiskey, is letting Austrian in on their information and telling him, in effect, that he is not to trust Chief Justice MacDonald. (This doesn't stop Austrian. To Harry's continued disgust, Austrian maintains to the end that MacDonald can be trusted. And, in the end, in one of the most incredible parts of the whole affair, we are going to see why.)

But notice again the juxtaposition here. The quick shift from the $10,000 to the position of MacDonald—which means, as far as the White Sox are concerned, MacDonald's relationship to Ban Johnson and the Johnson-Ball-Patterson Conspiracy.

This is not the first time the $10,000 figure has come up in the Black Sox investigation. It is the figure that Comiskey finally settled on as a reward for information that would offer positive proof that the Series had been fixed.

And that reminds you of something else about Phil Ball that should have had us wondering before. Ball owns the St. Louis Browns, the team Joe Gedeon plays for. (Gedeon was not only still playing in 1920, despite his admission that he had knowledge of a fix, he was having the only good season of his career.) When Gedeon popped up to claim Comiskey's reward, wouldn't it have been most logical for the owner of his team to have called him in and asked, in effect, "Hey, what's going on here?"

And isn't it more than probable that Ball would have immediately brought Gedeon's story to Ban Johnson and that realizing they finally had Comiskey in such an exposed and vulnerable position, they had sat down and hatched the plan to blast him right out of baseball?

It is quite possible, then, that Ball, out of a mischievous sense of humor, had sent someone around to collect the reward for Gedeon, a genteel form of blackmail.

Why would Ball get himself that deeply involved for $10,000, no great sum to him? Well, just what was the Johnson-Ball-Patterson plan? It was, after all, to wage a war of nerves against Comiskey, to use the Grand Jury hearing as a weapon to wreck the White Sox by destroying their team and, in the process, to so embarrass, frighten and discredit Comiskey that he would panic and sell out cheap. What better tactic, as the Grand Jury hearing was coming to an end, than to frighten him further—and show him how completely vulnerable he was—by hitting him with a quick little piece of blackmail? Johnson, remember, has no idea that Comiskey *knows* about their plan.

That kind of a deal would obviously carry a guarantee that Gedeon would keep his mouth shut. On October 27, two days after Harry has turned down Fleming's suggestion about striking the ice plants, Harry received information that after the witnesses finished testifying before the Grand Jury they were being brought into Judge MacDonald's private chambers to be questioned again. And Harry adds, in what seems to be a worried tone, "How about Gedeon?"

There is only one piece of information in Harry's journal that seems to go against the grain of this theory. If Ball had called in Gedeon there at the beginning, Ban Johnson would certainly have known about the fix—and about Redmon—immediately. There was a line about Johnson interviewing Redmon, if you remember, but it didn't occur until December 29, 1919, a month and a half after Gedeon and Redmon had come in to claim the reward.

But *that* disturbing point is cleared up at once:

Oct. 28. Saw Fleming, gave him data that Johnson knew all about the evidence of Redmon early in October. Johnson called on Redmon and Redmon told HG in December.

This seems to contradict the December 29 note until, looking back, you see that all Harry wrote at that time was "Redmon interviewed by Johnson." What Harry is saying now is that Johnson had called on Redmon back in October (shortly after the White Sox had bought his story from him) but that Grabiner *hadn't learned about it* until December.

This entry tells us something else too. Why, after all, is Harry telling Fleming about this almost a year later? Think about that a little. Fleming would have had to do a certain amount of ground work in arranging for the union to pull that strike on Ball. He would not only have made himself somewhat vulnerable but he would now owe something to everybody involved in setting it up. Fleming would want to know why the White Sox weren't going to take advantage of this opportunity. More than that, he had a right to know. Harry is telling him here that the White Sox are in no position, strategically, to take on Patterson and Ball.

This is all theoretic, of course. It could also be argued that Johnson had called upon Redmon under exactly the same set of circumstances that the White Sox had called upon him. Because Redmon had sent word that he had some information for sale. But the other theory not only holds together perfectly, it has one virtue that no other theory can claim. It accounts for Comiskey flinging that epithet "crook" into Ball's face at the joint meeting of the two leagues.

What interests us most here, though, is this bitter battle to name the Commissioner, a battle which very nearly left baseball with one 11-team league.

Sept. 29. Conference at Austrian of Stoneham, McGraw, Lasker, Wrigley, Ruppert, Frazee, Huston, CAC at which Stoneham, Ruppert and Frazee sign Lasker plan and National League agreed to stand by signers of this plan to the extent of refusal to recognize such American League clubs as do not agree on new form of Commission.

Two other American League clubs, the Yankees and the Red Sox, have joined with the White Sox in attaching themselves to the National League and supporting Landis. This is a vital development. Without the Yankees and the Red Sox, there would have been a complete deadlock: the National League plus the White Sox (who, under the conditions, would have been no great asset), against the 7 other American League clubs.

Again, we find one of those accidents of timing that slip into the picture to tip the scales. Why should the Yankees and Red Sox have turned against Ban Johnson? Well, later in Harry's diary, as he is reporting the 1920 American League meeting, he spends most of his time in writing about what seem to be insignificant and certainly irrelevant decisions about who was to pay what on the "Mays expense."

Carl Mays was a pitcher whom Harry Frazee of the Red Sox had sold to the Yankees late in the 1919 season. After the season was over, Ban Johnson invalidated the sale and forfeited all the games Mays had appeared in, a decision which would have dropped the Yankees from third place to fourth. The Yankees went into court for an injunction—it was a great year for court action—and Johnson was legally overruled. If Johnson's ruling had stood—and the Yankees probably wouldn't have gone to court if it hadn't been for that wholly unnecessary rider about forfeiting the games—then the sale of Babe Ruth to the Yankees a few months later probably would never have taken place. And if Johnson hadn't become so furious at the Yankees for challenging his authority that he talked the Giants into canceling their lease (and Harry's information seems to be good about this aspect of it), Jake Ruppert would probably never have built Yankee Stadium.

The other five owners, Frank Navin in Detroit, Connie Mack

in Philadelphia, Clark Griffith in Washington, Ball in St. Louis and Dunn in Cleveland stood firmly behind Johnson, proudly proclaiming themselves "the Loyal 5":

> Oct. 15. Lasker and Veeck willing to amalgamate or consider league without 5 clubs not agreeing on some plan of reorganization.

> Oct. 18. 10 A.M. Conference at Austrian with Huston, Frazee, Ruppert, CAC. Everyone satisfied to proceed along lines of working with Natl League on any basis that can be agreed upon regardless of the 5 remaining clubs of American League, tho these clubs should be given an opportunity to come along. NY club wanted to insert lease proposition.

In the afternoon, the hard core of Landis supporters got together to confirm their course.

> Oct. 18. Joint meeting. Records of work accomplished in written report. Met at 12 noon adjourned 12 midnight. Everything was agreed upon by committee then NY club and Boston wanted to make many unfair changes.

I have to smile at that last sentence because it is so typical of Harry. Any disagreement about a policy he favors becomes somehow a reneging on agreed policy and is, it goes without saying, eminently unfair. (Maybe that's why Harry and I got along so well. We looked at things the same way.)

> Oct. 19. [The afternoon of the day Austrian has proffered the $10,000 bill.]

> Saw Fleming and Soule later in day. Fleming thinks grand jury report will be framed to give Johnson wonderful send off and praise and place both he and MacDonald on high plane, thereby accomplishing two purposes, boosting MacDonald for Chairman of the Commission and placing Johnson in an enviable position in the controversy at hand. Fleming said he did not believe Mac-Donald was for us as he was continually with Johnson and nat-

urally to further his own end must be of the same belief. That Johnson was protecting himself and would try to implicate McGraw and Gleason account of former connection with book-making and gambling. There was another party but name was forgotten.

The following day, Harry paid Austrian the $10,000 and passed on Fleming's feeling about MacDonald. Harry is a sus-picious man, of course. His next line is: "Patterson no doubt has fixed the *Journal* for Johnson through Eastman which accounts for the articles that have been appearing the past few days. The parties have been taking place in the Loop in Sinek's room at the Sherman House. (*editor:* that would be Bill Sinek, who was a major stockholder in the Cubs before Wrigley.)"

This information seems to have come from the everpresent Fleming too, for there is an added note that "Heydler will go the limit if any litigation arises and has enough against Johnson to sink a ship."

> Oct. 20. Conference CAC and Austrian alone, regarding Mac-Donald and Johnson working together.

> Oct. 21. Conference with Austrian, he advised me regarding Veeck who stated he could secure 6 Natl League votes inc. his own for Landis, with McCarthy and Edwards as associate com-missioners. (*editor:* McCarthy was a minor-league representative and Edwards was a former Cleveland sports editor who finally ended up as secretary for the National League.)

> Austrian also stated he called on Landis regarding same and he (Landis) will take the matter up with his family and advise next Tuesday altho Austrian thinks the salary will not satisfy him unless around 50,000. Austrian stated he saw both the fore-man and the judge who intimated that they would go through and question Johnson regarding the conspiracy.

You can just see Harry demanding to know why the Grand Jury was ignoring the only thing worth investigating as far as he was concerned—Johnson's notorious and evil conspiracy against Comiskey. And you can just see Austrian, who has been breaking his back to try to limit the case to 8 dishonest players, *not* to spread it out to where it would touch his own clients, telling Harry what Harry wants to hear just to shut him up.

It is nice to know, though, that if Ban Johnson has access to the judge and foreman in what is presumably a secret grand jury hearing, then Austrian has access to them too. That's democracy in action. It is also Chicago in 1920, just before it fell to Al Capone.

And now comes a note that drives you up walls:

Oct. 22. Conference with Soule. Reports cover everything. [Oh, what I would give to see those reports.]

Oct. 26. Talked with Veeck who states that NY, Boston, Chicago, St. Louis, Phila, Pitts are all for Landis for Chairman. Bill does not know where Ebbetts and Herrmann stand as to candidates. Bill thinks Johnson and his five will try and hold out as before and have each league vote as a whole or unit thereby endeavoring to cause a deadlock but the new agreement provides that the majority of both leagues shall elect.

MacDonald while mentioned was given no serious consideration. From observation, the 11 have the situation well in hand and no doubt the minors would be pleased especially if McCarthy is given a place.

Oct. 27. Conference with Austrian who still believes in honesty of purpose of MacDonald. (See reports from Soule)

Austrian arranged to appear 2 PM before Grand Jury Friday, Oct. 29th also together with CAC, HG and Tip O'Neill.

Oct. 27. Talked with Rosenbaum who talked with Weaver. Weaver maintains that while he was at a meeting of the players who wanted him to take part in the throwing he being offered 5000 as his share he took matter under consideration but refused to be a party to same. Gandil told Weaver that the remaining players intended going through regardless of his connection still he refused to be a party to same, and tho he knew that he did not divulge anything to any one. He denied having received any money or of anyone leaving any package for him. Cicotte approached him first during the second trip to Boston. He also said that McMullin approached him during 1920 season to throw a game for 500 which he refused.

Oh, oh. That business about Cicotte approaching Weaver during the *second trip* to Boston puts an entire new light on the Series fix. The Black Sox scandal is always written up as a sort of last-minute affair in which everything got bungled. Cicotte, based on his own story, is usually represented as a man who was seduced by $10,000 tucked under his pillow. It becomes perfectly obvious here, however, that Cicotte was one of the ringleaders, along with Gandil, and that the players themselves had been planning to throw the Series all along. Did the gamblers seduce the players, one might ask, or did the players seduce the gamblers?

It also raises new thoughts about Buck Weaver. There is very little doubt that Weaver did remain honest through the Series but he was hardly faced, as had previously been supposed, with a difficult last-minute decision about whether to squeal on his friends. He had months to think it over and if he had come to a calculated decision not to go along with the fix, he had also come to a calculated decision to keep his mouth shut.

Having received that news from investigator Rosenbaum, Harry receives word from one Billy Hayes that the *Journal* is friendly to Johnson. Harry is outraged, of course, although he is not at all outraged that the *Examiner* has been equally friendly to Comiskey. Harry also seems to have some worthwhile contacts on the *Tribune*. His next entry that day reads:

JLDoherty of Tribune City Dept. says *Journal* has been given an underground direct from jury room as to all evidence testified and also that Johnson was in MacDonald's chamber when the various witnesses after testifying before the grand jury were brought to the judge and their evidence gone over.

Ban Johnson had a far better contact at the *Tribune,* though. As a matter of fact, Johnson seemed to have as good a friend in *Tribune* sports editor Harvey Woodruff as he had in Judge MacDonald. And for the same reason. After Landis had become Commissioner and consolidated his position, we find Harry writing:

> Fleming called up and said he ... pointed out to Woodruff how Johnson was duping him while promising the Commissionership and promising the same to MacDonald. Fleming said his argument had much weight with Woodruff and that Woodruff's policy and writing would be much changed from now on.

That's the way I always figure it too. If you can't be Commissioner, you might as well be neutral.

With the indictments in, the conspiracy is coming to a climax. Johnson knows by now that he's fighting a holding action, at best, as far as naming the Commissioner is concerned. He can only hope that he has Comiskey frightened enough or disgusted enough or tired enough to want to get out. The time has come to make his move and he sends the most innocent-appearing blind:

> Oct. 29. Cummings, president of Drovers Natl Bank (*editor:* where the White Sox banked) called HG on phone asking him to come over on some important business. HG went over at once and Cummings stated that a party of packing town men would purchase the Ball park if CAC felt disposed to sell out. His party understands that CAC was in ill health and disgusted.

> HG told him CAC would not sell but that he was disgusted with that business but would not as he (CAC) was interested only in cleaning up the present baseball filth and putting BB where it rightfully belonged under the control of *honest* men. This is the final episode of the conspiracy to buy at a cheap price after it was wrecked by the conspirators.

> Gave the above to Edw. Fleming.

There is a fascinating Freudianism to be found in there. This is the only place in his entire journal where Harry uses BB (in capitals yet) for baseball. Ban Johnson's initials were also BB, and Johnson was frequently referred to by those initials. What Harry is obviously thinking as he writes this is that he is putting BB Johnson where he rightfully belongs by taking away his power and bringing baseball under the control of honest men.

Lacking any action by the new Commissioner, Comiskey appears to be safe. There would now seem little left for the majority to do except to consolidate their power, elect Landis and let the Loyal 5 decide whether they really want to make a stab at going it alone.

But something else is going on at this time. The 1920 Presidential election is coming up on November 2. Lasker's name disappears from the journal for two full weeks. His plan for the Commissionership has obviously become a distinct second in his thinking. Still, everyone is aware that Harding is a shoo-in, and Lasker has been able to do a certain amount of baseball work along with his political work.

> Nov. 1. Attended conference at Austrian with Lasker, Veeck. Lasker had just returned from the East the latter part of the past week and stated that he had been in conference with Stoneham. Had seen Baker, Ruppert and Frazee, all were sincere upon going through with the plan as signed and agreed upon. Lasker stated that at least six in the National League were in favor of the following tribunal—Landis, Chairman, Edwards, McCarthy. Lasker is of the opinion that the minors should have representation and he would be in favor of even going as far as allowing the Loyal five to name one of the members providing Landis is the Chairman. Whatever is done by the Loyal five, Lasker stated that he was in favor of a fight to the finish regardless of the consequences.

Lasker, it becomes apparent, has not volunteered the information that they might give the Johnson people one of the associate Commissioners. He has apparently responded to a suggestion made by Alfred Austrian. Because here we see, on the day before the election, the hand of national politics reaching into baseball councils:

"Austrian stated that Hays, Republican National Committee, intimated that he did not feel as though the Federal Bench should be tampered with and he wished to use his good offices in behalf of MacDonald."

Wow! This is Will Hays, the Chairman of the National Committee. The man, in short, who is running Harding's campaign. This is about as strong as political pressure can be applied, and if the other side didn't have as powerful a counterbalance in Lasker, it could easily have been the end. The distinction between the Federal Bench (Landis) and the State Bench (MacDonald) is obviously sheer verbiage. Hays has to give some reason for stopping the favorite.

It is most interesting, too, is it not, that he is applying his pressure through the good offices of Austrian? There can be no doubt at all, at this point, that Austrian—the same man who carried his clients' offer to Landis—had been secondarily promising MacDonald that he would do what he could for him. In this respect, Harry's suspicions about him would seem to be correct. On the other hand, Austrian is only giving his *quid pro quo* here. He is keeping his promise. Austrian has maneuvered brilliantly for his client. By keeping a foot in both camps, he had got from MacDonald a voice in the Grand Jury hearing almost equal to Ban Johnson's. Most important of all, he had kept him from making the scathing indictment of Comiskey that Johnson had been angling for.

Still, Johnson is hardly out of the ball game. Not when he can wheel up as big a gun as Will Hays. Lasker now lets it be known that the Johnson crowd had seemed inordinately confident:

Lasker stated that Connery (*editor:* for many years owner of the St. Paul club) said he thought the loyal five had Landis licked and Lasker said if Landis were licked he would not oppose MacDonald.

They now apparently fell to wondering which of the 11 might be defecting. Lasker informed them that Ruppert had gone down to Philadelphia a week earlier at the solicitation of Connie Mack, a piece of information which came as no surprise to Harry since Soule had passed that little item on to him in one of his reports.

> Lasker said he personally thought Ruppert was the weakest one in the combination. That Ruppert was money mad and did not know if he would go to a finish, but further that Stoneham controlled the situation on account of the ballpark proposition in NY.

The next day, CAC called Lasker, just as Lasker was leaving for Marion, Ohio, to be with Harding on election day (and, we can presume, find out how high the backing of Judge Mac-Donald went). "Appointment made for Friday 11-5-20 Comiskey Park between 9 and 9:30."

> Nov. 5. Mr. Lasker called at Comiskey Park; went over the situation and suggested not to comment other than the plan as signed outlines procedure and that speaks for itself. Lasker does think that Ruppert was the weaker of the combination as he was in baseball for Ruppert alone. And might not want war if that length was necessary to go to. Lasker advises also that great influence was brought to bear on him to vote for MacDonald, but Lasker said he was for Landis, 1-2-3- but if Landis could not be put in he would not oppose MacDonald. Lasker said unless some form of government satisfactory to the majority of major-league owners could be installed that would restore baseball and protect same he would retire from baseball. that he did not want any more domination of Johnson who stood in the path of cleansing the game. Lasker said he had NY, Boston, St. Louis, Chgo, Pitts., Phila, and that the above were willing to take Landis as Chairman with Edwards, and for the minors to pick the 3rd man, or as long as Landis was secured as Chairman then the Loyal 5 could name one man and the minors the other.

> Lasker was told by Stoneham that Johnson came to him to secure the lease on the Polo Grounds in the name of the American

League and would place new owners in the American League in
New York that were satisfactory to Stoneham and Johnson would
even let Stoneham pick the new owner if he so desired and further that if Stoneham would give Johnson the above lease, Johnson would allow Stoneham to name the 3rd member of the
National Commission. Lasker will have Stoneham tell this to
Ruppert at the meeting to be held Nov. 7 Sunday.

And then Harry adds: "Lasker is of the belief that Johnson
was the person who forced the termination of the Polo Grounds
lease so that he could control the situation in New York. This
is in line with his conspiracy efforts to wreck the Sox and then
buy it at a 'cheap price.'"

The November 7 meeting is apparently preliminary to the
scheduled joint meeting of the American and National Leagues.
The question confronting the Landis backers is whether they'll
be able to break into the Loyal 5. The question facing the Loyal
5 is whether they're going to bother to show up.

Nov. 8. Meeting called 11 owners at 11 AM Congress Hotel.
other owners "Hungry 5" did not appear but Griffith acting as
spokesman wanted to have 11 appoint Committee of 3 to meet
with 3 from his faction and 3 from minors. said committee to
work out reorganization plan. He was told that if his 5 wished
to come into either a formal meeting or informal meeting the
11 would be glad to go over conditions. he carried his message
back to them and the answer from the 5 was brought back by
Miller [Johnson's attorney] who after a long talk said nothing as
usual, but in his closing remarks stated that he advised Johnson
to keep away from the directors meeting during 1919 and again
counseled against the 5 owners coming into the meeting at this
time. he was given the same message to take back to his clients as
was Griffith and the meeting adjourned for lunch and to wait
their answer that if they did not care to come to the meeting the
11 owners intended to proceed with the plans as outlined Oct.
18. About 4:00, the meeting again convened and Griffith came
back with nothing new so the meeting of the 11 decided to proceed without the other 5. After a little discussion, Judge Landis

was unanimously selected for the position of chairman at 50 thousand per year for seven yrs. and a committee appointed to tender the position to him consisting of Austrian, Ruppert Herrmann, Ebbets, Veeck ... after seeing Judge Landis he promised to give same his serious consideration and advise his answer in few days.

Note how shrewdly that committee was chosen. After Austrian, the lawyer, and Veeck, the personal friend, they were tying up the three weakest members of the combination; Ruppert, whose determination was suspect, plus Herrmann and Ebbets, the last two National League owners to fall into line.

While they were being so shrewd, they thoughtfully changed the rules to eliminate any possibility that Ban Johnson would be able to use his American League majority to exercise a veto:

> The meeting also decided that in the future all interleague matters shall be decided by a majority vote of the clubs of the 2 major leagues and that the Lasker plan was herewith endorsed that the minor league clubs could if they desired name one associate member of the Commission and the AL the other but what had been accomplished up to now cannot be changed and that man selected could in no wise be financially interested in baseball and that neither Commission associate could be at this time a president of any league.

> A drafting committee to meet with the minor league drafting committee was selected and was comprised of Ebbets, Dreyfuss and Herrmann.

With the minor-league meeting opening in Kansas City the next day, both factions rushed down to try to pick up support. Johnson, according to Grabiner, was deeply involved in trying to put his own man in as head of the minors over the incumbent John Farrell. "Johnson and Miller addressed the minor-league meeting and promised as usual everything but did not make any impression, as the minors know Johnson has been against them for 20 years, and now that Johnson can use them, he was addressing them to lead them on. . . ."

Unfortunately for Johnson, while he was politicking and speechmaking, his Loyal 5 were out on the floor collapsing. Not unsurprisingly, it was Clark Griffith, the man who had once formed the third leg of the triumvirate along with Comiskey and Johnson in the formation of the American League, who carried the message of surrender.

> Griffith approached Mrs. Ebbetts to pave the way for an interview with Mr. Ebbetts and finally solicited from Dreyfuss, Ebbetts and Herrmann an opportunity for the 5 to meet with the 11 owners in Chgo in an informal meeting on Nov. 12. The 5 owners practically admitting they did not want war and willing to agree that what had been done on Nov. 8 would stand.

After all the vows of unswerving loyalty and dedication, the grand rebellion hadn't lasted through one full day.

Harry then notes "frequent meetings," as the other 4 Loyal adherents come slinking back: "Navin stated Johnson's talk did not bind him, and he would handle his own affairs, this to Dreyfuss."

On the morning of November 12, the victorious 11 met at Austrian's office "to agree on plan of procedure."

At noon, the 16 owners finally came together, fang to fang, and after CAC had finished calling Ball "in his true name" they got down to business. In this most critical of all meetings, the one that set baseball on its current path, Harry becomes frustratingly brief and maddeningly laconic. There being little need to inform Comiskey of the byplay—since Comiskey was there—Harry contented himself with the bare facts:

> Meeting at Congress with 5 AL owners and final settlement on basis Landis, 7 yrs. at 50m per year, chairman. All inter-league matters to be decided as follows: All clubs to cast a vote then the AL to cast 1 vote and the National one vote and if deadlocked the Chairman of Nat. Com. to cast deciding vote. *It was finally*

agreed that if acceptable to Landis, no associate members would be selected but Landis to be sole judge. [our italics]

called on Landis at 4:10 PM

Landis accepted to take effect at once and at figure of 42,500 and Landis to remain on bench and to handle baseball affairs also.

No, Landis hadn't taken a cut. The other $7,500 was in the form of an expense account which, even in those days of relatively low income tax, was advantageous.

What really kills you here is Harry's sudden attack of reticence. After all that discussion about balancing the ticket with the associate Commissioners, not a word about how they finally came to the decision to make Landis the sole Commissioner. The first thought that comes to mind is that being unable to agree on the two associate members they decided it was not really worth arguing about. It is also possible that Ban Johnson, having been eliminated from the job in the new ground rules, exacted this one small concession to keep himself as close as possible to the seat of power. If so, he made his final mistake. By the time Landis got through interpreting his powers as Commissioner, there was nothing left over for Johnson or anybody else.

Nov. 13. Papers and owners in every league unanimous in approval of Landis and loud in praise.

CAC leaves for Excelsior Springs.

The crisis is over. CAC can now recline by the springs and bask himself in the most serene and soul-satisfying emotion known to man—the knowledge that you have gotten away with it.

Harry is laboring under one grave misconception, though. Believing that the White Sox have "their" man in power, he sets out to get Tip O'Neill the job as Landis's secretary. Despite

Austrian's attempts to warn him off, Harry insists upon trying to use his influence with the new Commissioner. Landis turns him down flatly, making it perfectly clear that he will not take into consideration "anyone who has ever had any baseball affiliations or connections with any one side."

As far as corruption in baseball is concerned, Landis is still feeling his way in these first weeks, distrusting one side as much as the other. In his search for an independent informant, however, his eye falls upon a most ironic source:

Dec. 3 11:30 AM

Was called on phone by Fleming who asked to have Mr. CAC and HG come over to his office

Upon arriving there Fleming said he had met with Landis who said to Fleming 12/1/20 "you know all about baseball and conditions and I would like to meet you so a meeting was arranged for Dec. 2 at which time Fleming told Landis everything from the start of the conspiracy.... Fleming clearly pointed out that the recent grand jury investigation was not started though Johnson had whatever he knew about the case as early as June but Johnson waited until MacDonald was made Chief Justice and then arranged, so Fleming thought, to have wires sent that opened with the Cubs-Philly matter and which was never referred to again. The real purpose of the investigation to go through with the conspirator plans and wreck the Sox so that they could purchase the plant.

Landis said he would run down all the telegrams and how sent and said it was a hell of a state of affairs when a judge on the bench could be secured to work with a matter of this kind and that he (Landis) would go to the bottom of this, Landis referring to Johnson as a sonofabitch.

(Harry's pleasure was unfounded. He would find soon enough that Landis referred to *everybody* as a sonofabitch.)

Johnson hadn't given up, even though it should have been obvious to even him by this time that he was badly outgunned.

As so frequently happens, Johnson turned out to be the best weapon Landis had, for by challenging the new Commissioner's authority he allowed Landis to define it.

With an American League meeting coming up, Harry hears that Harvey Woodruff, "Johnson's confidant," was going around saying that "Johnson was in the saddle and would ride regardless of conditions" because Johnson still had his 5 votes.

Johnson's basic error was that while he did have the 5 votes in league affairs, he did not have them where Landis was concerned. The Loyal 5 had accepted Landis, with his increased authority, and they were not going to renege. When the new major-league agreement was forced to a vote in the afternoon session—after Johnson had stalled through the morning session—it was confirmed by a 7–1 vote with Clark Griffith casting the sole vote against it.

Writes Harry: "Johnson by repeated attacks on the major agreements hoped to upset baseball conditions so that Landis would give up in disgust."

The great confrontation scene took place, finally, on January 12, 1921, when Landis presided over his first joint meeting:

> Johnson by the work of Killilea assisted by Herrmann changed the original agreement as to the powers of the Commissioner and endeavored to curtail the powers of Landis instead of action to one of recommendation only. Landis apprised by Dreyfuss of this in advance was primed and ready and he went over the matter in a talk that left no room for doubt in any one's mind. He told them that someone had changed and taken from the Commissioner the right to deal with all officials and that he would not stand for it as far as he was concerned.

That was all that was needed. A man with power has only to assert it. The first time Landis was challenged, he just stepped on the opposition and crushed it. Landis had taken Johnson's little plot to limit his authority and used it to establish his total control over baseball. Just as simple as that. Johnson could rant and rave around the countryside for the rest of his term—and he did—but Landis was firmly in control.

In the race against Johnson, Comiskey had made every post a winning one. But you can't teach an Old Roman new ways. His troubles, it became clear quickly enough, had taught him absolutely nothing. In a loose page of notes which Harry thoughtfully inserted into his journal we find, "Report that Pyotts signed [Dickie] Kerr for $5000. Took matter up with Landis."

In his notes for January, 1921, this unspeakable act of treachery is explained a little further:

> Talked with Landis about Kerr matter. Explained fully Billy Nieson in same so he would know him in any future plays. Landis ruled that if Kerr matter came before him for consideration he would rule that Kerr was obligated to play under contract signed in 1920.

In 1919, Dickie Kerr, as a rookie, had finished with a 13-8 record. In the Series, with his teammates throwing games all around him, he had won two beautifully pitched games.

Turning to Harry's salary list for the 1920 season, we find that Kerr has been rewarded with a big $4,500 salary. We also find the marginal note that the White Sox also have an option to sign him again in 1921 at the same figure.

Kerr's record in 1920 was 20-8. When Cicotte and Williams were suspended toward the end of the season, Kerr automatically became the ace of the staff. Nevertheless, Comiskey and Grabiner are insisting quite obviously upon holding Kerr to the option agreement for the coming year.

Billy Nieson was a guy who operated semi-pro ball clubs around Chicago. Which means that the semi-pros were willing to pay Dickie Kerr $500 more than a big-league team which had just finished, despite its troubles, the most successful season in its history.

Kerr did sign with the White Sox finally, and with the bare

bones of the old White Sox team he finished with a remarkable 19-17 record. Comiskey rewarded him by offering him a contract which Kerr found so attractive that he decided to play semi-pro ball back home in Texas.

There is one final note in Harry's journal that is of interest to us:

> Saw Landis regarding Johnson's statement. Suggested to refrain from giving interview in answer. He asked regarding players that I knew that were even mentioned in any wrongdoing so told him complete list on page 27. Also the report of games of final Cleve-St. Louis series, 1920; Cleve-Detroit series, 1920 and action of Gedeon.

The list on page 27 contains 27 names including two of my boyhood idols, Alexander and Maranville. Say it ain't so, Alex. Say it ain't so, Rabbit.

But the most interesting name of all is one that nobody would recognize. Packard. The record book shows a Eugene Milo Packard, a pitcher who had knocked around from club to club, ending with the Phillies in 1919.

Opposite Packard's name are the chilling words: "1918 Series fixer."

Oh boy. That was the Series where the players struck before the start of the fifth game for a higher share of the receipts.

Looking back through the years, you have to give Landis credit for the way he handled the swamp of corruption into which he stepped. Instead of setting out to make himself out to be a knight on white horseback, which is exactly what his critics have always accused him of doing, he did no more than the bare minimum that was necessary. He contented himself with barring the Black Sox fixers for life (even though they were all found not guilty of something or other when they finally came to trial). Gedeon never played again and neither did Hendrix. Presumably they were not offered contracts by their respective teams. As for the rest of it, he simply drew a line between the present and the past, granting an amnesty—if not necessarily immunity—to all who had sinned under the previous regime.

Landis' great wisdom was in understanding that any attempt to investigate all of the gambling and fixing of the past would not only be impossible from a purely administrative standpoint, but would open up a can of worms that would be eating away at baseball for the next decade.

He was quite content to let the skeletons rattle unheard in the closet and to fall upon anybody else who offended with a swift and dictatorial and unswerving punishment.

There was always the feeling that his sympathies lay with the players, even though they were the only ones who were punished. A player in trouble might tremble when called to Landis' office but he would leave with his problem solved and the final Landis admonition: "Don't go to those owners if you get into trouble, come to me. I'm your friend; they're no good." The happiest times of his life seemed to come when he was setting players free from their contracts.

In an indirect way he did punish Comiskey. When the players were found not guilty there is no reason to doubt that Comiskey would have been happy to welcome them back to the fold. It was Landis who moved swiftly to bar them.

It was not until 1927 when Cobb and Speaker, the two aging giants-become-managers, were accused of gambling on ball games that Risberg and Gandil, who were by then beyond the age where they could ever get back into baseball, came to Landis and blew the whistle on the 1917 incident about the $50 assessments on the White Sox players.

Landis, treating it as a new story, heard the evidence and was finally forced to rule publicly that he was not concerned with anything that had happened before he took office.

But Harry's journal tells us that the story had hardly been as complete a surprise to Landis as he pretended. On the same sheet where the Kerr matter is brought up, Harry wrote:

Austrian advises regarding Schalk-Landis conference.
And then: Feb 16, Schalk was out to Comiskey Park. Matter with
Landis regarding donation of $50 each by Sox in 1917.

As for Cobb and Speaker, they both lost their jobs as managers and shifted to other teams, Cobb going to Connie Mack
and Speaker to Clark Griffith. Both finished out their careers
as players in something less than disgrace.

Looking back at the Black Sox scandal from this comfortable distance it becomes easy to take another drag on your
cigarette and sneer that everybody did their best to cover up.
Everybody. From the Commissioner on down. The only figure
in all of baseball who did set out to expose the fix was Ban
Johnson, and he did it in his own way, in his own time and for
his own selfish reasons. His one great handicap—and his ultimate failure—was that his own record for dealing with fixes was
so sorry that he couldn't afford to really bust it open.

Lucky for us, we're living in more enlightened times, right?
It couldn't happen today, right? They were a particularly vile
kind of people in those days living in a particularly corrupt age,
right? Or, as our more sensitive historians always tell us, and
I quote: The nation, tired of the restrictions and idealisms of
war, loosed the bonds of conscience and suffered a moral
collapse.

So how come the gamblers were gambling and the players
were dumping in 1917 and 1918 while we were in the midst of
all that gallantry and idealism?

We're talking here about human nature which is unchang-
ing, not about history, which is only a contract negotiated by
the Alfred Austrians of the intellectual community. It is the nature of any organization in trouble to cover up its sins, to white-
wash itself when exposed and, in the final extremity, to try to
claim virtue for cleaning its own house when the Sanitation
Department is knocking at the door. Or have you forgotten
good old Charlie Van Doren, the intellectual's contribution to
the high moral climate of our own time?

Not too many months ago, we saw football's bright young Commissioner give this generation's best imitation of Red Grange as he weaved brilliantly through a broken field and—while everybody in football held their breath—got away with suspending two players for one year. One of the players had been gambling in the open for years and the other had made his announcement over television. In case I haven't made the point clear, the bright young Commissioner did only what had to be done.

I heard no great outcry from the press or the public to dig deeper, ever deeper. All I heard were a few stray attacks on Rozelle for suspending those two nice young fellows.

Anybody who thinks the moral climate of the United States today is higher than it was in 1919 hasn't looked out the window lately. Why, some of our more respected academicians could steal the scar right off Al Capone's face. Poor Al never did have the advantage of a higher education.

12

☻ ☻ ☻

The Carpetbaggers

I HAVE occasionally disagreed with baseball operators—publicly, privately and semiprivately, in print and out, in summer and in winter, in sickness and in health. I have called them backward, unimaginative and feckless. I have even been known to assail a few of the more worthy as greedy and rapacious. So how come they don't like me?

Despite these quarrels and an occasional mild rejoinder on their part—like kicking me out of baseball—I have never, until these past couple of years, felt called upon to apologize for having been associated with the National Game.

I have always believed that, at bottom, the operators did have some basic affection for and responsibility to the game and, when pushed to the wall, even some small affection for the customers who support it. It took the newest members of the exalted order of franchise owners, the Carpetbaggers of Milwaukee, to disabuse me. I was, quite frankly, incredulous when they first began to maneuver to pull their franchise out of Milwaukee. I was even more aghast when they were joined by Charles O. Finley, the Grand Old Man of Kansas City. Finley has cast his eyes southward to Atlanta, westward toward Oakland and now, it seems, northward to Milwaukee and its about-to-be-vacated County Stadium.

The boys are beginning to play it for farce. While the Carpetbaggers are being held prisoner in Milwaukee by a court order, Finley is aching to break in.

The Carpetbaggers did meet with some unhappiness in Milwaukee. They tried to foist off a stock issue on the public, and the public didn't bite. A non-biting public is to be deplored by anybody with an open mind.

They also say they lost around half a million dollars. They didn't. The loss was a bookkeeping loss only. On actual operations they made themselves a few bucks. But think how it must wound the ego of ambitious young men to have to admit to failure.

And then there was television. The income wasn't enough to satisfy them, a common-enough complaint. (My doctor tells me it's been going around lately.) The Braves' sponsor had a reasonable solution. He would pay them more money.

The Carpetbaggers had another solution. Their solution was to deprive Milwaukee of its franchise, leaving the good burghers with their park, a few tired memories and a bitter void. But the town will survive. It will survive quite nicely. The real loser will be the game of baseball. For what they are striking at, in this latest testimonial to the power of pure greed, is the very core of baseball's strength, the customers' feeling of identification with the ball club that presumably belongs to them and represents their city. Baseball's greatest asset, whether it knows it or not, is the sense of continuity that comes not only from the record books but from a long personal association.

Baseball's unique possession, the real source of our strength, is the fan's memory of the times his daddy took him to the game to see the great players of his youth. Whether he remembers it or not, the excitement of those hours, the step they represented in his own growth and the part those afternoons—even *one* afternoon—played in his relationship with his own father is bound up in his feeling toward the local ball club and toward the game. When he takes his own son to the game, as his father once took him, there is a spanning of the generations that is warm and rich and—if I may use the word—lovely.

What do you think made baseball the National Game? A geometric pattern? A few fairly simple techniques in throwing, catching or hitting a ball? If all the record books disappeared tomorrow, baseball would disappear with them. If the memories of our youth disappeared, we would look upon baseball as a rather dull game, hardly worth an afternoon of our lives. The secret ingredient is what the customer brings into the park with him. We put three dimensions in the field, and the customer supplies the fourth.

It takes a few years to reach three generations. Baseball has done a remarkable job of throwing it all away overnight. They began to throw it away when O'Malley took the Dodgers into Los Angeles. The job will be completed—utterly and irrevocably—when the Milwaukee Carpetbaggers go marching into Atlanta (a most appropriate city for Carpetbaggers) singing "We Shall Overcome."

It is gone. Greed took it away. Stupidity took it away. Silence —the silence of the operators who knew what was happening and chose not to fight—took it away.

As a hustler, you have to recognize that it is gone. You cannot insult your fans' intelligence by trying to sell them the idea that they have anything more than a ticket buyer's interest in the club. I have never been a believer in wrapping the game around the American Flag. Bogus patriotism is disgusting and, even worse, unprofitable. We have become too sophisticated for that. I did always try to create the feeling that we were all one big happy family, that we were all out to have a good time together. It was good business, yes; it also made the job more enjoyable.

It would be indecent to do it now, and no hustler has to submit himself to indecencies in order to make money. I would also run the risk of being wafted out of town on the waves of laughter. Scorn is the one emotion the hustler cannot survive.

The business has changed. It is possible that the television rights and the Big League label are worth more, in dollars and cents, than a mood and an attitude. I don't think so. A label wears thin and TV can always dump baseball. (Baseball happens to be a bargain. It supplies a daily 3-hour show, and provides its own location, its own actors and its own prepackaged audience. Television has to provide nothing except the cameras and the cameramen.) Times change. Tastes alter. If the ratings fall, TV will drop baseball without a qualm. Baseball has thrown away the permanent and is dependent upon the temporary.

If baseball ever does go under, future historians have only to turn to the story of baseball in the 1960s to find, in capsule form—encapsulated greed—the whole story of The Time of the Carpetbaggers.

After the carpetbaggers, the locust?

In order to understand why the Milwaukee move is different from all previous moves, we had better take a brief refresher course in the history of the winged franchise. Baseball has always been seasonal; it is only in the past decade that it has become migratory.

The man who started it all, the real villain of the piece, is me. (How many times do I have to tell you? Do as I say, not as I do.) I encouraged Milwaukee to build its stadium on the guarantee that I would either come charging in with the St. Louis Browns franchise or force Lou Perini, who owned the territorial rights, to move in with the Boston Braves.

In 1948, the Braves had won their first pennant since Rabbit Maranville was a bunny, and had set attendance records by going over the million mark for three straight years. By 1952, their attendance had dropped to 280,000, which is downright impossible.

The Braves moved to Milwaukee and immediately drew 1,826,000, a National League record. In case the point wasn't clear, Milwaukee went over the 2,000,000 mark for the next four years, climaxed by a record-breaking 2,215,000 in 1957. In their first six years, their average attendance was over two million. It was "The Miracle of Milwaukee," and nothing like it had ever been seen before.

Four years later, the attendance had dropped to 766,000 and Perini, who by this time had a keen instinct for a developing disaster, was looking for the way out.

This brings up a point that is occasionally overlooked. People who can operate can operate, and people who can't operate can't operate. Either Boston and Milwaukee were bad baseball towns with a freak attendance during those good years or they were good baseball towns which were ruined by inept operation. The kindest thing that can be said about Perini and his minions is that they proved rather conclusively that they had no capacity whatsoever for harnessing the enthusiasm of the winning years to carry them through the poor ones.

Is there any real reason to believe that the Milwaukee Carpetbaggers, who came into baseball for a fast buck, will view the world of baseball any differently in Atlanta than they do in Milwaukee? If they are bad for the game in Milwaukee—and I believe they are a disaster—they will be just as bad for the game in Atlanta.

Phase One of the floating franchises, then, covers the years 1953–1955. The teams were the Boston Braves, the St. Louis Browns and the Philadelphia Athletics.

The pattern was consistent, and rather rudimentary. Despite the understandable unhappiness in the cities that were losing a team, it was generally conceded that the moves were logical and probably inevitable. Under the changing economy, there was no room for two teams in St. Louis and Boston, or even in Philadelphia where the Mack boys had hastened their day of departure by providing nothing resembling a working model of a good operation.

Even the opposition ran to pattern. The King of the Mountain, in each city, was a man of inherited wealth: Tom Yawkey, Gussie Busch and Bob Carpenter.

No real controversy entered the scene, then, until O'Malley moved to Los Angeles in 1958. Here we were confronted with a situation that was unique and, even as we look back today, incredible. The Brooklyn Dodgers were a winning team and a profitable one. The Brooklyn fans had supported the team when it was a loser, and they had supported it so well as a winner that over the previous decade the Dodgers had been second only to the Yankees in attendance and profits.

The Brooklyn fans had become the symbol of the baseball fanatic. They were recognized by ballplayers throughout the league as the most knowledgeable in the country. The Dodgers were a part of the city's identification, a part of its pulse beat. The loyal rooters never doubted for a moment that their beloved Bums were as much a part of their heritage as Prospect Park. They discovered they were wrong. The Dodgers were only a piece of merchandise that passed from hand to hand. The Dodgers, it seemed, belonged to one man, to dispose of as he saw fit.

Walter O'Malley came into the Brooklyn organization as a lawyer, with a meager knowledge of baseball. But he was a lawyer with an instinct for politics and a genius for high finance.

In the confrontation between O'Malley the lawyer, and Brooklyn the borough, the debate was sharpened. If a lawyer who has come into control of the ball club wants to go elsewhere, do the fans who have supported the team and supported it well through almost a century have any vested interest that should be protected, either legally, in the courts, or morally, through baseball's own governing body?

Baseball's answer came back loud and clear. "Get lost, ya bum!"

In Phase Number Two, the floating crap game has begun. In the moving of franchises from this point on, the most important consideration is going to be the personal advantages that are going to accrue to the owner. O'Malley's flight to Los Angeles had nothing to do with league balance. It was a land grab.

It had been established from the first that the way for a city to get a team was to build a municipal stadium and guarantee a minimum attendance for the first two or three years.

Walter O'Malley's sights were set considerably higher. In his early negotiations with the mayor of Los Angeles, O'Malley discovered that the city was willing to give him real estate. Not build a park on which he would pay rent, but give him—*give* him—300 acres of choice real estate just outside the city of Los Angeles. Real estate that was worth more than the club itself and, in the long run, possibly more than the worth of all the clubs in baseball put together.

Walter O'Malley showed his colleagues how it was possible to use the ball club as a lever to extract real estate.

If O'Malley's rewards were so much greater, so were his problems. I keep reading these days that the city of New York built a park for the Mets after it had refused to build one for the Dodgers. That isn't true. New York offered to build O'Malley the same park, at the same site where Shea Stadium now stands.

But O'Malley was interested in real estate. Once he found what they were willing to give him in Los Angeles, not all the king's horses or all the king's men could have kept him in quaint, beloved old Brooklyn which he loved so well.

As transparent as it all was, O'Malley could make his arguments too. He could claim that it was necessary to move, unless he got his new park, because—and this gets funny here—he could not hope to compete with the unbelievable attendance they were drawing in Milwaukee. "They can use all that money to sign new players," O'Malley would say, "and in a few years they'll be winning all the pennants instead of us."

But even with the Giants leaving New York too, baseball could make the argument that it was still not leaving New York without baseball, since New York still had the finest team of all, the Yankees. Never mind that the loyal Dodger fan wouldn't be caught dead entering Yankee Stadium. Personal prejudices were no concern of baseball's.

There was also the promise, tacit to be sure, that New York would get another National League team as soon as there was an expansion program. If the second justification was in direct conflict with the first, so what? Nobody really believed what they were saying, or expected anybody else to believe them.

The logical rejoinder was that the National League should leave their teams in New York and expand into Los Angeles and San Francisco.

The answer to that is that the league wasn't doing any planning at all. O'Malley was doing the planning. Where was Warren Giles? Why, Giles was running interference for O'Malley. What else would you expect Giles to be doing? When Giles gets frustrated, he gives his umpires a bad time—the equivalent of kicking the dog. He has never been known to contradict a club owner, and he would rather switch to the American League than fight O'Malley.

And what about the legendary Ford Frick? Here was the time for the Commissioner, who presumably represents the interests of the fan, to step in and call a halt. You know better than that! The legendary Ford Frick had assumed his customary stance in times of crisis. He was locked in his closet, working on his eagerly awaited autobiography, *Armageddon Is a League Affair.*

The message to the fan was that all the fine talk that they have any rights or interest or claim upon their team was just conversation for the marks and the suckers.

This year, that statement of principle has been made even clearer. If the Brooklyn fans were the best over a long period of time, the Milwaukee fans were the best over a short distance of ground. For their pains, they are getting exactly what the Brooklyn fans got. And exactly what it seemed the fans of Cleveland (who still hold the American league attendance records) were going to get. Don't tell us what you did five years ago. What have you done for us *lately?*

Phase Number Three has been the most disturbing of all. The winter of 1964–65 was marked—*scarred* might be a better word —by threats of moves from Cleveland, Kansas City and Milwaukee. All three clubs have one thing in common. They are the only team in town. If they go, big-league baseball goes with them.

To make it more outrageous still, Milwaukee and Kansas City are both cities that have been moved *into*. The picture of the traveling carnival and the floating crap game has come unmistakably into focus. Swoop into town, bleed it dry, fold your tent and beat the cops to the nearest freight yard.

If Joseph E. Levine wants to film a horror story, I suggest that he take on "The Rape of Milwaukee," a tale of high intrigue in which the city of Milwaukee could easily be portrayed by Carroll Baker dressed in a Tyrolean hat.

The prospective departure from Milwaukee is, in its own little way, the most disturbing yet. Here you find a group of would-be hotshots, having no connection with the city and no particular background in baseball, coming in to make a quick buck. If their personal fortune depends upon taking a team away from the fans who had been the most delirious and openhanded of all time . . . well, that's free enterprise, folks.

To make it even more outrageous, Milwaukee has supported the team quite well by normal standards. The Milwaukee attendance in 1964—910,000—was quite good, particularly in the latter part of the season when the team began to improve. When you consider that the Braves had fallen apart because of bad trades, the most galling thing of all to baseball fans, and that absolutely no attempt was made to entertain them, the attendance held up surprisingly well. John McHale, the general manager who made the bad trades (just as he had made the trades that killed Detroit), seems to be a nice enough guy but he is dull, dull, dull. McHale is an ex-ballplayer who became a front-office figure overnight, another indication of the strange and wonderful way the game is run.

Lou Perini's role in the Rape of Milwaukee is bewildering. There is no reason, I suppose, why the man who had taken a club out of Boston, where he had roots, would hesitate to take the club out of Milwaukee where he had none. But Perini, the man who had profited so tremendously by those record-breaking years, seems to have gone out of his way to demonstrate that he owed them nothing.

Don't let the Carpetbaggers blind you to Perini's role in all of this. The Perini Corp. still owns almost 10 percent of the club, and Perini himself is a member of the Board of Directors.

Above and beyond that, it was Perini who seems to have made the first move toward Atlanta. It is definitely on the record that McHale visited Atlanta during the season of 1962, just before he signed the final 3-year lease to play at the County Stadium. The lease that was running out had run for 10 years. McHale wasn't signing for another 10 years, though. Three years was as far as he was willing to go. As it turned out, he went one year too far.

By this time, it was already known that the Braves were on the market.

There is no doubt at all that there were offers from perhaps half a dozen Milwaukee syndicates, because three groups that I remember contacted me about running the team for them. They weren't insubstantial figures either. Joe Uehlein of the Schlitz Beer family was one of the interested parties. By coincidence, I bumped into him one night in Rochester, Minn., and we had dinner together. Joe was willing to work out all the arrangements so that I would have something like 30 percent ownership, but I had to tell him that I didn't feel you could go back to a city a second time. You can't go home again, because you're in the position of competing against yourself, against the *memory* of yourself and, worst of all, against an *idealized* memory of yourself.

Now, Perini had been having his troubles with the county board over the rental figure, and perhaps he was incensed that the citizens had stopped supporting the team in the record-breaking manner to which he had become accustomed. On the other hand, this was a city that had welcomed him when he came limping into town, and it had hardly left either him or his construction company any poorer.

Perini had kept me and the Browns out of Milwaukee. He

had made a fortune there. Although, it should be added, he has given much of that fortune back to the city in the form of charity. Still, one might have thought, by standards of ordinary street-corner loyalty, that if he wanted to get rid of the team he'd sell to local people. He didn't. Instead, he almost pointedly sold the club to a syndicate composed of half a dozen young hustlers from Chicago, led by Bill Bartholomay.

I know most of them. They are all from Chicago and all cut from the same bolt of tweed. They are the pampered sons of wealthy families: the ivy-type education, the finance-oriented backgrounds, the family firm. They are all so similar, so indistinguishable really, that there is no particular value to listing them by name. They have one final characteristic in common too: the sum of their total knowledge of baseball is zero.

No, wait a minute. There is one exception, Del Coleman, who runs the Seeburg Jukebox Company. Coleman made his own money and he has a sizable personal income. Coleman is like the social-climbing wife who is accepted into a charity organization run by the socialites because there has to be someone, after all, to do the hard, dirty work. Although Coleman is a more able guy than the rest of them put together, it seems to flatter his ego to be allowed to associate with them.

It was Don Reynolds who came to Hank Greenberg and me back around 1960 with an offer to buy our 54 percent interest in the White Sox. We had been unable to buy Chuck Comiskey's minority interest (of great importance to us for reasons that will become apparent when we get into the Milwaukee financial structure), but these guys did not seem to have any doubt that Chuck would be more receptive to them. These guys, you have to understand, feel they are *entitled* to have everything fall into place for them, because it has been their experience—as it had been Gussie Busch's—that the lower classes, for reasons undoubtedly having to do with the wisdom of the Divinity, bow down gratefully and low.

Where Chuck Comiskey was concerned, they very well may have worked out something at that.

Even after we turned Reynolds down flat, he seemed to have told his pals he still thought we'd sell. At any rate, his son was around letting everybody know that his daddy had bought the White Sox.

When Hank and I sold our stock to Art Allyn Jr., they made the same offer to him and got turned down again. That didn't discourage them. They went to Chuck Comiskey and bought the minority 46 percent from him. By refusing to sell to us—or at least to sell enough to give us the 80 percent we needed to reorganize—Chuck had cost the club a tidy little $1,300,000 in taxes. The Bartholomay group quite obviously felt they would wage a battle of nerves against Arthur and force him to sell his majority holdings to them.

Boy, did they underestimate Arthur. Giving them their due, they were not alone. Everybody in Chicago had underestimated Arthur for years. Including me.

Arthur's father, Art Allyn Sr., was one of the fabulous figures of Chicago. Art was a big, jovial, happy man with a fringe of white hair. He smoked a big cigar, wore a flower in his lapel and had a big booming laugh. He looked like Scattergood Baines, and he was a complete delight.

He was also widely known as the most astute financier west of New York. He had single-handedly built A. C. Allyn Co. into one of the most successful investment companies in the country. If there was any big deal in the works around Chicago, you could be sure that Art was in it.

Art had helped me put all my deals together beginning with the purchase of the Cleveland Indians in 1946. In Chicago, where he had something like 20 percent of our 54 percent, he had asked us to put the stock in Arthur Jr.'s name and give him a place on the Board of Directors.

As you may have gathered by now, the unpredictability of the human being has always fascinated and amused me. To find illogic in a logical man, to find the screw turned slightly awry where you'd least expect to, is one of the wonders of life. Great men—and Art Sr. was a great man—are more unpredictable than average men. Their follies are greater than the ordinary man's follies and their idiosyncrasies are more idiosyncratic.

Art Allyn had his one great idiosyncrasy. Chicago's great financier hated real estate. Hated it! He had once come out of a deal as the owner of the Sherman Hotel, and his money had been tied up for years before he was able to work anything out.

The White Sox owned Comiskey Park, a situation which made him most unhappy. If he had his way, we'd have given it away to some unsuspecting street peddler. Hank Greenberg would get Chuck Comiskey on the edge of selling every now and then, and Art would always tell him, "Give him the ball park, too. The ball park's no good. It's real estate. Throw it in." His attitude always seemed to be that it would serve Chuck right.

Well, let me tell you something. Big Henry is no slouch when it comes to high finance either. Once Hank got himself involved in operations, he studied finances with the same loving care and dedication with which he used to study pitchers. Big Henry wasn't about to give Chuck Comiskey any ball park.

(Art Jr. put a $3,000,000 mortgage on the park when he took over, so you can see that it was not totally worthless.)

The point I am making is that when you talked about Art Allyn in Chicago, everybody knew whom you meant. You didn't have to say *Senior*. That other Art Allyn—he was just a quiet, pleasant guy, in his early forties, who hung around.

Shortly after Art Allyn died, I became ill, and Arthur Jr. bought us out. The Carpetbaggers, in their debut as financiers, were among the first to discover that Arthur Jr. had some steel in him.

Arthur Allyn Jr. is, in his own quiet way, as intriguing a figure as his daddy. For all Art's surface mildness, the man who spent so much of his life practically blotted from sight by the shadow of his father is out to show Chicago—and, more to the point, himself—that he is fully capable of equaling his father as an operator and—yes!—of eclipsing him. He could not have found a more perfect instrument than the White Sox. For one thing, the purchase of the Sox has been, I am sure, the best investment he has made. For another, it is a business which automatically draws public notice upon himself. Most important of all, though, he runs no risk whatsoever of being compared unfavorably to his father because his father was never more than a minority stockholder in the club and a relatively silent one.

Art can therefore compete against his father without feeling that he is being disrespectful to his memory and what more could any man ask?

He has been far more effective, frankly, than I for one would have expected. He has been so effective, in fact, that it is not beyond the realm of possibility that if the Yankees' demise continues, Arthur will end up as the strong man of the league, which—taking nothing away from Arthur—is a rough indication of the competition.

The most interesting part of it all is that Phil Wrigley, across town, has always been influenced just as strongly by the shadow of his own powerful and brilliant father, and he has reacted in a completely opposite way. Mr. Wrigley, who could have been the strong man of the National League at the flex of his little finger, deliberately eschewed all power. Mr. Wrigley has spent his life running away from any comparison with his father. The Cubs were left to him in his father's will, as a special bequest, and while he has accepted his father's wishes dutifully, he has sometimes left me with the impression that he has taken it on as a particularly oppressive burden. Almost as a penance.

So while the Carpetbaggers may have thought they had a little lamb in Arthur, perfect for their purposes, they were really nothing more than targets for Arthur to practice on, perfect for his purpose. Arthur told them quite bluntly that he not only had no intention of selling them his stock but that he had no intention of voting any stock dividends.

This left the Carpetbaggers with a couple of million dollars tied up in the White Sox, earning nothing. The only comfort they did have was the prestige and publicity that came from being stockholders in a big-league club. But when they showed up at Sarasota in the spring ready to cavort with the ballplayers, Arthur barred them from the field. Your little boy could go out on the field but they couldn't.

Here you have as good a definition of power as any. The man with the stock can go out onto the field and sweat like one of the hired hands. The manager will even tell him he has all the natural ability to have made a great third baseman. If you haven't got the power you can only sulk in the stands and adjust your cap (since Arthur couldn't prevent them from buying caps at the concession stand) in a way that will lead people to think—you hope—that you're an athlete.

Arthur had them boxed in nicely.

The Carpetbaggers came back from spring training somewhat subdued, and within a month or so they sold their stock to Arthur for the same price they had paid Comiskey.

Actually, their money had been eaten into in three ways. They had to pay bank interest (since it was, of course, mostly borrowed money), the legal fees had been considerable, and they had lost the profits they could have made if the money had been invested elsewhere.

With this triumph behind them, they brushed themselves off and, ever undaunted, looked around for new fields to conquer. Just to the north, there were those rumors that Lou Perini, the Lochinvar from the East, wanted out.

The financing of the Milwaukee purchase is of interest to us here because it is directly related to the move to Atlanta.

The Carpetbaggers bought the ball club from the Perini Corp. for $5,737,847. With the brokerage fee, the assumption of existing liabilities and the agreement to turn back to the Perini Corp. some money that was due, the total cost of the purchase came to $6,218,480. That's the figure we will be working with from here on in.

And now for the financing: To pay for the club, they were able to borrow $3,000,000 from the First Wisconsin National

Bank *on behalf of the club.* I would assume that Lou Perini helped them get that loan.

They also borrowed $900,000 from the Marshall & Ilsley Bank on a 120-day note.

Put in general terms, they had mortgaged the team to the extent of $3,000,000. The other $900,000 was an unsecured note, but it too had been borrowed on behalf of the Milwaukee Braves, not on behalf of the Carpetbaggers themselves.

As soon as they reorganized and formed their own company, the Carpetbaggers sold back 15.4 percent of the stock to the Perini Corporation for $310,000.

When everything shakes out, we find that the Carpetbaggers had a personal investment of $1,700,000, borrowed from the Chicago banks and probably guaranteed by Del Coleman. (The other $300,000-odd, you will remember, is in the form of liabilities and deferred assets already on the books.)

Not a thing wrong about this, students. On the contrary, I want you to absorb these figures because it is the proper way to buy a ball club or anything else. The more you can borrow in the name of the company, the greater percentage of the total stock you are able to buy for a limited amount of money. This is known, in dugouts and locker rooms throughout the land, as leverage.

But the Carpetbaggers' financing has another twist. The 120-day note was due on May 1, 1963, which seemed to mean that our boys would still have to go out and borrow another $900,000 on their *own* names. That kind of thing doesn't help the leverage at all.

But they had that figured out too. Their plan was to pay it back and give themselves a little working capital by selling 115,000 shares of stock to the citizens of Wisconsin at $10 a share. (The same price they and the Perini Corp. had paid.) It is plain that Perini had to be in on this phase of the financing from the beginning since the new stock was diluting the Perini Corp.'s share of ownership to 9.8 percent. The public would own 36.4 percent and the Carpetbaggers would still have a controlling interest of 53.8 percent.

It was confidently anticipated, apparently, that the fans would be so overjoyed at this opportunity to become part-owners of their ball club that they would snap up the stock. From everything I heard, the Carpetbaggers fully expected the offering to be oversubscribed.

It didn't happen that way at all. Their basic premise about the stock issue was just as bad as their basic premise that Arthur Allyn was a lamb.

As much as I hate to say I-told-you-so, I said at the time that they'd be lucky to sell 10 percent. They did better than that. They sold something around 15 percent.

Chicago is the last place on earth anybody should come from if he wants to sell stock in Milwaukee. Milwaukee has such an inferiority complex where Chicago is concerned that anybody from Chicago is suspect. If you do have the misfortune to be from Chicago, it would be just as well if you are not part of a phalanx of polished young financiers. The whole deal had the uncomfortable smell, to Milwaukee, of the city slickers coming in to take over the country yokels.

There was another handicap that was almost as bad. Perini had *already* given the Milwaukee citizenry an opportunity to buy a financial interest in the team. When the Perini Corp. went public, he had put the ball club into the corporation as a way of giving the offering a touch of glamour.

The Perini Corp. came out at the end of the bull market in new issues, however, and was caught in the subsequent slide. The issue was offered at something like 13, opened at around 11, and very quickly plummeted to 3½.

Anybody who had wanted to own a piece of the Braves had already bought it. All he had to show for it was a loss. Any impulse to buy it a second time was not difficult to restrain.

This was a blow to the Carpetbaggers. Under the terms of the stock issue, they were obliged to buy any of the stock that had not been snapped up, which meant they had to run back to the Chicago money marts to borrow another million dollars or so at what I would assume were considerably less than prime rates. (Even if they had not been forced to buy the stock, they'd have had to dig up the money in order to pay off that 120-day note.)

The stock issue laid such a bomb that it should have been obvious to the Carpetbaggers that it had not been a very bright idea from the beginning. It seemed to convince them, instead, that Milwaukee was no longer interested in supporting a big-league team. That's not an unnatural conclusion to reach, I suppose, once you have assumed that you and the team are synonymous. If they are not interested in supporting you and your stock issue they are not interested in supporting you and your team. It is quite possible that the Carpetbaggers, in a pet, turned their shiny eyes toward Atlanta the next morning. Why not? Perini and McHale would already have the preliminary information to pass on to them.

The original plans were for the city of Atlanta to fix up old Ponce de Leon Park so that the Braves could move in the following year, 1964, while the new Municipal Stadium was under construction. (Just as San Francisco had played in the old minor-league park and Los Angeles had played screen-o in the Coliseum while their parks were being built.) A commitment was made to pay Bill McKechnie and his minor-league team $250,000 for territorial rights, and arrangements were made to indemnify the league.

I can't swear that the contracts with Atlanta were ever signed but I do know that they were drawn up. The way I know indicates why it is so difficult to keep anything secret in baseball.

The stock issue bombed in April. In July, a New York lawyer with whom I am friendly phoned to pass on a piece of information he thought might interest me. He had been in Atlanta on routine business, he said, and on the day he was leaving he was having a farewell lunch with four or five attorneys from the firm with whom he had been dealing.

With lunch over, they had immediately got up to leave, explaining—by way of apology—that they had to hurry back to the office to get the papers ready for the Milwaukee move to Atlanta.

I immediately called Russ Lynch, who had been the sports editor of the Milwaukee *Journal* when I was there. Russ, a close friend, had become the paper's conservation writer.

Russ found the story exceedingly difficult to believe. Rumors had been floating around for some time, he told me, and he assumed they had simply floated, in somewhat exaggerated form, over to me in Easton, Maryland. "Russell," I said, "you can take my word for it. They're going to move that ball club. Unless somebody does something, the papers are going to be signed within a day or two. I'm calling to warn you that you had better mobilize your forces at the *Journal*."

It pains me to say that because they know me so well in Milwaukee, I am always suspect. "What's his angle?" the management of the paper wanted to know. "What does he want out of this?"

I tried to tell him that I didn't want to see the team leave Milwaukee because I have some thought of getting back into baseball myself some day and I could see where this constant moving, this lack of stability—to say nothing about the impression being created of a certain lack of honor—would have to hurt everybody.

Having helped to get the County Stadium built, and having coerced the Braves into moving in, I also felt some responsibility for seeing that the stadium wasn't left to rot and turn to weeds.

I called Bobby Uehlein of Schlitz, who were about to take over the TV sponsorship. Bobby Uehlein is on the Board of Directors of the First Wisconsin, where the Carpetbaggers have their loan (it is known around the Midwest as the Uehlein Bank) and even he couldn't believe they were dealing that seriously with Atlanta.

Nobody wanted to believe me. I must confess that my confidence in the therapeutic value of a hustler's life did not soar in those twenty-four hours.

By coincidence, the majors were holding a meeting in Chicago that same day, and Jim Enright, the fine sportswriter for the Chicago *American,* had picked up a tip of his own.

Enright ignored the meeting and concentrated on the projected move of Milwaukee. Nosing around among his sources, he learned that the Braves had talked to all the other clubs, off the record, and that they already had unanimous, if unofficial, permission to go to Atlanta.

The story came back to the Milwaukee *Journal* from Chicago. Now that they had the same story from what seemed to be a totally different source, they decided it had to be legitimate. Immediately, the *Journal* began their campaign to stop the Carpetbaggers from packing.

When you're in a situation where you know you want to leave a city, and yet you also know you're there for the rest of the year, you have to tread carefully. When O'Malley was in that spot, he kept saying how heartbroken he would be if an unfeeling city administration forced him to leave his beloved homeland. When L.A. officials, unable to contain themselves, kept breaking the news that the Dodgers were theirs, O'Malley would make clever comments about the reliability of politicians in an election year, sprinkling his words with grins and winks. It was a strategy which served O'Malley well. He never went on the record with a flat denial, and he conned everybody into thinking he was merely using Los Angeles to force the N.Y. politicians into giving him what he wanted.

The Carpetbaggers didn't have an O'Malley among them, of course, because the O'Malleys don't travel in packs. "We didn't buy the Milwaukee franchise to move it to Atlanta," Bartholomay said. "How do those things get started?"

Said McHale: "Absolutely nothing to it. We recognized when we bought the club that we had a rebuilding job to do. Any city which can average attendance around a million and a half for ten years as Milwaukee has, and average two million for five years, must certainly have a basic baseball interest. It's up to us to stir it up again."

The *Journal's* campaign apparently caused everybody to pull back. At the very least, it ended any thought of trying to move while there was only a minor-league stadium—and a bad one, at that—to play in. Even when a stadium miraculously began to go up in Atlanta, the Carpetbaggers continued to act as if the whole thing were a complete surprise to them. "I can't picture the Braves representing any city but Milwaukee," Bartholomay said. "We bought this club to play in Milwaukee, not in Atlanta, or Seattle or San Diego . . ."

On September 23, with the 1963 season coming to an end, McHale read a formal statement on behalf of the Carpetbaggers: "The Braves will be in Milwaukee today, tomorrow, next year and as long as we are welcome." To connoisseurs of this kind of thin-ice skating, it was apparent that the Carpetbaggers were going to set their own standards as to how many paying customers constituted a wholehearted welcome.

The following February, with another season about to begin, Bartholomay said, "We are not going elsewhere no matter what you hear. . . . I think the day of transferring franchises is pretty well over. . . ."

As the season progressed, it became apparent that while the Braves might not be going anywhere, some of their property was. For some reason, too baffling for the human mind, the Braves shipped some of their concession books down to Atlanta. Simultaneously, their own items at County Stadium began to carry the neat and simple word BRAVES instead of the complex and vulgar MILWAUKEE BRAVES.

The scoreboard for the Atlanta stadium, it was learned, was being decorated with Brave emblems, and the mayor of Atlanta had offered the contractor a $700,000 bonus to have the park ready by Opening Day of 1965.

If we didn't have Bartholomay's word for it, it would almost have seemed as if the Braves intended to transfer their franchise.

For their part, the Carpetbaggers continued to be bewildered by all the malicious talk. On July 2, McHale said, "We have definitely made no commitment of any kind to any other city. We have a commitment with the County extending through 1965 and we intend to keep it. . . . How many times do we have to keep answering?"

Two days later, the Braves cut off all promotions of their front office and maintenance personnel.

On July 14, Bartholomay, still puzzled by the ugly rumors, said, "Only our Board of Directors could make a meaningful commitment of this magnitude. This matter has never come up for a vote nor is it scheduled for any future board meeting."

In August, a wire service quoted an Atlanta advertising man as saying he had an appointment with representatives of the Braves to discuss sponsorship on Atlanta radio and television. "It's the wildest of the wild," said Bartholomay, dismissing the statement with the good-natured contempt it so obviously deserved.

"It's the same old story we've been hearing for months and years," said McHale, beginning to weary of his hopeless battle against calumny.

But somehow when the Schlitz Brewing Company offered the Braves a three-year radio and television deal, McHale sang a different song. "There are many other factors and considerations which we must study in the overall picture of major-league baseball here," he said.

The words may have been "Hello, Dolly" but the actions were "Goodnight, Irene, Goodnight."

As late as October 11, 1964, Bill Bartholomay could say, "We didn't buy the club to sell it and we didn't buy it to move it either. If it works out that way, it will be a personal disappointment."

Three days later, Bartholomay, not struggling noticeably to hide his personal disappointment, announced that the Braves were "considering" the move to Atlanta.

Who'd have thought it?

Actually, I had felt from the beginning that they would not be moving. At the end of July, when there was a flurry of stories about both Milwaukee and Cleveland pulling up stakes, I went to Milwaukee for ABC's *Wide World of Sports* and fearlessly predicted that neither team would be moving the next year.

I was right about Milwaukee, but I was right for all the wrong reasons. There was never any doubt that they could have been stopped in their tracks by even a token opposition within the National League, and I was sure that the opposition would come from Phil Wrigley. Mr. Wrigley has a vested interest in having a team in Milwaukee, because of the natural geographic rivalry. If you live in Chicago's northern suburbs, you can get to the Milwaukee ball park quicker than you can get to Wrigley Field.

Without the slightest attempt to exploit the rivalry, Milwaukee has outdrawn every other team in Chicago, except the Los Angeles Dodgers. The same situation obtains when the Cubs play in Milwaukee, since nothing makes a Milwaukeean happier than the sight of his team beating anything wearing a Chicago uniform.

But that wasn't really why I thought Mr. Wrigley would insert himself into the picture. Mr. Wrigley is a peculiar man. While he is not sensitive to promotion *per se*, he is most sensitive to public relations and—as a result of his own background —to the public-image phase of advertising. Having studied him carefully since the time I went to work for him as an office boy, I knew that he would be far more sensitive than any other owner to the press reaction and the public outcry. (Walter O'Malley would be concerned too, but O'Malley is hardly in a position to make any impassioned speech against moving a franchise.)

One word from Wrigley and the Carpetbaggers would have been stopped in their tracks. Not, to make this perfectly clear, that I thought Wrigley would threaten to put the heat on them in Chicago, their home base. That kind of tactic is so foreign to Mr. Wrigley's nature that it would never even occur to him.

All Mr. Wrigley had to do was to voice his objection at a league meeting, and he is so respected that he would easily pick up the votes he needed to stop them. One of the reasons he is so respected, though, is because he *never* asks for anything. It is his nature to go his way and permit others to go theirs.

The Carpetbaggers remained in Milwaukee, not because of Wrigley but because they had a contract which nailed them to the County Stadium through 1965. In a roundabout way—and how this amuses me—they remained in Milwaukee because of the friendly little spats I used to have with the city fathers in Cleveland.

Normally, a tenant wishing to break a contract would only have to pay the amount the landlord would have received and he has satisfied the legal definition of performance.

Something else was involved here, though. One of those accidents of life that make life so bearable.

When the Braves came to Milwaukee, the Cleveland Indians were the only team to have played in a municipal stadium. Since I had been indirectly connected with the building of the stadium, Bill McGovern, the head of the county board, asked me if I could send him a copy of my old contract for a guide.

Now, in my first year in Cleveland, I'd had an occasional squabble about the facilities, and I had always exerted pressure —and got myself some publicity—by threatening to move back to our own park, League Field, although between you and me they couldn't have forced me to go back there with a gun.

When the contract came up for renegotiation, the city cruelly stripped me of that weapon by inserting a sentence that the Indians would schedule "all their home games on its American League schedule at the Stadium. . . ."

In writing their contract with the Braves, the lawyers for the county inserted the sentence whole—changing only the name of the team and the league—although it had no relevancy whatsoever to their situation.

Because of that wording, the Braves had done more than simply contract to rent the premises. They were legally committed to play at the Stadium *and no place else.*

Despite a game attempt at wriggling out of Milwaukee, the Braves were finally told in court that, regrettable though it might be, they were going to have to live up to their contract just like ordinary folk. There's nothing better for the National Game, of course, than to let it be known that it takes a court order to make baseball owners live up to their contracts.

The league did its own level best to make a bad situation worse by voting unanimously to permit them to go to Atlanta in 1966.

I am about to ask a foolish question:

Question: Where was Ford Frick during this time of disrepair?

Answer: I don't know, but I'll give you a hint. There was one meeting where the Governor of Georgia was trying desperately to talk to him, and Frick was trying just as desperately not to be talked to. This is the one thing he is able to do exceedingly well, since the owners have never shown any particular desire to talk to *him*. They don't consult him beforehand, they just tell him after it's all over. Or maybe he reads about it in the paper.

During the early talk about the Milwaukee situation, Frick had dropped into town and stated with unwonted fervor that he would "insist" the team be offered to Milwaukee interests before he would permit it to move. Fortunately for Frick, not even the most passionate Milwaukee adherent took him at all seriously. As Paul Richards, a man of few words, said, "Malarkey."

Lord knows that I don't want to say anything that might be construed as critical of the Commissioner. To attack him is to belabor the obvious. The man was a bad choice at the beginning and a bad joke at the end. I had my say about him the last time around, and I took a vow that this time I'd leave him alone. But the man is just incredible. Having reigned over the decline of baseball for 13 years, he went to his last meeting and told the owners that nobody had better blame him for the mess the game was in because he would have been a great and powerful Commissioner, just like Judge Landis, if only they had let him.

So the owners said, "Well, gee, fella, if that's the way you feel about it, then all right. You can have all the power Landis ever had. Go on out there, Ford, and clean this mess up."

When the press somehow got wind of Frick's revolt (I think it was because Frick called them in to tell them), they sharpened up their pencils and asked, "What are you going to do, O great and powerful Commissioner just like Judge Landis? Have you got any immediate action in mind?"

And Commissioner Frick, converted now into a figure of thunder and lightning said, "No."

What? You're not going to do anything about Milwaukee? You're not going to do anything about CBS?

But what could the poor fellow do? Sure, he now had the power to make the rain to fall and the sun to shine, but all those other things, why, they're league affairs.

A Milwaukee sportswriter, apprised of Frick's new powers, put in a hasty phone call to find out what he was going to do about reversing the league's approval of the Braves' move to Atlanta come 1966. "I could have done something about it if I had my new authority before the shift was approved," Frick said. "But what has been done is done."

Frick also implied, coyly, that he had been against it all along, although he could not comment further because "there are suits pending."

Asked if he meant that his sympathies were with Milwaukee in its time of tribulation, he said, "You said it, I didn't. But remember that there are certain American fundamental rights such as the one to sell and trade property that can't be violated. I don't care how much authority you have. There are normal procedures in selling or buying property that must be observed." (I love the use of the word "American" in there.)

Though his sympathy lay unmistakably with Milwaukee, Frick had to say, "I can't do anything now because my power isn't retroactive."

Can't you just picture the scene where the assembled owners, trembling before Frick's demand for more authority, told him, "OK, Ford, but remember, your authority isn't retroactive."

Giving a man like Frick authority is like giving a hitter like Sandy Koufax a bigger bat. If you can't hit, you can't hit.

As for his former disabilities, back in those prehistoric, unretroactive days, the power of the Commissioner had been cruelly limited by clauses which restricted him to investigating "... upon his own initiative, any act, transaction or practice charged, alleged or suspected to be detrimental to the best interests of the national game of baseball, with authority to summon persons and to order the production of documents and in case of refusal to appear or produce, to impose such penalties as are hereinafter provided."

If that weren't bad enough, all he could do after these investigations was "to determine ... what preventive, remedial or punitive action is appropriate in the premises and to take such action either against Major Leagues, Major League Clubs or individuals, as the case may be."

How can anybody operating for 13 years under such severely circumscribed regulations be expected to do anything except draw his $60,000 per annum? The poor fellow was in handcuffs.

Frick has always had all the authority he needed. Every owner knows it. Every sportswriter knows it too, including those old buddies who try so hard to defend him.

It is Frick's misfortune that he came upon his true vocation too late in life. His real field is undoubtedly foreign policy, as he so conclusively proved in the recent squabble between Horace Stoneham and Japan. Frick was rougher on the Japanese than General MacArthur was during the surrender ceremonies on the *Lexington.*

But, then, Japan doesn't contribute a yen to the Commissioner's salary.

The Carpetbaggers cannot help but make money in Atlanta, because they have a TV contract that guarantees success. In Atlanta, the sponsors are hitting the entire Southeast. In Milwaukee, where they are jammed between Chicago, Minneapolis and Detroit, the market area is severely limited.

But even with the enthusiasm of having a big-league team and the support of the business community, they are not going to draw much over 1¼ million people. They'd have done that in Milwaukee with any kind of promotion.

In their contract with the city of Atlanta, the Carpetbaggers are being given the concessions, the right to set their ticket prices (not to exceed the highest price anywhere else) and 6,000 of the 8,000 parking spaces. The city is also putting up $500,000 for moving costs, $280,000 to buy the territorial rights from McKechnie and the remainder to be applied toward the indemnity to the league. If that seems as if McKechnie has profited from his extra year, forget it. The original $250,000 would have been pure profit for Bill. Given the one extra year, he managed to lose more than his territorial rights will bring him.

There has been a lot of conversation around that Coca-Cola (one of the TV sponsors in Atlanta) has agreed to underwrite whatever losses the Braves may suffer in their final year in Milwaukee. My information is somewhat different. What Coca-Cola did agree to do, as I understand it, was to purchase a portion of the telecasts of the Braves' games into Atlanta this year, so that the Carpetbaggers could operate in Milwaukee for another year without having to borrow any fresh money. I have also heard that the Carpetbaggers have been negotiating new loans in Atlanta to cover their existing loans in Chicago and Milwaukee.

I have carefully spelled out the Carpetbaggers' financing because it is directly related to the moving of the club.

The big loan, you will remember, is the $3,000,000 at the First Wisconsin Bank. The first payment ($500,000) would have fallen due on June 1, 1966, the second a year later, and the final $2,000,000 on June 1, 1968. There had to be profits or the poor chaps would have had to pay for the club themselves, a fate too terrible to contemplate.

It is almost impossible not to make money on a baseball club when you are buying it new because, unless you become inordinately successful, you pay no income tax at all. It is, in fact, quite possible for a big-league club to go on forever without *ever* paying any income tax.

Look, we play the "Star-Spangled Banner" before every game. You want us to pay income taxes too? There are those chronic critics who are forever complaining that baseball is a favored business because of our special exemptions from the antitrust laws. Given certain very pleasant conditions, we also have a tax write-off that could have been figured out by a Texas oilman.

It wasn't figured out by a Texas oilman. It was figured out by a Chicago hustler. Me. But it was perfected by Nate Dolin, to whom I sold the Cleveland Indians.

I should probably keep my mouth shut about it because I may be buying another club myself some day. If I'm going to explain this, though, I might as well do it right. Besides, it's the kind of financial gimmick that is worth the best efforts of all would-be hustlers.

I will keep the historical background brief and, let us all hope, decently lucid.

Historically, when you bought a ball club you bought the ballplayers as part of the inventory, just as you'd be buying the machines in a manufacturing plant.

In liquidating the old company and forming your new company, you simply transferred the players, like any other assets, from their books to yours. When you bought a new player yourself, you charged him off as an operating expense like any other operating expense.

It seemed to me far more logical in forming the new company

to *buy* the players from the old company before you liquidated, in distinct and separate transactions. Once you did this, they were no longer simply an existing asset, which the previous ownership had already written off at the time of their original purchase, they were an expense item. It said so right in your books.

The purpose of all this maneuvering was to enable you to *depreciate* the cost of the players over a period of time that can run anywhere from three years to ten. If you expect to make a lot of money fast, you're better off being able to write them off as quickly as possible. If you don't expect to strike a bonanza, the longer you can spread it out the better. OK?

The first thing you have to decide, then, is how much of the purchase price you can attribute to the players. Since they are the same players, no matter what valuation you place upon them, the more you can charge off against them the better.

OK, what are you buying when you buy a big-league ball club?

You are buying three things: the franchise, the players' contracts, and a place to play; i.e., either a park or a lease that allows you to play in somebody else's park. (The park can be depreciated too, but this is covered by a statute and takes 33⅓ years.)

At any rate, Milwaukee, our case in point, played in the County Stadium, and so no park was involved.

That leaves only the franchise and the players' contracts. The less you can charge off to the franchise, the more you are paying for the players. It has become customary in recent years to place the worth of the franchise at $50,000—almost a token figure. The Government has not wholly accepted this evaluation, and has, in fact, challenged it in New York, Cleveland and Detroit. (You will notice that in expansion there was no charge for the franchise at all. The initiation fee took the form of exorbitant prices for lousy ballplayers.)

Still, $50,000 was the price which the Carpetbaggers, following the general practice, used. Everything else was attributed to the players.

Everything means *everything*. It means not only the price that was paid to the Perini Corp. but the entire cost of the acquisition (including the $160,000 broker fee, the bills they were taking over from the Perini Corp. and the accounts receivable that still belonged to the Perini Corp.)

After the $50,000 had been deducted, the figure came to $6,168,480.

Being aware that the days of the 2,000,000 annual attendances were over, the Carpetbaggers depreciated the players over the full ten-year period.

What all this means, students, is that for the first ten years of their operation, they have an annual tax write-off of $616,848.

Put in a slightly different way, they will pay no federal taxes on their first $616,848 profit. Since the corporate tax is now set at 50 percent, they would be saving $308,424 per year. If you want to be cynical you might even say that the Government was paying half of their purchase price for them.

After that original $616,848 profit, they do pay taxes, right? Well, if they're silly, they do. In baseball, the cost of player replacement is a very considerable item. I would suspect that anybody who was unable to find a way to spend his surplus profits on new players is in the wrong business.

After ten years, though, you *are* on your own. Right? You have written off almost the entire purchase price, and you have been charging off your new player purchases as a normal operating expense. The time has come to face the world without the aid and comfort of the Bureau of Internal Revenue.

You haven't learned a thing, have you? After ten years, you sell! And the guy you sell to can start depreciating *his* entire purchase price (less $50,000) all over again.

Because here's the thing: As a seller, you are selling more than just the franchise and the players. *You are selling the right to depreciate.* This is the real reason the price of ball clubs has been going up, up, up into the stratosphere.

The more the price goes up, the more the ballplayers are worth and the higher the tax write-off becomes. But as the price goes up, it also becomes more and more difficult for an individual to buy a ball club. Even with a syndicate like the Carpetbaggers the cost of borrowing money gets to be something of a drag. As a result the corporations have been moving in. CBS is the horrible example, but Autry, Fetzer, Busch *et al.* have all bought their clubs on behalf of a corporate empire. A corporation not only has the money, *but it can use the depreciation write-off on its total corporate profits even if the ball club itself hasn't made enough profit to cover it.*

The old-line owners like Phil Wrigley and Tom Yawkey didn't enjoy this kind of write-off, of course. On the other hand, they bought their clubs at a fraction of what they go for today.

As new owners put their clubs up for sale once their write-off period comes to an end, or as old sportsmen die, the corporations will take over completely.

Private syndicates like the Carpetbaggers will move the club before they will lose those tax-free profits.

Because there is that one catch to the write-offs. You have to make those profits before they become tax-free. If you make no profits you save absolutely nothing.

The Carpetbaggers, with their huge bank loans, were not making any money in Milwaukee. They were not losing what they claimed to be losing either. Their book loss in 1964 was about $45,000 but since the interest on their loan came to $150,000, it is obvious that they really had a net income from operations of more than $104,000.

What they were losing were all those beautiful tax-free dollars. No one can sympathize with them more than me because I know that those 100¢-dollars are the hardest ones to lose.

By the end of 1965, a total of more than $1,800,000 will quite probably have slipped away.

Ah, but not completely. The money has not yet gone down the drain. The tax laws allow you to carry forward this kind of capital loss over a five-year period. When the Carpetbaggers go marching into Atlanta, with their ragged band of Braves, they should really be singing "We Shall Overtake." They still have three years to overtake the first year's write-off, four years to overtake the second year, and five years to overtake the third.

In those first few years at Atlanta, when enthusiasm will be at a peak—and profits quite probably guaranteed—they will not only be getting their fixed annual depreciation, they will be picking up the three years they have lost.

In the first four years, they will be able to take seven years' worth of write-offs. If everything goes as well as expected, they can make more than $4,200,000 without paying any taxes. That's a million dollars a year, buddy, tax-free. Get that, tax-free.

Why should they stay in Milwaukee under those conditions, you ask? They're in the game to make money, aren't they? Would I, you are entitled to ask, turn my back on that kind of money?

I don't know what I'd do. My resistance to money has not always been inspiring. There's one thing I do know, though. I do know that this floating crap game is bad for baseball. I do know that the Milwaukee situation has disgusted the entire nation. Few men in baseball want to stop them, because too many owners are thinking of moving themselves. That leaves it up to the Commissioner, who is presumably there to represent the interests of baseball when those interests come into conflict with the understandably selfish interests of individual owners.

The Commissioner prefers to plump for the owners' unfettered property rights.

Let us take the Commissioner at his word. Let us consider this entire matter as nothing beyond a conflict of property rights. All right. What about the Wisconsin citizens who bought stock in the Milwaukee Braves? What about their property rights?

Let us think about that very carefully for I do believe that Milwaukee, by wheeling up a little free enterprise of its own, can prevent the Carpetbaggers from leaving. Or, at least, prevent them from leaving on anything except Milwaukee's terms.

Suppose you were such a miserable human being that you were not particularly interested in enriching spoiled brats. Suppose you were so miserable that you were even against enriching spoiled brats as a matter of personal philosophy. How would you stop them?

Suppose, on the other hand, you were a kindly fellow like me, and you thought it would be beneficial to the Carpetbaggers, spiritually, to keep them in Milwaukee where they belong. Not out of anger but of love. It would be good for their souls, good for Milwaukee and good for baseball. How would you stop them?

I think it can be done. With a new Commissioner coming in, the timing is perfect. Baseball is well aware that it has to hire a man of personal strength to take the taste of the Frick years out of everybody's mouth. A strong Commissioner would welcome the opportunity to begin his administration by solving a vexing problem and, at the same time, demonstrating to the country that he is not only strong but fair.

Because of my own personal interest in baseball and in Milwaukee, I have been a volunteer adviser in setting up the strategy of defense. I think it is important for some city to make a stand. From every conceivable point of view Milwaukee is in the best possible position to fight back.

When they did fight back by insisting that the Braves honor their contract at the Stadium, it was to be noticed that baseball officials came running into town to offer the city advice. Such an old and valued friend as Lou Perini felt called upon to warn them, out of the goodness of his heart (his 10 percent ownership had nothing to do with it), that they would ruin their chance of getting another major-league team if they held the poor Braves in the city through 1965 and then failed to support them. While the violins were playing "Old Faithful" in the background, Lou ruminated that "We'll probably do all right in Atlanta, but we don't want to see Milwaukee hurt."

Perini was so concerned about the city's good name that he

had a plan for its redemption. Milwaukee would let the Braves depart in peace, see, and the National League would send some *other* teams in there to play 36 games. All Milwaukee then had to do was to show its gratitude by filling the park every time. "Then the next team would say, 'If they can do that in only 36 games, look what we could do in 81.'"

Lou was afraid that if Milwaukee held the Braves to their contract and failed to support them, "they could scare the day-lights out of everybody who is interested in putting a team there." The identity of these mysterious strangers who seemed so interested in putting a team back in Milwaukee was not divulged. It wasn't Perini. He was the guy interested in pulling the team out.

All that talk about lawsuits wasn't doing the city any good either, Lou told them sternly. "What Milwaukee needs," he informed them, "is a constructive attitude. . . ."

Oh.

John Quinn, the former general manager, advised Milwaukee to let the team go for its own good, too. "The city's national image would be greatly enhanced and all of baseball would also have to admit there are real big people there . . . you people would be ingratiating yourself with the rest of the country by being big about this thing."

You know, I once tried that with my local loanshark (I have a friend on Pier 18). "Rocco," I said, "you just forget about that money I owe you and I'll let everybody know what a real big guy you are. You'd be ingratiating yourself with debtors all over the country."

Rocco looked at me rather oddly.

Milwaukee would have no baseball team if it had followed all that selfless advice, but it would have an honored plaque in Cooperstown and be placed in nomination for the Harvard Medical School's coveted Pickled-Brain Award.

The Braves are playing in Milwaukee this year only because the city fought it out in the courts. The strategy should now be to exploit the infinite complexities of the law, with all its agonizing delays, to the limits of human ingenuity.

Between the delays and the appeals and the new motions and the appeals, a case can be held in court indefinitely. I don't know how many years the deportation of Frank Costello was delayed (until they finally found a technicality on which to forget the whole thing), but I see no good reason why a Milwaukee court should be any less considerate of Milwaukee's rights than a federal court is of Frank Costello's.

I wonder, to put it bluntly, if there is a judge sitting on a Milwaukee bench who would want to go down in local history as the man who let the Braves depart.

There is a theory that a court proceeding is a gentlemanly contest between brothers at the bar. This is a theory advanced by lawyers doing public-relations work for the Bar Association and accepted with a simple and touching faith by people who have never been inside a courtroom.

We have rule by law instead of rule by force, only because it is a somewhat less bloody—and considerably more intriguing —way of conducting our affairs. Next to the confrontation between two highly trained, finely honed batteries of lawyers, jungle warfare is a stately minuet.

When you get into this kind of a court fight, where delay is as good as victory, you must be prepared to be dirty, cunning and malicious. If you haven't got the stomach for it, just remember that the other guy would do it to you, and he would probably do it with glee.

As the 1965 season began, Milwaukee was in as much of a bind as the Carpetbaggers. They didn't want the attendance to be real good because they didn't want to give the Carpetbaggers any money. They didn't want it to be real bad either for fear they would be written off completely as big-league territory.

(A certain euphemistic approach has been used in this regard. Everybody knows that Milwaukee is a good baseball city. What is really meant is that if Milwaukee punishes the Carpetbaggers [and the visiting clubs] by not supporting them in their final year, then baseball will punish Milwaukee by never giving them another team.)

My plan was to form Baseball Anonymous, an organization which would encourage season ticket holders to pass up 1965 and purchase their seats for 1966. Whenever any degenerate fan felt like going to a game during the season, he would buy a ticket for 1966. If his willpower faltered, he could call us at Baseball Anonymous—available any time, day or night—and we would rush a member over to entertain him, talk baseball, read old Burt L. Standish novels to him and—in the final extremity—get him drunk.

In the end, the prospective backslider (he's not really bad, just sick) would buy a ticket for 1966 and lay his head peacefully upon his pillow at night, content in the knowledge that he had done the right thing.

The beauty of this plan was that it would take the city completely out of its bind. The Carpetbaggers would take a financial beating and the advance sale for 1966 would grow and grow. If Baseball Anonymous had an advance sale of a couple of million dollars for anybody who wanted to come in with a ball club, the area would look mighty attractive.

Meanwhile, the money would be in the bank gathering interest. If no club came in, the bank interest would pay the cost of mailing it back.

I pushed this plan on some of my Milwaukee contacts. There was some interest but it never really got off the ground.

They will probably end up in the courts. The Milwaukee County Board got things started very nicely by voting to hit baseball with an antitrust suit. This is a frontal attack with heavy cannon and is therefore to be highly commended.

Not that we should ignore the darting thrusts of the cavalry. Just to keep the enemy lawyers on their toes, there might also be a series of suits by a vengeful army of individual stockholders. (I am a wounded veteran of this kind of guerrilla warfare. In St. Louis, where the previous owners had sold stock for

$3 a share, a gentleman with 9 shares was granted a temporary injunction against us. In order to deliver the club to Baltimore, it cost us $50,000.)

That stock issue the Carpetbaggers offered to Milwaukee residents could turn out to be even more ill-fated than anybody thinks. Since the issue was limited to residents of Wisconsin, they were quite obviously selling more than an investment. They were selling pride in the local team.

In the prospectus, it was made clear that the team drew its customers from the metropolitan area of Milwaukee. "All Braves home games," it said, "are played in Milwaukee County Stadium."

In attempting to get out of Milwaukee, the Carpetbaggers' attorneys insisted that the Stadium had broken "an implied covenant" with their tenants by failing to throw ticket scalpers off the premises.

That's a nice artful phrase, "implied covenant." It has a sweet legal ring to it. Let's steal it from them. It would seem to me that there was most definitely an implied covenant between the buyer and the seller of that stock that they were being sold a rooting interest in their local team.

The Carpetbaggers would undoubtedly argue that the stockholders would be benefiting from the move to Atlanta because the value of their stock would undoubtedly rise.

But that isn't the point at all. Since it was made perfectly clear in the prospectus that no dividends could be expected in the foreseeable future, it should be clear to any Milwaukee jurist that the stockholders had purchased the stock for reasons of pride, prestige and fun.

An even more telling case can be made by a stockholder who owns a business which profits directly from the presence of a big-league ball club in the city. Such a stockholder might well have bought his stock because of the value the ball club held for him personally. Is it possible that his own Corporation will now be permitted to damage him personally by picking itself up and removing itself from town?

Nor is it particularly difficult to demonstrate the extent to which he stands to be hurt. The value of a big-league club, in dollars and cents, has been well documented—ironically enough —by the Milwaukee Chamber of Commerce.

The report was so well done that it has been widely distributed not only by the Chamber of Commerce but by baseball itself. By the Commissioner's office! The best witness of the great harm that is being visited upon this innocent stockholder and, indeed, upon the entire city of Milwaukee is baseball itself.

Unless we have degenerated into a country where the majority is allowed to run roughshod over the interests of the minority, the claims of these stockholders would be very difficult to overlook.

There is always the question of whether a Wisconsin court has jurisdiction over out-of-staters, but from what I have been reading, this should not pose any insurmountable problem in this case. Each visiting team is getting a percentage of the gate, which means it is doing business in Wisconsin. (Technically, anyway. Fnancially, is something else again. Financially, the business has been so inspiring that it has inspired the Carpetbaggers to offer the county $400,000 to be allowed to decamp at once—thereby changing their theme song to that earlier-day chant *Let My People Go*—with another million thrown in so that Teams, Inc. would get right to work to convince some other group of freebooters what a great baseball city Milwaukee really is. And if they don't believe Team, Inc. they can presumably be referred to Carpetbaggers, Inc.)

At any rate, the plan, as I understand it, is to serve the traveling secretary of each club as his team comes in to play a series. Since all traveling secretaries are listed as officers of the ballclub this would most certainly constitute sufficient service.

Maybe before Milwaukee is through, baseball will be happy to give Milwaukee an expansion team in return for letting the Braves go.

And here is where Milwaukee's battle would serve the common good. You can't just add one new team, you must add a second team for purposes of scheduling. If the National League adds two new teams, the American League will have to add two new teams too.

With four new cities welcomed into the fold, there will be almost no place left for an adventurous club owner to fly off to. The real reason baseball would not accept Branch Rickey's Continental League, in case you didn't know, was because our boys were not about to let outsiders come in to grab off New York and swallow up all those other promising new areas. Not when they might feel in need of refuge themselves some day.

With expansion, each league would have 12 teams, broken down to two 6-team divisions. With no place for a disgruntled owner to fly off to, stability would return to baseball.

This may not be the statesmanlike approach that Bill Bartholomay spoke of so glowingly. Its only real virtue is that it would work.

13

☻ ☻ ☻

Epitaph for a Hustler

NOW that you are all gathered here, in cap and gown, to receive your diplomas, I have something—ahem—to tell you. The hustler has become an anachronism in baseball. You have become the victims of corporational obsolescence.

Hustlers and corporations have always been so hostile that personnel managers break out into a heavy sweat at the sight of you. Hustlers, I do not have to tell you, make dreadful employees. They tend to have ideas of their own, a practice which is frowned upon, and they have this nasty habit of moving in on the command post, fomenting insurrections and seizing the president's chair for themselves.

But the corporation is wary of even the most benign of you. Corporate people don't have to be identical, they just have to be interchangeable. Corporations want tractable personnel who will fit neatly into their assigned slots whether the slots be in Rochester, New York; Rochester, Minnesota; or Rochester, Manitoba.

Unsatisfactory as he may be as an employee, a hustler makes an even more unsatisfactory employer. In order to be effective, the hustler has to have full, freewheeling control. Once he feels the hot breath of the Board of Directors wafting over his shoulder he tends to turn sulky and fractious and bolt to the outside of the track.

This means you can function only as a free-lancer, and the

free-lance hustler has been priced out of the baseball scene. I'm sure you all understand by now that the prices for ball clubs could never have gone much higher than five million dollars—give or take a million—if the clubs had remained in the hands of individuals. As long as the prices remained around five or six million dollars, the hustler who knew his way around the banking houses, was able to raise a couple of million, keep 30 to 35 percent of the ownership for himself, and form a syndicate of congenial chaps to put up the rest of the money.

But that's the least of it. Even if I could raise my share of the $15,000,000 that CBS paid for the Yankees, the club wouldn't have been worth it to me. It is the tax structure, far more than their bulging cash drawers, that allows CBS to pay $15,000,000.

We all know about the player-depreciation dodge by now. I could have formed my own corporation and depreciated the players but that wouldn't have changed the basic situation. I would be in precisely the same position the Carpetbaggers found themselves in. The only way I could take advantage of the depreciation would be out of the ball club's profits, and there is almost no way for the profits to be great enough to justify that price.

CBS doesn't have to worry about the Yankees' profits. For one thing, they are not borrowing money and paying interest. On the contrary, they are paying the money out over a period of time, which means that some of that money is sitting in their own bank account, *earning* interest.

Far, far more important, though, CBS doesn't have to worry about the Yankees' profits because CBS knows it is going to be able to write off the player depreciation even if the Yankees don't make a cent for them. The Yankees are only one small principality in their empire, and no matter how badly the Yankees might do, they will still be able to write off the depreciation against the entire corporate profit.

When everything is broken down, then, CBS isn't really paying $15,000,000 for the Yankees, it is paying something much closer to $5,000,000.

Of the 10 clubs in the American League, only two—Cleveland and Minnesota—are not tied in some way or other to established profit-making institutions which can absorb either the player depreciation or the operating losses and pass 50 percent of the price on to the government.

But I don't want to leave you on such a discouraging note. While the opportunities in baseball may not be unlimited, they are not as hopeless as they seemed to be only a short time ago. After the CBS-Yankee deal had shaken down, the American League seemed to be even more monolithic than ever. The low point came when Art Allyn stood absolutely alone on the vote to approve Iglehart's stock trust. Charles O. Finley, his erstwhile comrade in arms, had become very friendly with Iglehart. Finley had apparently come to the conclusion that while it was nice to battle the big boys, a rebel could easily spend the rest of his life in Kansas City. Since his vote was essentially meaningless anyway, Charles O. decided to be reasonable. Reasonable men can end up in Oakland.

CBS not only seemed to be taking over the Yankees' mace of power, they seemed to be wielding it even more efficiently. After Clearwater, the lineup went like this:

Fetzer (Detroit) and Autry (Los Angeles) were tied to CBS by common television interests, and Iglehart (Baltimore) was tied to them by his former close relationship. Johnston (Washington) was in solidly as a member of the financial world, and Yawkey (Boston) and Griffith (Minneapolis) were a package deal deliverable by Cronin. That gave the Yankees the complete East Coast, plus Detroit, Los Angeles and Minneapolis, a firm bloc of 7 votes.

Gabe Paul's attendance in Cleveland had been so low that he had to have the goodwill of the majority in case he found it necessary to ask permission to leave, and so Cleveland had become a sort of loose satellite. That made eight. Finley had begun to woo Iglehart even before the Clearwater meeting, and now there were nine.

That's why it was so important to encourage Iglehart to disgorge himself of his Baltimore stock. With Iglehart gone, Jerry Hoffberger became the controlling voice in Baltimore, giving Art Allyn a natural ally. But something else was happening too. By some remarkable trading, Gabe Paul had come up with a team that was not only colorful but good. With a contending club on his hands, Gabe (the only poor man, relatively speaking, among the millionaires) is free to move toward Allyn and Hoffberger, who are his natural allies, temperamentally and philosophically. Add Finley, who seems to be back among the rebels with the departure of Iglehart, and you have a good working minority block.

There are also increasing indications that CBS will not have the stultifying influence of the old Yankee owners. Since they are in the entertainment business, they do not sneer "Bush" whenever any new idea is presented. Besides, baseball is not that important to CBS. The same week they bought the Yankees, they bought a guitar company for even more money.

And, finally, the Yankees no longer have the ballplayers to dispense. George Weiss traded off the minor-league surplus, refused to pay the bonuses to the new kids, and came up almost empty on the free agents he was able to get cheap. What Weiss has sown, Ralph Houk and CBS are reaping. The Yankees are no longer dispensers of largesse, they are the *nauvre pauvre*, proud but needy.

Their leadership is based upon the power of CBS itself, and while CBS can still undoubtedly summon the support of the Solid Seven on any matter they consider vital, they are in no position to crack the whip too often.

And so while the opportunities in baseball are, at the moment, negligible, the future is not wholly without hope.

As we unleash you on an unsuspecting and defenseless world, trained to deceive and distort, to sack and to pillage, we can only encourage you—with every other commencement day orator—to take heart and be of good spirit. If baseball does not appreciate your peculiar abilities, there are opportunities waiting in abundance elsewhere.

This one promise I will make you.

If you will hold The School of Hustlers' two slogans close to your heart no harm can ever befall you:

1) *Victita volup!* *
2) *Ne unquam aliquid raptes quod tibi non ferat superbiam raptando.* * *

---

* Have Fun!

* * Never Steal Anything You Will Not Be Proud of Having Stolen.

Bill Veeck (1914–1986) grew up in Hinsdale, Illinois, and learned about the business of baseball when his father, William Veeck Sr., became president of the Chicago Cubs. After schooling at Phillips Academy and Kenyon College, young Veeck worked as club treasurer for the Cubs before purchasing the American Association Milwaukee Brewers. There and later as owner of the Cleveland Indians, the St. Louis Browns, and the Chicago White Sox, he brought a flamboyant, fan-oriented entrepreneurship to the game. He is best remembered for his innovative promotion of baseball and for his publicity stunts that brought fans to the ball park. He also wrote, with Ed Linn, *Veeck as in Wreck* and *Thirty Tons a Day*.